A Window into History
Family Memory in Children's Literature

D1520875

A Window into History
Family Memory in Children's Literature

by
Eleanor Kay MacDonald

ORYX
1996

The rare Arabian Oryx is believed to have inspired the myth of the unicorn. This desert antelope became virtually extinct in the early 1960s. At that time several groups of international conservationists arranged to have 9 animals sent to the Phoenix Zoo to be the nucleus of a captive breeding herd. Today the Oryx population is over 1000 and over 500 have been returned to the Middle East.

© 1996 by The Oryx Press
4041 North Central at Indian School Road
Phoenix, Arizona 85012-3397

Published simultaneously in Canada
Printed and Bound in the United States of America

∞ The paper used in this publication meets the minimum requirements of American National Standard for Information Science—Permanence of Paper for Printed Library Materials, ANSI Z39.48, 1984.

Library of Congress Cataloging-in-Publication Data

MacDonald, Eleanor Kay.
    A window into history : family memory in children's literature / Eleanor Kay MacDonald.
        p. cm.
    Includes bibliographical references (p.) and index.
    ISBN 0-89774-879-4 (pbk.)
    1. Children's literature, American—Study and teaching. 2. Memory in litera-ture—Study and teaching. 3. Family in literature—Study and teaching. 4. Children—Books and reading.
PS490.M24 1995
810.9'9282'07—dc20   95-40621
                                                                        CIP

In memory of my mother, Lorna C. Bruhn, who understood the importance of families and taught me to love good stories.

C O N T E N T S

• • • • • • • • •

PREFACE

• • • • • • • • •

A *Window into History: Family Memory in Children's Literature* is a resource and activity guide to books and videos that connect the reading child to the universal experience of family stories. All families share stories informally and unconsciously: "*Did I ever tell you about . . . ,*" "*That reminds me of the time . . . ,*" "*Remember when Uncle Charlie. . . .*" The instinct to share a unique moment or vivid memory is strong—it permeates our daily conversation and is one of the ties that hold families together. It is not surprising that authors and illustrators who write or draw for children are increasingly turning to their own families for the stories they choose to share, creating a rich and varied body of work.

This publication presents a selected list of 203 books and audio cassettes that are derived from family stories. They range from picture books based on a single event to novels or series of novels detailing the entire texture of individual lives. All have been given structure and literary polish and many are richly illustrated, but at the center of each lie the thoughts and feelings of a living individual, not a fictional creation. Even if the reader remains unaware that a given story is that of a real person, this unique source material gives the stories an immediacy and integrity that draws readers in and allows them to participate directly in another time. This sense of participation is reinforced in this book by the inclusion of enrichment activities that are designed to encourage children to explore both storytelling and history in a direct and personal way. I have attempted to emphasize this personal exploration by directing the instructions to students rather than teachers. The list of books and the enrichment activities offer teachers a flexible resource for materials in both social studies and language arts and for the connections between them that are encouraged in whole language curriculums.

This book is also a unique resource for libraries, answering the need for primary sources on historical events. Most of the titles can be used to fill requests for historical fiction and will be especially helpful in locating historical materials for younger readers. The titles featured here are particularly rich in the kind of picture books that can be used for a variety of purposes—from a simple read-aloud at home to a lesson on the home front during World War II.

CRITERIA FOR SOURCES

Nearly all the books recommended in this bibliography are based on direct, firsthand experience or are a recounting of the experience of a family member or close friend. Some stories have been told directly by a participant to the author. Others stories have been passed down through a family or have been discovered in a diary or some other primary source. Many of the books are based on the authors' own childhood memories. Like all good stories, these have been structured and polished, but the core of these works remains experiential. Because many works of fiction draw on the authors' personal experiences to one degree or another, care was taken to identify the source of the material in these works and to cite works that are most directly related to actual events. Books were eliminated from the list, even when the story or characters seemed to be based on the author's own life, if major characters or events had been altered. While this criterion eliminated many outstanding works, it also ensured that the titles in this book represent real families and real events.

Selection has also been made on the basis of literary quality, historical accuracy, and the way the book conveys a sense of time and place to young readers. While recognizing that these stories are from the past, children should be able to connect emotionally to their characters and events. It is equally important that illustrations enhance the text and convey additional detail and enrichment.

Another, somewhat arbitrary criterion was to center the materials around the American experience. I am aware that this eliminates some outstanding literature, but I've chosen to focus my attention on the large percentage of material available to teachers in this country that deals with the United States and Canada and their shared history of immigration, frontier life, and urban development.

Using these criteria, I assembled a list of works describing a variety of circumstances: lives spent in spacious countryside or cramped inner cities, lives of wealth or poverty, lives spent in the midst of large families or as solitary children. However, because of a lack of available materials, I was not able to find representative works describing families from many minority cultures. The good news is that there is a growing awareness of this gap and many fine works of fiction are now being published to fill it. Some of these newer books also represent an awareness of family stories, and with encouragement, these stories may begin to emerge from each minority group in this country. It is the author's hope that children who read these books will see the value in such stories and begin collecting and writing their own family histories. As children begin to see themselves in the role of historian, author, or illustrator, teachers can help them find a voice for these stories and ways to share them with others.

Family stories, memories, and the instinct to share them are centered around the points in a life that are unusually vivid or intense. This is why many of these books are clustered around historic movements or events (i.e., times of change and movement for families). There are compelling descriptions of immigration to the New World and the settlement of frontier lands, followed by rich descriptions of life in America's cities, small towns, and isolated farms. The details in these stories come from memory rather than research. The emotions are those of the teller and the sensory texture that of actual experience. This gives these stories an immediacy and integrity that draws children in. The lives described may be very different, but the emotions are universal, allowing the child to realize, "I feel like that too!" This revelation connects children directly to a past that is either unknown or previously perceived as little more than a series of dates and events.

ACTIVITIES

The enrichment activities and projects included in each chapter are designed to encourage children to make similar connections to their own family pasts and the stories that lie within them. References to nonfiction books that give additional ideas and information precede the activities, which have been set in boxes to highlight them for the reader. The projects, on the other hand, are not associated with a specific nonfiction title.

Many of the research and writing activities involve oral history—interviewing older relatives or friends and learning firsthand about their lives. Because these activities require children to deal directly and personally with their own family histories, teachers need to be aware that this could lead to an unhappy or uncomfortable experience for some children. Children who are adopted, living in foster homes, or estranged from a parent may need an alternate choice for such activities. Such a choice should be prepared in advance and offered to all children as part of the assignment so that no child will feel singled out. An ideal alternative would be to interview another adult volunteer who is willing to share his or her family history with a student. Volunteers could be recruited in advance through senior citizen organizations or other community groups.

Through reading, directed research, family trees, and interviews, young readers will become aware that members of their own families share many of the experiences of the families they are reading about. Students will begin to see themselves as part of the continuity of a history that is more than dates and places. They will recognize that each family, including their own, has a story to tell.

Other projects in the book re-create the physical tasks of a time when families, working together, raised their own food, made many of their own clothes and household furnishings, and created their own entertainment. Since the gentle nostalgia of the stories is balanced by detailed descriptions of the hard work required by many families simply to survive, the experience of cooking, making simple household objects, and inventing new games will give students a direct understanding of what childhood was like for their ancestors. Other activities encourage children to really look at the world around them, track the changes in their communities, and explore the physical evidence of earlier times. The exercises will help children focus on changes in architectural styles, household objects, and popular culture, as well as compare many things from the past with their own lives.

The instructions for the activities have been addressed directly to the students to create a sense of immediacy and discovery. I hope that this will also help busy teachers as they adapt the activities for their own students. With the exception of Chapter 7, the activities are grouped at the end of each chapter along with references to nonfiction books that give additional ideas and information. The activities refer back to specific titles on the recommended reading lists only when pertinent. Additional, particularly apt titles are also included with the activities. The intent is to present a variety of ideas to be used in a number of ways. Because teachers always adapt ideas to meet the needs of their own classrooms, the suggestions were kept as open-ended as possible.

The exception to the pattern of a single recommended reading list followed by a single group of activities is Chapter 7. In this chapter the books and activities are clustered around single themes dealing with ways to save and share family stories. While the majority of recommended titles in this book are based on the authors' personal memories, Chapter 7 contains some that can be considered purely fictional. These books were included because they illustrate the subject so effectively. The annotations for the books that come from family stories contain information on the source.

Finally, the titles included in this book cover the full range of the American experience yet never move away from the intimacy of personal storytelling. The materials allow young readers to compare their experiences with those of children of the past and to see what has changed and what has remained the same. They also open the door to an increased awareness of the roles their own families have played in history. Young readers can begin to see themselves as part of the continuity of a history that is not just dates and places but a fabric of families, each with its own story.

ACKNOWLEDGMENTS

• • • • • • • • •

My sincere thanks to everyone in the Children's Department at the Beverly Hills Public Library for their suggestions and enthusiastic support. I also gratefully acknowledge the patience, understanding, and support of my family.

A Window into History
Family Memory in Children's Literature

CHAPTER 1

Coming to the New World: The Immigrant Experience

T hough other sections in this book are devoted to the variety of family stories created by the American experience, this chapter tells a story common to all American families, that of immigration. For Native Americans that story is ancient, existing in the realm of myth and legend. For recent immigrants the story is current and directly told. For others the story is recalled by aging relatives, found in family diaries, or shown in fading photos, with details only dimly remembered. Despite these differences, these family stories have an amazing similarity. In reading them one learns of the hardships that forced these people from their homelands, the dangers and frequent humiliations of travel, and the sense of adventure combined with the frustrations of starting a new life. They arrived with exaggerated hopes and limited English into an impatient and frequently hostile new world. It is easy to understand the pride that underlies these works, which are tributes to the courage, tenacity, and eventual success of American immigrant ancestors.

RECOMMENDED READING

Bartone, Elisa. *Peppe the Lamplighter.* Illustrations by Ted Lewin. Lothrup, Lee & Shepard Books, 1993.

Source of Material: The story is loosely based on a story the author heard about her grandfather.

Location: Little Italy section of New York City.

Dates: 1890s.

Grade: 2 to 6.

This richly illustrated picture book tells the story of Peppe, the only son in a large family of Italian immigrants. His father is sick and his mother is dead, so Peppe sets out to help support his seven sisters. He is young and jobs are scarce, so he is thrilled when he is offered a job lighting the gas street lamps in his neighborhood each night. Everyone is pleased but Papa, who is angry that his only son should take such a menial job. As he lights the lamps each night, Peppe makes wishes for those he loves, seeing each light as a small flame of promise for the future. However, as Papa continues to turn away from him in shame, Peppe begins to lose his joy in the work. One night he just stays home, leaving the streets of Little Italy in the dark. When Assunta, the youngest daughter, does not come home, Papa finally begs Peppe to light the lamps. Peppe lights the lamps as he searches for his sister and finds her under the last streetlight, waiting for him. When Peppe carries her home, Papa is waiting to admit to Peppe that he was wrong and is proud of him and the job he does.

Ted Lewin's lush watercolor paintings vividly convey life in Little Italy at the turn of the century: shops and bars, crowded streets filled with pushcarts and pedestrians, hanging laundry, and dark tenements. Lamplight is the recurrent motif. Peppe's lanterns light the busy streets as well as his young and hopeful face, and he returns home to the light of a single lamp. The warm glow against the oppressive darkness makes a strong visual symbol of one boy's hope for the future. Ted Lewin has portrayed with love and documentary accuracy the crowded, energetic life of this immigrant neighborhood and one family that was part of its story.

Bresnick-Perry, Roslyn. *Leaving for America.* Pictures by Mira Reisberg. Children's Book Press, 1992.

Source of Material: Author's childhood memories.

Location: Russian town of Wysokie-Litewskie.

Dates: 1920s.

Grade: 1 to 3.

In this colorful picture book the author recalls the days when she and her mother prepared to join her father in America, leaving behind a loving family and many memories. As they say good-bye and pack, they are given advice and comfort from all in their village. For Roslyn, the most difficult parting was with Zisl, her cousin, best friend, and co-conspirator in various adventures. When everything is finally packed, she says good-bye to her beloved grandfather who reminds her to be a "true Jewish daughter" to her people.

The rather matter-of-fact telling of this story is enlivened by the vigor and color of the full-page paintings that illustrate the book. Both the pictures and the surrounding borders are filled with details: family portraits, beloved objects, and sunny gardens—all the memories of a childhood left behind.

Cech, John. *My Grandmother's Journey.* Illustrated by McGinley Nalley. Bradbury Press, 1991.

Source of Material: Based on the experiences of Feodosia Ivanovna Belvtsov.

Location: Russia.

Dates: 1914 to 1945.

Grade: 2 to 5.

The bright colors and folkloric quality of the illustrations in this book are in sharp contrast to its tale of a life shattered by revolution, war, and exile. Cech based this book on the experiences of his wife's mother, Feodosia, told in first person, much as she shared them with his daughter. As a young girl in Russia, she has two memorable encounters with the gypsies: one in which she is healed and another in which she is given a dire prophecy of hunger, weariness, and pain. When the revolution comes, she loses everything—family, land, and shelter. She and her husband wander the countryside as exiles, hiding in the forests and finding work wherever they can. Their daughter is born on the banks of a river, and they carry her with them, "the one gift of hope we had in those days." Small acts of kindness by others and their own determination keep them moving until they are captured by German soldiers and taken to work in the factories. Peace finally comes and they eventually migrate to America where Feodosia can once again eat bread in a warm house and rest her feet.

The illustrator uses folk motifs containing a multitude of patterns in bright colors and decorative borders that convey the Russian origins of the storyteller. While the borders define both text and illustrations and symbolically echo the story, there are some images that recur throughout: birds, fish, flowers, and smiling angels. For the most part, the figures are stylized, flattened, and vividly patterned and more successfully show the action of the story than the emotions of the couple and the grim realities of war and revolution. While the illustrations are attractive and show how folk motifs can be used to symbolically tell a story, their persistent cheerfulness is at odds with the drama of the story.

Hesse, Karen. *Letters from Rifka.* Holt, Rinehart & Winston, 1992.

Source of Material: Based largely on the memories of Lucy Evrutin, the author's great-aunt.

Locations: Russia; Poland; Belgium; Ellis Island, New York.

Dates: 1919 to 1920.

Grade: 5 to 7.

Twelve-year-old Rifka flees Russia with her family to protect one brother from the draft and the other from a firing squad. With no opportunity to say good-bye to a beloved cousin, she begins a series of letters to her in the margins of a volume of poetry by Pushkin. These letters record the fear of capture, humiliating examinations by doctors, deadly typhus, and finally the heartbreak of being left behind while her family joins her older brothers in America. She has contracted ringworm on her scalp and will not be allowed to board a ship until she is officially cured. She spends months in Antwerp, living with a kind family and receiving treatment at a convent. Though her beautiful golden hair has fallen out and she cannot speak Flemish, she begins to venture out, making friends and learning independence. Finally the ringworm is cured, and she is put on a ship to America. The journey begins well, but the ship runs into a disastrous storm that sweeps away a shipboard friend and cripples the ship. When Rifka finally arrives in America, she meets yet another obstacle: her baldness makes her an undesirable immigrant and she is placed in a hospital on Ellis Island for a waiting period. There she makes herself helpful, nursing a baby with typhus and befriending an unhappy Russian orphan. She is finally able to convince the authorities that both she and her young friend are acceptable immigrants, and the book ends as she joins her family and begins life in America.

Though this is very much the story of one individual, this book also encompasses much of the immigrant experience: the prejudice that drove people from their own countries; the callous treatment by government authorities; the real dangers of the journey; and the development of independence as young immigrants faced obstacle after obstacle. Rifka is a well-realized character with a lively mind and quick tongue. Her evolution from a somewhat sheltered youngest child to an independent and courageous young woman is believable, and the reader is left knowing that this immigrant will thrive in the New World.

Kherdian, David. *The Road from Home.* Greenwillow Books, 1981.

————. *Finding Home.* Greenwillow Books, 1979.

Source of Material: Story of author's parents, particularly his mother Veron Kherdian.

Locations: Turkey; Greece; Racine, Wisconsin.

Dates: 1910 to 1925.

Grade: 6 to Adult.

In *The Road from Home*, David Kherdian tells the story of his mother Veron Kherdian's tattered childhood, years of exile, and journey to America to become the picture-bride of a man twice her age. The oldest child of a successful trader, Veron's early childhood in an Armenian village is happy and secure. She is seven when the Turkish government removes her family, along with thousands of others, to the Arabian desert. At first her father is able to spare them many of the worst horrors of the journey, but her brothers and sisters die of cholera, her mother of a broken heart, and her father of sheer exhaustion. At the age of 11, she is left an orphan, hundreds of miles from her home. She goes from relative to relative, school to orphanage, and endures the final hours of Smyrna when the city is burned and everyone driven to the sea. Veron and her aunt are rescued and taken to Greece where she is offered the chance to go to America as the picture-bride of Melkon Kherdian.

Finding Home, which switches from the first-person account of *The Road from Home* to third person, tells of Veron's journey to America and the first awkward months when she must not only marry a stranger, but learn the language and ways of a new world. Though the author gives some insight into "Mike's" fears and unease about this marriage, the story continues to be dominated by Veron's point of view. As her confidence grows, she gradually establishes herself in an independent home, finds her place in the community, and makes friends of her own choice. Though she remains committed to the Armenian community, especially its church, she—unlike her husband—is eager to move beyond this group, give up old customs, and become part of this new world. As the story ends, she has finally found a home through which she reclaims the beauty and sense of peace she lost so long ago.

The compelling drama of this story gives it a strong force, but it is also rich in memorable characters, especially women: Veron's gregarious mother, philosophical grandmother, and two aunts, one selfish and bitter and the other generous and courageous. Veron is the strongest, and as the story unfolds, her life changes her from a happy child to a "burning orphan" to a woman with the strength to take advantage of every opportunity, quietly change the rules, and find her own place in the world.

Kopelnitsky, Raimonda, and Kelli Pryor. *No Words to Say Goodbye: A Young Jewish Woman's Journey from the Soviet Union to America: The Extraordinary Diaries of Raimonda Kopelnitsky.* Translated by William Spiegelberger. Hyperion, 1994.

Source of Material: Based on author's diaries.

Locations: Ukraine; Italy; Brooklyn, New York.

Dates: 1989 to 1992.

Grade: 6 to Adult.

Simultaneously with her family's decision to leave the lingering radiation and growing anti-Semitism of the Ukraine, 12-year-old Raimonda reads Anne Frank's diary. She decides to do what Anne had done: keep a diary to help her remember what she left behind and record the changes that were to come.

The clear voice of this diary records all the fears, frustrations, and joy her family experienced. Raimonda describes the months of waiting in Italy when tension was expressed in endless family quarrels; the shock of arrival when they were housed in a dirty welfare hotel; and a new life of uncertainty in which dreams of a crystal country are tempered by the reality of life in a tiny apartment in a tough Brooklyn neighborhood. She writes with great insight of life in America and how the freedom she cherishes is balanced by an uncertainty never experienced in the Soviet Union. She longs to see her grandparents again and regretfully loses her memories of the city and friends she left behind, but she works hard and embraces new opportunities with enthusiasm. Though financial security remains elusive and her parents particularly feel the frustration of language obstacles and limited opportunity, they slowly begin to create a life where success seems possible. The contemporary setting and the wit with which Raimonda describes her family and her life as an inner city student give the book authenticity: "I saw a horror movie and then the news. I like to see horror movies because they aren't as terrible and crazy as the news from New York."

Lehmann, Linda. *Better Than a Princess*. Thomas Nelson, Inc., 1978.

————. *Tilli's New World*. Elsevier Nelson, 1981.

Source of Material: This story is based on the life of the author's mother.

Locations: Germany to Missouri.

Dates: 1880s.

Grade: 4 to 7.

The arrival of a letter from her mother starts Tilli on a journey full of surprise and adventure. It confirms her secret belief that cold, demanding Mother Baelk is not her real mother—her real mother lives in America and has sent for her. As she is taken from the only home she remembers, she meets a frightened little girl, Melia, who is her sister, and a tall, self-confident boy, Albert, who is her brother. With Albert in charge and guided only by the tags attached to their clothes, the three are escorted by officials from a riverboat to an ocean steamship and then to a train for the final three-day journey to their parents in Missouri. As they travel, their fellow immigrants take the "happy orphans" to their hearts, making sure they are fed and reassuring their fears. Tilli begins to remember fragments of her past and wonders if her mother will be the rich and elegant princess she has dreamed of. Although the farm in which their father takes such pride is a simple cluster of log buildings and the woman in front of the stove is nothing like she imagined, Tilli has learned from her fellow immigrants that a mother who loves you and sacrifices for you is better than a princess. Tilli has a home, and that is better than dreaming.

This novel takes the reader inside the adventure and fear that accompanied children who faced the immigration experience alone. Though the journey went as planned and the three were cared for by sympathetic adults, Tilli was unprepared, and her confusion and fear are vividly conveyed, along with her joy at being released from the harsh life she was leaving. This compelling story will fascinate young readers.

Tilli's New World begins exactly where *Better Than a Princess* ends, with Tilli's arrival at her parents' new farm in Missouri. Far from being wealthy, Tilli's parents are barely making a living on the farm they have just bought. When they discover that the seller has cheated them of the corn crop they counted on, the situation becomes even more difficult. Their father finds work in town, and their mother struggles to keep the farm going and tend sickly baby Victor. The children help as they can. Tilli learns to milk the cow, and Albert learns to harness the team and help his father. Tilli longs for school, which is too far from their farm. Her parents manage to stay in town one winter, but Tilli must leave them to work for wealthy ladies in town in exchange for a few hours to attend school. One kindly woman offers to adopt her and keep her in school, but a tragedy at home makes Tilli realize that her place is with her family; she is needed and she knows that like her parents, she will have to get an education on her own. She returns to the farm and, with her sister Melia, saves her baby sister Rosie from nearly drowning in the well.

This book clearly illustrates the immigrant's struggle to adapt to a new land. Though Tilli's father has worked for years to buy this farm, language barriers make him susceptible to being cheated. The children have to learn the unfamiliar tasks of farming, and the demands of this new life keep the family apart, both physically and emotionally. Yet the family survives the hard work, the death of two babies, and the sacrifices they must all make to be together. By the end of the story, Tilli has realized her family is more important than her dreams of leading a more comfortable life in another home.

Lehrman, Robert. *The Store That Mama Built.* Macmillan, 1992.

Source of Material: Author's family history.

Location: Steelton, Pennsylvania.

Date: 1917.

Grade: 5 to 8.

Twelve-year-old Birdie Fried's father was on the brink of realizing his dream of opening his own grocery store when he died of influenza. Now his family faces a choice: open the store or return to the sweatshops and cockroach-infested apartments they left behind in New York City. The children long to stay in the small Pennsylvania mill town, but can Mama, who barely understands English, manage the store? Papa's Uncle Izzy thinks so and is willing to help. So is Mama's sister Esther, who comes from New York. They all pitch in; Joe helps Mama with the orders and bookkeeping, Heshie prints flyers in the school print shop, and Birdie helps him distribute them. But it is Mama who makes the tough decisions, even going against Uncle Izzy's advice. She extends credit they can't afford and welcomes African-American families to the store despite the objections of an important supplier. In the end, her trust is repaid and the family can see that the store Papa dreamed of and Mama built will be a success.

  This book gives a clear picture of how immigrant families worked together to overcome obstacles of language and poverty. It also points out the generational conflict between the traditional religious practices of immigrant Jews and their children's desires to become real Americans. This conflict influences Mama's choices about the hours the store will be open, the meats that will be sold, and finally the dilemma of taking much-needed payments during the Jewish Sabbath. She surprises even her children on occasion, and Birdie comes to respect both the traditions that mean so much to her mother and the courage it took to move away from them for her children's sakes.

Lester, Julius. *To Be a Slave.* Illustrated by Tom Feelings. Dial Books for Young Readers, 1968.

Belinda Hurmence, editor. *My Folks Don't Want Me to Talk About Slavery: Twenty-one Oral Histories of Former North Carolina Slaves.* John F. Blair, 1984.

Michele Stepto, editor. *Our Song, Our Toil: The Story of American Slavery as Told by Slaves.* Millbrook Press, 1994.

  Source of Material: Oral histories and other slave narratives.

  Location: Southern slave states.

  Dates: 1790s to 1870s.

  Grade: 6 to Adult.

The memories collected in these books were compiled from a number of primary sources. Throughout the history of slavery in this country slave narratives, written or collected from those who had escaped to freedom, were published. As the debate over slavery intensified, more and more interviews and narratives were gathered. Because white abolitionists were anxious to confirm the equality of slaves, most of the accounts from this period were rewritten to conform with literary standards of the time. The experience survived but the speaker's individually was often lost. After the Civil War, interest in gathering this material dwindled until the 1930s when researchers from the Federal Writer's Project systematically collected the memories of the last survivors of the slavery period, trying to preserve both the memory and unique voice of these people. Together, these accounts present a vivid picture of the experience of slavery in North America.

Many of the most central and searing memories of these peoples are of the imposed separation when family members were sold and taken away with little or no warning. Slaves never forgot the pain of this loss. The accounts describe a variety of experiences. While some owners were careful of their slaves health and well being, there were also masters of unthinkable cruelty. Slaves experienced endless hours of labor, minimal food and shelter, and loss of self and family. They remember with satisfaction all the ways they found to survive and occasionally triumph over a system designed to keep them docile and ignorant. They even found strength in the white man's religion, taking stories of freedom and courage from the bible. Though the accounts are brief, the books are filled with the courage and endurance that allowed these forced immigrants to survive in a system that was entirely hostile to their humanity.

Lester's book is the most complete account of the entire slavery experience. He starts with accounts of capture in Africa, the passage across the Atlantic, and the confusion felt as new slaves were sold and separated. Other accounts describe plantation life, how slaves were treated, and the forms of resistance taken by the slaves. He shows both the joy and frustration of Emancipation, as old attitudes were allowed to survive after the Civil War.

The Hurmence book focuses on a smaller group, people who experienced both slavery and the uncertainty of Emancipation. Their accounts are longer but less representative of the whole experience. *Our Song, Our Toil* covers the same material as *To Be a Slave* but has fewer accounts and more explanatory text, introducing each account and giving brief explanations of unfamiliar terms. It provides a less compelling but more accessible introduction to the experience of slavery.

Levinson, Riki. *Watch the Stars Come Out.* Illustrated by Diane Goode. E. P. Dutton, 1985.

————. *Soon Annala.* Illustrated by Julie Downing. Orchard/Richard Jackson, 1993.

Source of Material: Stories from the author's family.

Locations: Atlantic Ocean to New York City.

Dates: 1910 to 1911.

Grade: 1 to 4.

In simple words, a grandmother tells her granddaughter the story of her mother's journey to America. The courage of two young siblings, traveling alone for many days, and the hardships of the voyage are quietly understated. The story is related as a child would experience it, and events are simply told:

there are too many steps down in the hold to count, the old lady who accompanies them dies, they travel alone for 23 days, she misses the stars and feels sad. They arrive at last, go through the bureaucracy of Ellis Island, and are finally reunited with their parents and older sister. Their new home is a three-bedroom apartment where she is bathed in the kitchen sink, given cookies and tea, and tucked into a bed where she can once again watch the stars come out.

The text is subtle and low key, but the illustrations give physical reality and emotional resonance to the story. The colored pencil drawings show the brother and sister, distinct in matching blue, amidst crowds of people busy with their own lives; one can almost hear the noise and confusion. The background, showing the ship, Ellis Island, the ferries, and the crowds on Hester Street, is historically accurate and filled with a sense of life and human energy. Though in color, the drawings are primarily in brown and blue-grays that give the impression of old sepia photos or faded prints. There are wonderful details that children will enjoy, such as a doll the girl clutches throughout the journey. The same doll turns up at the end of the story on the bed of the granddaughter who is looking at photos with her grandmother and listening to this story.

Though the change in illustration style is a bit confusing, *Soon Annala* is a sequel to *Watch the Stars Come Out*. The little girl from the previous book, whose name we now learn is Anna, has settled into her new life in America and is learning English in school. She helps pull out the long white basting stitches of her mother's endless sewing at home and has collected enough thread to make 48 balls to hang on the end of her bed. She longs to show them to Sammy and Elly, the little brothers they left behind. Everyday she asks when they will be coming, only to be told, "Soon . . . soon." Finally, a letter arrives form their aunt indicating the name of the boat the family is traveling on, and then Papa brings home a newspaper listing the expected arrival date. Seven days later, they go to the harborside to wait for the ferry. Anna recognizes the Lady with a Crown, but ferry after ferry comes without her brothers. Papa picks her up and holds her close to comfort her through the long wait, until a ferry arrives with two little boys and a man and woman holding a baby. The family is together at last! After supper and special prayers of thanks, Anna takes her little brothers to her room to show them the white balls she has made and teach them to count the emerging stars in English.

The story is simpler and more intimate than *Watch the Stars Come Out*, and the illustrations are softer and less crowded. Though a few illustrations show the school and crowded streets, this book centers around the family, their apartment, and the table where they eat. Mama sews and they gather to read important letters and papers. In contrast to the first book, these illustrations convey the warmth of the family and less of the crowded living conditions and economic struggles of reuniting immigrant families.

Levitin, Sonia. *Journey to America.* Illustrated by Charles Robinson. Atheneum, 1970.

———. *Silver Days.* Atheneum, 1989.

Source of Material: Based on the life of the author and her family.

Locations: Berlin, Germany; Zurich, Switzerland; New York City; Los Angeles.

Dates: 1938 to 1943.

Grade: 5 to 8.

Journey to America is the story of a German-Jewish family's flight from Nazi Germany as seen through the eyes of Lisa Platt, the second of three daughters. First Papa goes, leaving in the middle of the night as if this was a regular business trip. Because he can take nothing with him, the family must wait for him to earn the money to arrange their passage to America. For a while they remain in the uncertain comfort of their Berlin apartment, then, when Papa feels that is too dangerous, they go to Switzerland. They, like Papa, are allowed to bring very little, and as the months pass, they face poverty and even hunger for the first time. When their mother becomes ill, they are taken in by kindly Swiss families until Papa can send for them. It has been almost a year and four-year-old Annie doesn't remember Papa at first, but by the end of *Journey to America,* the family is reunited and ready to start a new life.

Silver Days tells of the family's first years in America. Lisa's dreams of her new life are grand, but the family has left everything behind and is struggling with a new language. Papa sells ties and Mama works at a series of menial tasks to make ends meet. Finally Papa decides to start again, this time in California. After a difficult beginning filled with humiliations and bad news from Europe, things begin to improve. Papa finds a partner and once again begins to manufacture fine woolen coats, Lisa finds a way to continue her dance training, and the family moves into a house with a real garden. Then Mama becomes ill when she hears that her mother has been sent to Auschwitz. For a while the family falters, but a message of courage from an old friend gives them hope and brings them back together.

This story recounts the fear that drove prosperous Jewish families into a life of uncertainty and the struggle they faced in a new country. The characterization of the family is believable. Mama endures poverty without complaint but cannot hide her fear of events in Europe. The girls have moments of strength and courage, but they also complain and show insensitivity toward their struggling parents and each other. When events threaten to overwhelm them, they band together, and at the end, one senses this family will survive and flourish in America.

Lim, Sing. *West Coast Chinese Boy.* Tundra Books, 1979.

Source of Material: Author's childhood memories.

Location: Vancouver, British Columbia.

Dates: Early 1920s.

Grade: 3 to 6.

In colorful prints and vivid prose, Lim recalls his childhood in Vancouver's Chinatown during the 1920s. Though he was born in Canada, his parents had immigrated from China and continued to live as Chinese in Canada. Despite poverty, hardship, and constant discrimination, these memoirs are filled with the richness of Chinese life and the foods, mischief, and celebrations of Lim's childhood. His home was a large apartment complex with a courtyard that was shared with other families, groups of music-making bachelors, and a variety of shops. His favorites were the Chinese herbalist and the poultry shop with its collection of live chickens and ducks. His favorite adult was Uncle Jing, a restaurant owner who let him hang around the kitchen, took him to the Chinese opera, and made him a participant in the numerous feasts he prepared for the community. The descriptions of food and cooking are fascinating, as are those of celebrations including Chinese New Year; Ching Ming, with its feast and offerings for the dead; a celebration for one-month-old babies called "Baby's head shave"; and elaborate funeral parades complete with two bands, one Western and one Chinese.

The text is filled with humorous incidents and is enlivened by the sketchy and comic quality of the pen-and-ink drawings on each page. There are also 22 full-page monotypes with vigorous line and color. Though the book is dedicated to the artist's mother, sister, and Uncle Jing. It is interesting to note in the drawings the dominance of men in immigrant Chinese communities and in the life of the artist, who has shared his memories of a rich and varied culture.

Lord, Betty Bao. *In the Year of the Boar and Jackie Robinson.* Illustrated by Marc Simont. Harper & Row, 1984.

Source of Material: Author's childhood memories.

Locations: China; Brooklyn, New York.

Date: 1947.

Grade: 4 to 6.

Traveling with her mother and bearing a new "American" name, Shirley Temple Wong journeys from China to Brooklyn, New York, to join her father.

Their new home is a small apartment that is up four flights of stairs but equipped with all the labor-saving devices mother will need to learn to cook, clean, and wash clothes. In school Shirley is put in the fifth grade with students who are not only older but much bigger than she. She struggles to learn English, keep up her schoolwork, and carry out her parent's charge that she be a good ambassador for all Chinese, but what she really longs for are friends. After an initial wave of friendship, the children find it easier to ignore her than try to include her in games she cannot play or understand. Later, she unexpectedly proves herself, gains acceptance to the group, and discovers the Brooklyn Dodgers, becoming an avid fan. She spends the summer following the team's fate on the radio, helping her father, and baby-sitting. Though she misses her Chinese family, Shirley feels herself being drawn away from them and becoming more and more American. When school starts again, Shirley is no longer a stranger; she makes a new friend and is given the opportunity to meet her idol, Jackie Robinson. Standing in front of the school, he reaffirms to her that America truly is a land of opportunity.

This is a touching and humorous portrait of one child's struggle to become part of a new place with a new language and customs. The story has the authenticity of real experience and is filled with vivid characters and engaging humor. Both the humanity and humor are reinforced by the illustrations at the beginning of each chapter. The pictures show a tiny, earnest girl: bowing to a group of larger children to whom she is as invisible as she feels; squeezed onto the corner of a piano bench; and hunched under an umbrella. Later, she is depicted in a store with a group of children listening to the World Series, and you know she has become one of the group and part of the vigorous and diverse energy of her Brooklyn neighborhood.

Say, Allen. *Grandfather's Journey.* Houghton Mifflin, 1993.

Source of Material: Author's memories of his grandfather's life.

Locations: Japan and the United States.

Dates: Early 1900s to present.

Grade: 2 to 6.

With full-page luminous paintings and single lines of text, Say tells the story of his grandfather's love of two countries: his native Japan and the America he discovered as a young man. He travels throughout America, seeing the wonders and meeting all types of people before settling down in California with his Japanese bride. However, he never forgets Japan, and when his daughter is nearly grown, the family returns to his homeland, where his daughter marries. Once settled, he begins to miss the rivers and mountains of California. He plans a trip back to America, but World War II comes first, destroying their home and making the trip impossible. Though he never returns to his adopted home, he passes on his love for America to his grandson who, like his grandfather, moves from one country to the other, always homesick for the one left behind.

The text tells the story in clean, simple prose, but the real story is told in Say's paintings, which have the studied formality of postcards and family photo albums. They show a young man, first in traditional Japanese clothing, then clutching a bowler hat on the windy deck of a ship. He is shown throughout his travels, usually dwarfed by the overwhelming size of America's landscape and industry. The landscapes are grand and scenic, while family life is depicted through a series of studio portraits and posed "snapshot" vignettes. Despite the illustrations' formality, the affection between grandfather and grandson is clearly seen. The last picture shows the author, now a young man, posed against a distinct California background of palm trees, bringing the story full circle.

Although both the writing and illustrations have a structured formality, they nonetheless combine to create a moving portrait of a beloved grandfather.

Telemaque, Eleanor Wong. *It's Crazy to Stay Chinese in Minnesota.* Thomas Nelson Inc., 1978.

Source of Material: Author's childhood memories.

Location: Minnesota.

Dates: 1950s.

Grade: 6 to 9.

Ching Wing, the only daughter of a Chinese immigrant family, helps her parents in their restaurant, moons over movie magazines, and longs to be a real American. Her father's passions are Generalissimo Chang Kai-shek, the Wing family tong, which he heads, and their struggling restaurant. She doesn't understand why her father continues to feed a succession of free-loaders when *The Canton* is running in the red. She also doesn't understand her mother's refusal to learn English or join in the life of the community. Ching wants to go to college in the fall but knows her father has business problems and there is little money for education. Meanwhile, her mother is busy looking for a rich husband for Ching and finalizing a plan to bring her nephew from China, a difficult and expensive procedure involving bribes and false papers. Then a newcomer arrives. Bingo Tang, the handsome son of a local tong leader, spends the summer with them, helps in the restaurant, and lives in their home. Looking at her world through his eyes, Ching begins to see that the Chinese community respects her father as a man of honor and that her mother's stubbornness contains a fierce determination to succeed in this new country. She sees their dreams die when her mother's nephew dies in China and her father loses the lease on his business. Her father swallows his pride, settles an old quarrel, and makes a new start in San Francisco. Ching is able to go to college, starting a life that will be different from her parents but still Chinese.

Though there are some comic moments, the center of this story is Ching's need to reconcile her own experience with that of her parents', to understand their values, and find her own way. The novel is filled with memorable characters, ranging from assorted restaurant customers to Auntie Tong, a formidable Chinese woman full of advice and bent on improving Ching's life by finding her a rich husband. This is a fascinating view of the way Chinese immigrants survived in a country that was both culturally and politically hostile to their presence.

Yep, Laurence. *The Star Fisher.* Morrow Junior Books, 1991.

Source of Material: Childhood memories of the author's mother.

Location: Clarkesburg, West Virginia.

Dates: 1920s.

Grade: 5 to 8.

When her parents decide to move to West Virginia and start a new laundry business, 15-year-old Joan Lee finds herself operating as interpreter between her traditional Chinese parents and a hostile community. Papa was trained as a scholar and Mama is the practical one, but she speaks no English. While her younger brother and sister make friends easily, Joan finds herself ignored and isolated. She feels as alone and strange as the Star Fisher's daughter in one of Mama's stories. Joan encounters prejudice because she is Chinese then discovers that a fellow student is shunned because her family are theatre performers. She realizes that prejudice must be faced head-on and pride should not stand in the way of genuine offers of friendship. She helps her mother understand and accept the help offered by Miss Lucy, their indomitable landlady. When vandals repeatedly paint racist warnings on their fence, it is Miss Lucy who drives them away and rallies the town to show the Lee family the real face of the community that will become their home. Joan's mother finds her way when she stubbornly learns to bake an apple pie for a church social. Her success after many failures is their first step into the community.

The story told here is not unusual for the time. Immigrants who ventured beyond their own communities were often subject to isolation and prejudice. The book is defined by strong characters, especially women. The conflict between Joan and her proud, traditional mother is clearly defined, as is the

love that holds the family together. Miss Lucy is another memorable character—her house is filled with the remnants of family hobbies and her own vivid
memories of the past. The theme of the story is shown in the way these three
women put aside their fears and pride and use their strengths to help each
other. As the book ends, Joan knows that her parents will succeed, that this
town can become her home, and that, like the Star Fisher's daughter, she is
finally free to fly.

SPECIAL PROJECTS AND ENRICHMENT ACTIVITIES

The projects included in this chapter are designed to give students an appreciation of the experiences of their immigrant ancestors, pride in their own
cultural heritage, and an understanding of the way all cultures have combined
to create a richer, stronger whole. The critical thinking exercises specifically
target new immigrants and the ways their experiences compare with those in
the past.

Background Sources

These background sources to reinforce the recommended reading and give
information for all the activities in this chapter.

Freedman, Russell. *Immigrant Kids.* E. P. Dutton, 1980. **Grade:** 3 to 6.

This book is a photo essay that documents the lives of immigrant children
starting with their journey and arrival. Centered primarily in the tenement
neighborhoods of New York, Freedman shows these children at home, school,
work, and play. Using first-person accounts and well-selected photos, Freedman shows the crowded conditions and hard work that greeted most families,
along with the simple recreations these children enjoyed.

Koral, April. *An Album of the Great Wave of Immigration.* Franklin Watts,
1992. **Grade:** 4 to 8.

This large-format book with its large-type text and array of fascinating photos
gives an excellent overview of the immigrant experience and serves as
preparation for the oral history project featured in this chapter. In simple
straightforward language it details the political and economic factors that
caused immigrants to leave Europe, the conditions under which they traveled, and the difficulties they faced on their arrival. The writing is concise and
accessible to all but the youngest readers, while the photos give a human face
to the facts.

Kurelek, William. *They Sought a New World: The Story of European Immigration to North America.* Tundra, 1985. **Grade:** 4 to 8.

The illustrations and many of the comments in this picture book are provided by Kurelek, a child of immigrants who became a well-known painter in Canada. Part of the text gives the basic facts of immigration, while Kurelek's comments and paintings give emotional insight into the physical hardship and struggle of immigration. Though some of the paintings deal with sweatshops and industrial work, the most compelling come from Kurelek's own background in the Canadian prairie. One sees bewildered immigrants facing the sheer enormity of the Canadian wilderness and the labor involved in taming this empty land. Many of the paintings illustrate compelling personal narratives, but the stories of hardship and loss slowly give way to those of family meals, church gatherings, and holiday celebrations. Kurelek shows the success of independent businesses built by families working together and points out that most immigrants fulfilled their dream of a better life for their children.

PROJECT   Oral History—Learning About Your Immigrant Ancestors

The various aspects of this oral history project can be combined to help students learn about their families, the accomplishments of their ancestors, and to connect stories from the past to those of more recent immigrants. Though immigration is the most basic American experience, the responses to these exercises will be varied, and teachers will need to be conscious of a number of issues when planning this project and developing questions with their students. In addition to the sensitivities of adopted or foster children discussed in the introduction, one needs to be aware that the families of recent immigrants may be reluctant to discuss their status, and some children may not be comfortable being set apart as newcomers. African-American children, whose ancestors were forcibly removed from their homeland, may need to develop a special project, collecting the fragmentary records that exist of that experience from libraries and other sources. Children whose families immigrated long ago may have an equally difficult time finding enough information in the semi-legendary memories passed through many generations. An alternate for children with these situations could be an opportunity to interview a friend, a neighbor, or a willing older person whose memories are closer to the experience or neutral to the child's family situation.

Though the initial source of information will be direct family members, students can be encouraged to combine the memories of several generations to create as complete a picture as possible. Some families have a member who is particularly interested in family history, and that person can be a treasure trove of information and an enthusiastic assistant in the project.

Once an interview subject has been determined, students should do some basic research on the immigrant experience and then spend some time

SAMPLE ORAL HISTORY INTERVIEW QUESTIONS

What is your full name?

When and where were you born?

Tell me about your family.

How old were you when you came to this country?

Why did you or your family decide to leave your old home and come here?

How old were you when you came here?

Tell me what you can remember about the journey?
>How long did it take?
>How did you travel?
>Who came with you?

What did you bring with you when you came here?

What was hardest to leave behind?

What do you miss the most?

What can you remember about arriving here?
>Where did you arrive?
>How were you treated?

Was anyone here to help you when you came, and how did they help you?

Did you speak English when you came?

How did you learn to speak English? Who helped you?

Where did you live when you first came here?

How did you (or your parents) find a job?

Were you (or your parents) able to do the same kind of work you or they had done before?

What was the scariest or saddest thing about this experience?

What was the happiest thing about this experience?

developing a series of questions for their interviews. The children could work as a group to develop both basic questions and individual questions for the people they have chosen to interview. The books listed in Appendix 1 give a number of suggestions on the ways to structure and record an oral history interview. The exercises that follow can be used to structure the questions as well. Remind students to ask questions that call for full explanations, not simple "yes" or "no" answers. It is also important to be flexible. If one question leads to a wonderful story or a different response than you imagined, remember that the memories you are collecting are more important than the list of questions you have prepared.

Where Did I Come From?

For this project you will need a simple outline world map that shows national boundaries. You may also need to look at historic maps since the boundaries and names of some countries have changed. Talk to your parents and grandparents or any other family member who can tell you about your ancestors. When did your family first come to America? Which countries did they come from, and when?

As you gather information, begin to mark on the map all the places your family lived before they immigrated. If you are locating members from both your mother's and father's family, you may need to develop a color code to show all the different countries or different branches of the family. If that becomes too confusing, make a separate map for each family. Make the map locations as accurate as possible, though in many cases all that will be remembered is an ancestor's country of origin, not the city or region. As you ask questions and learn more, keep notes on *everything* you have learned.

Now that you know where your ancestors came from you can begin to find out about the countries they left. What does the country look like and how do the people live? What was happening in the country at the time your ancestors left? Many people immigrated because there were wars, lack of opportunity for their children, or religious persecution. What does your research tell you about the reasons your ancestors immigrated? If you lived in that country today, would you choose to immigrate as your ancestors did, or have conditions changed so that you would want to stay?

The Journey

As you talk to family members about their immigration experience, find out as much as you can about their actual journey to America. When did they come? Who came with them? How old were they? What did they choose to bring with them into their new life? What was left behind? Who was left behind?

Can you find out how they traveled? Many immigrants traveled long distances to get to ships and even longer distances after they arrived in America. Is there any record of your family's journey? If not, do some research to find out how people traveled during the time your ancestors traveled; try to determine the methods your immigrant ancestors might have used and how long their journey would have taken. How expensive was travel in those days? How long did it take them to save the money for the journey? Again, remember to make notes of any stories or memorable events that happened during the journey.

You can record and share the information you have gathered in a number of ways. You could write a research report about immigration, focusing on the experiences of immigrants from your ancestor's country. You could also write a fictional story about a journey to America using what you have learned about your ancestors and the times in which they lived. Incorporate some of the stories about your own family into this fictional account. Perhaps the story could be in the form of a fictional diary, written by your ancestor during the journey.

The Arrival

Levine, Ellen. *If Your Name Was Changed at Ellis Island.* Illustrated by Wayne Parmenter. Scholastic, 1993. **Grade:** 4 to 8.

Using a simple question-and-answer format, this book describes the experiences of millions of newcomers who passed through the immigration station at Ellis Island. The book describes the entire immigrant experience but focuses on the procedures and examinations that immigrants faced before they were admitted to the United States. Well-chosen details and quotes from children and adults along with colored paintings give a good picture of this experience and will help develop questions for oral history interviews and further research.

The book listed above details the experience shared by many immigrants upon their arrival in New York. Combined with other sources, it is a useful reference for information and questions about this part of the experience. Talk to your immigrant ancestors or another older person and find out where they arrived and what the experience was like. How did they feel at the end of the journey? How were they treated? Were they happy or disappointed by what they found?

After your ancestors were formally admitted to the country, where did they go and what did they do? Did they have friends and family to help them, or were they alone? What did they do to make a living? Was it different from what they had done in their home country? What problems did they encounter in the first weeks and months after they arrived? Did they feel welcome, or did they encounter prejudice? Did they speak English, and if not, how were they able to make themselves understood? When and how did they learn English?

Using what you have learned, write about your ancestors or another immigrant in the form of a fictional story or diary. Use your research about your ancestors and your imagination to tell the story of an immigrant's arrival into this country, how he or she felt, and some of the problems he or she may have had. Remember to include historic details so the reader will understand the time period you are writing about.

Cultural Heritage

When people immigrated they brought their culture with them. Although much of this history has been lost and intermingled with other experiences, surprising fragments remain within the family group. These projects will give you a chance to rediscover the culture of your ancestors and share it with others.

Recipes

Albyn, Carole Lisa, and Lois Sinaiko Webb. *The Multicultural Cookbook for Students.* Oryx Press, 1993. **Grade:** 5 to Adult.

Divided first by continent and then by country, this collection offers brief introductions of each continent or region and describes the foods and meals typical of each country. There are 337 recipes from 122 countries, with at least 2 recipes included for each country. This single volume provides an unusually complete introduction to the foods of many countries.

Cooking the [various countries] *Way.* (Easy Menu Ethnic Cookbooks). Lerner, [various dates]. **Grade:** 4 to Adult.

This series provides an introduction to each country and the role both the physical land and custom play in the choices of food. Typical menus are given, followed by recipes, including diagrams where necessary. Colorful photos will help entice readers to try the 20-plus recipes included in each book.

Food in [name of various countries]. (International Food Library). Rourke Publications Inc., [various dates]. **Grade:** 4 to Adult.

The emphasis in this series is on the ways history and regional differences have influenced the choice of foods in a variety of countries. There are also descriptions of specific customs and festivals and 10 to 15 recipes to prepare both festive and typical meals.

ACTIVITIES

1. Using the above books and series, learn about food and cooking in the countries of your ancestors. What foods are grown or produced in these countries? What are popular foods and what are special foods for holidays? Ask older members of your family what foods they remember as being particular family favorites. Do any of these come from your country of origin? Does someone in your family still prepare some of these dishes? If so, try to get the recipe or find a similar recipe in a cookbook. If it's not too complicated, try cooking it yourself. If it's too hard, try an easier recipe from one of your research books.
2. With others in your group or class, plan a potluck feast featuring food from your various countries of origin. Make a collection of all the recipes used in the feast along with notes on where each recipe came from. This collection of recipes and the other information you gathered might be combined in a book to be shared outside your class or group.

Music and Dance

Beginning Folk Dances Illustrated. Directed by Kevin McDonnell. Distributed by High/Scope Press, 600 N. River Road, Ypsilanti, MI 48198. **Video.**

This series of four videos is intended to be a visual learning and teaching tool for beginning-level folk dance. A variety of international folk dances are demonstrated by adults, teens, and children.

Carlin, Richard. *English and American Folk Music.* Facts on File, 1987. **Grade: 6 to Adult.**

This book traces how music traditions from the British Isles merged with those of other immigrants to create a number of distinctly American styles.

Dances of the World. Produced by Folk Dance Videos International. P.O. Box 470907, Charlotte, NC 28247. Distributed by Cambridge Career Products. 90 MacCorkel Ave., SW South Charleston, WV 25303. **Video.**

Each tape in this series features folk dance groups from a single country or region. Interspersed with the performances are commentaries by experts, describing the dance origins, costumes, and the history of each group of performers. Though the tapes are a bit too long and repetitive for classroom use, they are an excellent introduction to the folk dance traditions of a wide variety of countries. One of the series, *Folk Games*, features dance/games from a variety of countries for children and adults of all ages.

Silverman, Jerry. *African Roots.* Chelsea House Publishers, 1994. **Grade:** 5 to Adult.

This book includes 28 African songs with notes on the origin of each, brief information on the countries of origin, and photos of African performers.

Yurchenco, Henrietta. *A Fiesta of Folk Songs from Spain and Latin America.* Illustrated by Jules Maidoff. G. P. Putnam's Sons, 1967. **Grades:** 4 to Adult.

This collection of songs includes a brief explanation of the story or game, words in both English and Spanish, plus an extra line for ease of pronunciation.

ACTIVITIES

1. Using books and recordings, learn about the music from the countries of your ancestors. What instruments are played in these countries, and what kinds of music was and is popular? Ask family members what kinds of instruments and songs were common in their area. Using the library or other sources, find and listen to recordings of music from those countries. Are any of the songs familiar? Are they still sung in your family? Do you know anyone who plays the traditional instruments of the country? Perhaps they will let you make a recording of this music. Make notes on the information you find and compile a collection of personal and family favorites from the music you have found.

2. Does anyone in your family remember the traditional dances from their countries of origin? If possible, have family members or someone in your community show you how to do some of these dances. If you can't find someone to teach you personally, you can find videotapes of folk dancing and recordings with music and dance instructions in the library. Many communities have special festivals featuring music and dance from different parts of the world. Watch for opportunities to see live performances of traditional dances and learn these dances yourself.

3. With other members of your class or group, plan a music and dance festival featuring the songs and dances of the various immigrant groups in your community. You can perform the music and dances yourselves, find groups in the community to perform them, or have a mixture of both. As part of the festival, the group can prepare a written program, using the information you have learned about the music and dance of the countries of your ancestors.

Games Around the World

Millen, Nina. *Children's Games from Many Lands.* Illustrated by Allan Eitzen. Friendship Press, 1965. **Grade:** 5 to Adult.

This book includes brief descriptions and rules for games from every continent plus a special section on the regional games of North America.

Sierra, Judy and Robert Kaminski. *Children's Traditional Games: Games from 137 Countries and Cultures.* The Oryx Press, 1995. **Grade: 5 to Adult.**

This book contains descriptions of popular games from 130 countries and cultures, including over 20 games from native America.

Writer's Program of the Works Progress Administration in the State of New Mexico. *The Spanish-American Song and Game Book.* A. S. Barnes and Company, 1942. **Grade: 5 to Adult.**

Though this book is older than many titles, these songs and games were collected during a period when the Spanish culture was still very strong in New Mexico. The text includes rules, songs in both Spanish and English, and a division into three distinct age levels.

ACTIVITIES

1. Using the books listed above and others from your library, look for information on the games children played in the country of your ancestors. If possible, interview someone from that country, possibly someone in your own family. You can also find information in the library on children's games from many countries. What were the rules for playing these games? How many could play, and how were the players chosen? Are any of the games you play similar to games you play now? Compare notes with others in your group. Did you find that the same game is played in many countries with only slight differences?

2. Try playing some of these games with your friends. Decide which ones are the most fun and which are not so much fun today. Think about why some games are played in only one part of the world but others are popular everywhere. Vote on which are your favorites.

3. With others in your group, make a book about the games you found. For each game, list the number of players, the rules, and all the places the game is played. What special equipment is required? Can some games be played only in summer or winter? If so, tell why, and think of ways to adapt it to your situation.

Critical Thinking and Writing: Comparing Experiences

The experience of immigration is not one that existed only in the past. Every year thousands of people arrive in America seeking a new life. Some of these people may now be your friends, classmates, or neighbors. Which of their experiences do you think are the most like those of earlier immigrants, and which have changed?

Ashabranner, Brent, and Melissa Ashabranner. *Into a Strange Land: Unaccompanied Refugee Youth in America.* Dodd, Mean & Co., 1987. **Grade:** 5 to Adult.

Bode, Janet. *New Kids on the Block: Oral Histories of Immigrant Teens.* Franklin Watts, 1989. **Grade:** 5 to Adult.

Dawson, Mildred Leinweber. *Over Here It's Different: Carolina's Story.* Photographs by George Ancona. Macmillan Publishing Co., 1993. **Grade:** 5 to Adult.

The books listed above describe the experiences of present-day immigrants, focusing on the personal stories and experiences of young immigrants. Compare their stories with those of earlier immigrants you have read about or known. Make a list of all the things that are the same as those in the past and all the things that are different. Consider factors such as the reasons immigrants leave their own countries, the ways they travel, and their experiences when they arrive. Do you think it is easier or harder to be an immigrant today? Why?

ACTIVITY

Into a Strange Land is about children and teenagers who arrive in refugee camps with no parents or other adults to care for them. Compare their stories to those told in *Better Than a Princess* (see p. 6), and *Watch the Stars Come Out* (see p. 9). How are they the same, and how are they different? Imagine you are traveling alone to a new country. Write a story about what you would say, do, and feel if you were in that situation.

Fassler, David, and Kimberly Danforth. *Coming to America: The Kids' Book About Immigration.* Waterfront Books, 1993.

This book poses a list of brief questions which children have answered using simple words and drawings to describe their experience in adjusting to a new country and culture. The book is designed to be used interactively by parents, teachers, and counselors to help immigrant children be more comfortable when writing or talking about this experience. Because many of the experiences of moving, leaving loved ones behind, and adjusting to a new place will be shared by nonimmigrant children, the book can also be used to help nonimmigrant children understand their classmates.

ACTIVITY

After you have learned more about the stories and experiences of children you know, compare their experiences with those of past immigrants, starting with the ways they traveled, how they felt as they traveled, and what problems they had to solve when they got here. How are these stories the same, and how are they different? Do you think it is easier or harder to be an immigrant today?

CHAPTER 2

Opening the New Land: The Frontier Experience

The experience that defines and separates the history of the Americas from the more ancient and settled world is the relatively recent frontier and the pioneers who came from various circumstances to make the new frontier their home. There is a universal recognition that this experience was unique; that as the pioneers shaped the land to suit their needs, the struggle defined and shaped them as well. The mystical, heroic elements of this story are a staple of popular culture, not only here, but around the world. However, one does not have to look very hard at the legend to find, beneath it all, the actual families who made it happen.

Look at the fading photos and read the diaries and you find evidence of courage and hard work, combined with a great sense of adventure. They were looking for a better life, but there was no room on the frontier for the weak, the lazy, or those with short-term goals. Starting with the journey itself, this was an enterprise that required much and rewarded in surprising ways. Those who were children at the time have left surprisingly detailed accounts of this experience, including the daily chores that at first meant survival but ultimately made possible a rich and fulfilling life.

Children have always been interested in how things work and how they are made, and perhaps their attention was focused by hunger for the food that was prepared and anticipation of a new home and furnishings after weeks on the road. In any case, a common thread in these memoirs is that of exact description. One can learn how houses were built, how wells were dug, and how simple furniture was made with rough logs and hand tools. One reads mouth-watering descriptions of women preparing simple meals over fires and wood-burning stoves and preserving food for the long winter to come. One senses the real joy of a child attending school with classmates after months on a solitary homestead and the importance of the simplest recreations. These books give the history of the frontier a face and a meaning, allowing readers to participate in a world different from their own. For some children, these books can also link them to their own family history and grandparents who shared many of these pioneer experiences.

RECOMMENDED READING

Brink, Carol Ryrie. *Caddie Woodlawn.* Illustrated by Kate Seredy. Macmillan, 1935.

————. *Magical Melons: More Stories About Caddie Woodlawn.* Illustrated by Marguerite Davis. Macmillan, 1944.

Source of Material: Stories told by author's grandmother.

Location: Wisconsin.

Dates: 1863 to 1866.

Grade: 5 to 7.

Though their home is the frontier of Wisconsin in 1864, Caddie and her six brothers and sisters lead a comfortable life as the children of a prosperous miller. Mother and older sister Clara miss Boston, but Caddie and her brothers Tom and Warren love exploring the surrounding wilderness, making friends with the Indians, and testing the limits of every restriction. Though tomboy Caddie is the despair of her mother, her father is proud of the fact that letting her run wild with the boys has turned Caddie from a frail toddler into a healthy 11-year-old. His confidence in her gives her the courage to try new things and stand up to bullies. In one memorable chapter, Caddie warns her Indian friends of an impending attack. The book is filled with small daily events and adventures: a special valentine, a fight and a fire at the one-room school, the decision on spending a prized silver dollar, and several family storytelling sessions. A visit from a city-bred cousin leads her to disgrace and a new view of herself. Then an unexpected letter arrives, and the whole family must decide whether their future belongs in Wisconsin or aristocratic England.

While the drama of the situation and the setting give the story force and flow, one of its strong points is the characterization. Each member of the family has a distinct voice and personality, and it's clear how conflicts are created and resolved. Caddie in particular grows from a stubborn child into a maturity that allows her not only to see her mother's point of view, but to also recognize younger sister Hettie's loneliness and begin to include her in her adventures.

The pioneer setting is well developed and gives a good picture of a time in which farms were well established and people generally prosperous, but the wilderness was never far away. Both the fear of Indian massacre and the treatment of an Indian wife and her half-breed children show the prejudice and potential for conflict that marked the pioneer experience. This is an entertaining and believable account of pioneer life in the 1860s.

The sequel, *Magical Melons*, is a less structured group of individual stories and episodes about the Woodlawn family and their friends. Though it lacks the dynamic drive and dimension of the first book, the stories have humor and charm. Caddie seems older and more mature, though one story tells how she leads a battle against the school bullies armed with cattail swords that explode into clouds of fluff. There are stories about friends, including a whole chapter about one friend, Emma. Another chapter features the adventures of a pioneer circuit rider. Clara gets a beau, and Hetty finds a special friend. Like the earlier book, these stories grew from personal memories and have the feel of family stories, lovingly recalled and carefully crafted for young readers.

Harvey, Brett. *My Prairie Year: Based on the Diary of Elenore Plaisted.* Illustrated by Deborah Kogan Ray. Holiday House, 1986.

————. *My Prairie Christmas.* Illustrated by Deborah Kogan Ray. Holiday House, 1990.

Source of Material: Memories recorded in a notebook by the author's grandmother.

Location: Dakota Territory.

Date: 1889.

Grade: 3 to 6.

Both of these books are based on the vivid memories the adult Elenore Plaisted wrote for her daughter, the author's mother. *My Prairie Year* begins with simple descriptions of their house on the prairie, their arrival from Maine, and the day-to-day routines that marked the weeks for them. Much of the time is spent in housekeeping, laundry, mending, gardening, and preparing food. In the afternoons, the children sit in the shade and do the lessons Mother gives them, and on Sundays, Elenore is allowed to ride Dolly, the gentle horse bought for Mother, who never has time to ride. There are the great seasonal events: communal plowing, threshing with teams of workmen, and neighboring women preparing food. They survive several common crises: a fierce tornado, a prairie fire, numbing cold, and blizzards that lock them inside for days. Just when they think spring will never come, a box arrives filled with real fruit, books to read, and a package of paints and canvas for Mother. Mother sits right down to paint apple blossoms and blue skies, and though they are still homesick, they agree with Mother when one spring morning she tells them, "We are home."

As the author says, her grandmother's account was full of vivid images, beginning with the description of the house on the prairie. . . "like a white ship at sea." There are sensory descriptions of the way things looked or felt, especially the weather and simple joys of daily life. These are reinforced by Deborah Kogan Ray's simple, low-key drawings. The horizontal format and page layout reinforces the impression of immense space and sky that almost overwhelms the settlers. The family is generally depicted at a distance or with their faces turned away: busy, occupied, and somehow detached from the present. The drawings are realistic and frequently filled with the drama of the moment, yet softly impressionistic as well.

My Prairie Christmas focuses on the family's first Christmas on the prairie away from Maine and the familiar joys of a traditional celebration. Elenore worries about Christmas, but Mother has good ideas, and Papa has spotted some cedar trees just outside of Britton. The shiny ornaments were left behind in Maine, but Mama shows the two of them how to make dolls and animals from twisted corn husks and long chains of popcorn. Everyone is busy making simple but secret presents, and Mother has planned an Indian pudding to be made from cornmeal. Two days before Christmas, Papa leaves to get the tree, but a sudden storm comes up, and by suppertime he has not returned. Mother resolutely tells the usual Christmas story, and in the light of the next morning, takes the children out to cut a cottonwood sapling, which they decorate with the dolls, chains, and fine cottonwood silk. Just as they finish, Papa returns. He has no tree but has brought a Christmas barrel from home, filled with gifts, including a shiny star to top their prairie tree. As the happy day ends, Elenore and her parents go out into the snow to see the millions of stars in a sky so large it makes her shiver.

This sequel's illustrations are not only in color, but they also move closer to the family, showing much more detail and individuality than those of My Prairie Year. Though a few double spreads show the immensity of the prairie and the family's isolation, much of the story takes place in the house, and these illustrations are single page. The square format and depictions of the warmth of stove and candlelight give intimacy and immediacy to the story. Ray's picture of the mother and her three little children crossing an unmarked white plain and the vigorous way the mother chops at the cottonwood show the courage and determination of pioneer mothers. Throughout the book, the illustrations skillfully portray the warmth of the family.

Henry, Joanne Landers. *Log Cabin in the Woods: A True Story About a Pioneer Boy.* Illustrated by Joyce Audy Zarins. Four Winds Press, 1988.

Source of Material: *Log Cabin in the Woods* is a retelling of Oliver Johnson's boyhood reminiscences, which were collected by his grandson Howard Johnson and published in a book, *A Home in the Woods.*

Location: Central Indiana.

Date: 1832.

Grade: 3 to 6.

A month-by-month chronicle of a year with 11-year-old Ollie Johnson and the life he and his family lead in a log cabin, some four miles from the village of Indianapolis. The oldest in a family of three girls and four boys, Ollie spends much of his time helping his father tend the animals, plant crops, and clear the land for even more crops. The format gives a good picture of the variety of tasks required to maintain a family on the frontier and the high level of responsibility children were expected to take. In the course of the book, Ollie travels alone to the mill, helps tap the trees and boil the sap for maple syrup, helps clear and plow fields, and helps his father make new benches for the family table. Two chapters describe the way neighbors helped each other—all working together for one day to complete a major task—in this case, log rolling and cabin raising. The description of community cabin raising gives exact detail on how log cabins were built—from the shaped, notched logs to the shake shingles for the roof. It all happened in one day—with no nails. Though the point of view centers on male activities, Ollie's mother manages her share of the household in a brisk manner and is depicted preparing meals over an open fire, doctoring a broken arm with homegrown herbal remedies, making candles, and growing and preserving vegetables.

While the book is rich in details of daily life, the characters are never fully realized and the language tends to be stilted and static. There is little sense of being inside the experience; rather, it is a look back with the uncritical eye of nostalgia.

Much of the story is conveyed by the black-and-white illustrations, starting with a map that locates the Johnson farm in relation to the landscape of forest, streams, and other farms. The items and activities described in the text are clearly illustrated in the pictures that appear on every double-page. One sees the stacked rail fences zig zagged over the country, the working of a mill, plows, guns, cooking utensils, and the manufacture of entire houses and furnishings using simple tools and materials at hand. Like the text, the characters are generic but their daily activities are clearly and accurately rendered.

Keith, Harold. *The Obstinate Land.* T. Y. Crowell, 1977.

Source of Material: Based on the experiences of the author's grandparents and extensive research in historic archives.

Location: Oklahoma Territory.

Dates: 1893 to 1896.

Grade: 6 to 9.

The Romberg family leaves Texas to try their chances in the Oklahoma land run of 1893. Frederic, a German immigrant, is an experienced farmer. He wants his own farm, despite opposition from the ranchers who want to keep the range open and the difficulties of the land itself. He has already picked his spot, but when the Rombergs arrive, another family, the Coopers, has reached it first, settling early and illegally on the land. With no law enforcement available, they are forced to choose a less favorable spot. They ignore the Cooper family and a hostile rancher but become close friends with the Pattersons, sharing work and helping each other. The early chapters detail the backbreaking labor of building a sod dugout, plowing and planting, and struggling to find fuel and water, scarce commodities in the area. They improvise, save, and start over again when the weather destroys their crops. Despite an earlier animosity, they share fuel with the Cooper family, and the Coopers' eldest daughter Mattie repays them with her skills as a "doctor."

Then Frederic is caught in a sudden winter storm and dies of pneumonia, leaving eldest son Fritz to fulfill his dream. Though disaster looms at every turn, 14-year-old Fritz is not only a hard worker, he is also willing to sacrifice and take risks for the sake of his family's future. He turns orphan calves into a small herd, acquires a choice piece of property, and convinces a banker to back him in developing it with windmills (a new technology) and strong fences. When he wins over a neighboring rancher who has tried repeatedly to drive him out, it becomes clear that the future will belong to Fritz and people like him who have proved to be as obstinate as the land.

The story is told from Fritz's point of view. The family, while realistic, is a bit larger than life. One of the strong points is the depiction of homestead life and the endless tasks involved, but there is enough action and conflict to keep the story moving. Much of this is centered on the tension between homesteading farmers and ranchers who were forced to give up free range to them. This is most keenly felt in the character of Yoakum, a cowboy who befriends and surreptitiously helps the family but becomes an outlaw rather than accept the Romberg's tamer life. There is also a strong sense of the locality, the town, and the social life, including a cowboy shindig and a box supper. As the story ends, 16-year-old Fritz is thinking of marriage and finds himself making a surprising choice.

Kinsey-Warnock, Natalie, and Helen Kinsey. *The Bear That Heard Crying.* Illustrated by Ted Rand. Cobblehill Books/Dutton, 1993.

Source of Material: Story about an ancestor of the author.

Location: Warren, New Hampshire.

Date: 1783.

Grade: 2 to 5.

This unusual story was found when Helen Kinsey was doing genealogical research and found the story of an early ancestor who had been lost in the woods, protected by a bear, and found through a dream. Three-year-old Sarah Whitcher is lost in the woods in June 1783, and after wandering all day she meets a "big black dog" who licks her face and feet and lets her sleep on his shoulder. In the meantime, her parents realize Sarah is missing, and all the settlers for miles around leave their work to join in the search for the child. When searchers find her footprints next to the tracks of a bear, they give her up for lost, but Mama begs them to try just one more day. The next day a man named Mr. Heath arrives and says he saw the child in a dream and a bear was guarding her. The searchers lead him to the place he described, and they find Sarah, sleeping under a pine tree. There are bear tracks all around her, and she tells them all about the "big black dog" who stayed with her every night. When Sarah is brought home, Mama faints at the news, Papa holds her tight, and everyone joins in a joyous feast of celebration.

The tension and joy of this story is dramatically reinforced by Ted Rand's luminous watercolor paintings. The title page features a full-page portrait of the bear, standing and sniffing the air. Rand then moves to the family and the tiny lost girl walking through the forest, happily unaware of the dangers around her. She greets the bear with joy, and a double-page spread shows the two of them peacefully asleep. The pictures then cut to the search and show clearly the dense forest, the frantic anxiety of the settlers, and the dynamic joy that greets the returning child. A final small picture shows the bear wandering away alone, unaware of the drama. The crisp storytelling and large-scale illustrations make this an ideal story to share with groups as well as individuals.

Knight, Amelia Stewart. *The Way West: Journal of a Pioneer Woman.* Adapted with an introduction by Lillian Schissel. Pictures by Michael McCurdy. Simon & Schuster, 1993.

Source of Material: Amelia Stewart Knight's diary of the journey.

Locations: Iowa to Oregon on the Oregon Trail.

Date: 1853.

Grade: 2 to 5.

This richly illustrated picture book excerpts the diary entries of a pioneer woman, Amelia, to show the difficulties and dangers of overland emigration to Oregon. The journey described in this journal begins in the rain of early April and ends in September. The brief, almost shorthand entries tell of sickness, bad weather, crowded trails, dangerous river crossings, and assorted encounters with Indians. One son falls from the wagon, and in a later entry, he is nearly run over. A young daughter is left behind and retrieved by a following train. Near the end of the journal, Amelia casually mentions the birth of her eighth child.

This dramatic but low-key account is illustrated with colored scratchboard drawings that add details and dimension. They clearly show the heavily loaded wagons, stolid oxen, and busy family (who appear more vigorous than attractive in these pictures). The physical difficulties of crossing rivers, climbing

steep mountains, and surviving fierce storms is expressed through the drawings' angular tension and their depictions of the straining bodies and faces of
the pioneers. The scratchboard technique reinforces the crisp vigor of the text.
There are also moments of tenderness and peace, and the final pictures show
the joyous family running toward their new home, "a small log cabin and lean-
to with no windows."

MacLachlan, Patricia. *Sarah, Plain and Tall.* Harper & Row, 1985.

    Source of Material: Based on a true event in the author's family history.

    Location: North Dakota.

    Dates: Early 1900s.

    Grade: 3 to Adult.

In quiet, stately language, MacLachlan tells the story of two prairie children
and the emptiness left when their mother dies. Sarah is the tall, plain woman
who answers their father's advertisement for a wife and mother. They first
meet her through a series of letters that reveal not just information but each
writer's hopes and fears. Sarah finally agrees to come for one month, "just to
see." She arrives in the spring, looking as she has described herself, plain and
tall, wearing a yellow bonnet and bringing a cat named Seal. Gradually,
eagerly, they come to love her; but Sarah is from a different kind of place and
the children watch her, knowing that she misses something they cannot give
her. The book is a series of moments captured as the weeks go by: Neighbors
come with gifts, Sarah teaches the children to swim in the cow pond, and she
cuts their hair, scattering the curls for the birds. They sing, draw pictures, and
survive a sudden squall. Sarah learns to ride, drive a team, and demonstrate
both her independence and her skills as a carpenter. Then she goes to town by
herself, and the children wait and think of all the reasons she could decide to
leave. The day drags on and at last she returns, with candles and seeds and
colors for her pictures of the sea. She will stay and they will be a family.

    Much of the power of this story lies in the way the reader is allowed to
discover the isolation and quiet of the prairie. Also powerfully conveyed are
Anna and Caleb's loneliness, Sarah's affection and fierce determination to
remain herself, and the way these elements work together to create a quietly
powerful conclusion.

Russell, Marion. *Along the Santa Fe Trail: Marion Russell's Own Story.* Adapted
by Ginger Wadsworth. Illustrated by James Watling. Whitman, 1993.

    Source of Material: Memoirs collected by Marion Russell's daughter-in-law
and published as *Land of Enchantment: Memoirs of Marion Russell Along the
Santa Fe Trail.* This story was adapted from that text.

    Locations: Independence, Missouri, to Albuquerque, New Mexico.

Date: 1852.

Grade: 2 to 6.

Marion Russell is seven years old when she and her mother and brother set out from Kansas to try their luck in California. Mother earns their passage part of the way cooking for two army officers, and they join a large wagon train following the Santa Fe Trail west. They soon became accustomed to the daily routine of travel, but there are always new wonders to be seen: huge herds of buffalo, endless miles of prairie grass and wildflowers, sunsets of unbelievable beauty, and fierce storms that briefly halt the train . At night, the 500 wagons are parked in two great circles with the mules inside and the space in-between a no-man's-land, which the children use as a playground. Though the coyote's eerie cry frightens her at night, Marion learns to bravely stamp at tarantula spiders, daring them to come out of their holes. After two months of travel, there are several days of rest and trading at Fort Union in New Mexico and in the old adobe city of Santa Fe, where their driver leaves them one evening to go to a *baile* (a dance). In Albuquerque their plans are shattered: mother's money has disappeared and they must leave the train. They rent a small house and begin to take in borders, bringing to an end the first of many trips on the Santa Fe Trail.

A double-page map clearly shows the route the travelers followed, and the text is enhanced by detailed watercolors that accurately depict the daily life and natural beauty of the wilderness. In several paintings, the horizontal format of the book is used effectively to show the sweep of the prairie. There is a strong sense of realism in the pictures of the wagon train; the crowded activity of the travelers and settlers is in marked contrast to the serene landscape through which they pass. Though the author does discuss the hardships of the trail, what dominates here is her sense of joy and discovery, feelings that would lead her to take many more trips on the Santa Fe Trail.

Scott, Lynn H. *The Covered Wagon and Other Adventures.* University of Nebraska Press, 1993.

> **Source of Material:** The stories and sketches were originally created by the author as an informal family memoir.
>
> **Locations:** Nebraska to Thermopolis, Wyoming; Medford, Oregon.
>
> **Dates:** 1906 to 1910.
>
> **Grade:** 6 to Adult.

What an extraordinary person Lynn Scott's father must have been. A small man, missing one arm, crippled in one leg, and suffering from chronic asthma, he describes himself as half a man, but thinks nothing of loading his entire family into a couple of wagons and setting off to a new place. He is seeking new opportunities, a better climate for his asthma, and a cure for son Don's crippling rheumatism. Lynn Scott, the book's author and illustrator, is the youngest son. He describes two of the journeys the family made. The first section, "A Trip to Thermopolis," describes a 600-hundred-mile journey from Nebraska to Thermopolis, Wyoming, where there is a hot spring. Traveling in two wagons are Pa, Ma, sister Beck, and the four youngest boys. Scott casually describes the details of traveling by wagon, hunting as you go, and cooking over a camp stove. On arrival, they camp for a while. The kids entertain themselves with various games and mischief, while Pa and Don try the hot spring. Ma gets Rocky Mountain Spotted Fever and nearly dies. Once she recovers, they start back to Nebraska, where Pa buys a ranch with a log house and pasture land. There they spend the winter getting things in shape while Pa buys and breaks in a herd of horses. Then they start off again, back to the "home place," taking the herd with them.

At the beginning of the second section, "McKee's Mill," Pa sells off their horses and they take off again, this time by emigrant train, for Medford, Oregon. They camp near a river while Pa searches for a new place. He settles on 280 acres of timber and some old buildings called McKee's Mill, which the owners are happy to sell. It comes complete with everything but clothes and blankets. Here they do well, but Pa's health is not improving, so he sets off again. At the end of the book they get a letter from him: he has traded the farm for a house and one acre in Pamona, California, and they are to pack their clothes and bedding and join him there.

Much of the charm of these accounts lies in Scott's portrayal of a warm and likable family. While Pa is clearly the boss, Ma is resourceful and cheerfully accepts the challenge of Pa's frequent moves. Together they fend off Indians (who are convinced sister Beck is one of them), potential horse thieves, and neighbors who mistake Pa for an eastern greenhorn who can be intimidated. The author's drawings are surprisingly accurate despite their primitive quality. The writing is vivid and humorous, capturing the language and life style of an unusual frontier family.

Strait, Treva Adams. *The Price of Free Land.* J. B. Lippincott, 1979.

Source of Material: Based on author's memories of the three years during which her parents complied with the terms of a government offer for free land.

Location: Western Nebraska.

Dates: 1914 to 1917.

Grade: 4 to 7.

Treva Adams was five years old when her parents selected the 160 acres of land they would claim and live on for three years, making the improvements the government required as the price of free land. First her father has to "race" for the land, driving his stakes next to each of the four designated corner markers. They have to live on the claim, and the first winter is spent in a strong tent, though one of the first improvements is a storm cellar that enables them to survive a tornado. There are numerous details of daily life: hauling water, boiling clothes with homemade soap, and gleaning and hauling potatoes for the first winter. Gradually they acquire the makings of a real farm: a walking plow, a wagon, and two horses. Mama's birthday present is a roll of linoleum to replace the burlap sacks on the dirt floor. Summer brings a huge garden and a new barn, and in the fall, Treva joins her brother on the two-and-one-half-mile walk to school. As winter approaches, Papa begins work on a sod house. The whole process is described, from plowing the slabs of sod to the day when friends come to help put on the roof. It is Mama who discovers how to turn sod into plaster and papers the finished walls with striped wallpaper.

Strait, as a child, must have been quite observant of the work going on around her, and consequently, her descriptions are clearly detailed. She also tells of her own child life—going to school, the way her wet curls froze in winter, playing with her younger sister, and the birth of a new baby sister. This is a fairly straightforward account of homestead life. The author relates the events as they happened with little sense of emotion. While the picture of the work involved is clear, there is little sense of individuality or feeling to draw readers inside the story. Illustrations are minimal: family photos and catalog prints of items described in the story: a base burner, a walking plow, and a farm wagon.

Van Leeuwen, Jean. *Bound for Oregon.* Illustrated by James Watling. Dial, 1994.

Source of Material: Mary Ellen Todd's daughter, Adrietta Applegate Hixon, wrote down her mother's stories, and after her death they were published in her book, *On to Oregon! A True Story of a Young Girl's Journey Into the West.*

Locations: Arkansas to Oregon on the Oregon Trail.

Date: 1852.

Grade: 5 to 8.

In the spring of 1852, nine-year-old Mary Ellen Todd sets off with her family to make the long journey to the Oregon Territory. Though warned of the dangers ahead, her father is convinced that a family that is careful and well prepared can safely make the journey. Mary is the eldest of three girls, and they are joined by John, a local boy who works for their father. Though they are well prepared, they have their share of difficulties. There are dangerous river crossings; shortages of food, fuel, and water; and they are attacked by Indians.

Some emigrants get discouraged and leave the wagon train, while others decide to move faster or try a different route. Mary makes friends only to see them leave when her father slows down to spare his oxen for the end of the journey. Cholera sweeps through the emigrant trains, and Mary Ellen's younger sister nearly dies. The children of another family are orphaned by fever and taken in by a widow. On one dreadful day, only Mary and John are well enough to keep their wagon moving. Toward the end of the journey, Mother gives birth to a son, Elijah, and Mary is proud that she helps drive him over the last mountains into the rich valleys of Oregon. They have made it through. Father is able to rent 40 acres with a cabin, and they have time to plant a crop for spring. The end of the book finds the family celebrating their first Christmas in Oregon, thinking of all the others who made the journey and feeling grateful that they made the journey safely.

This book is based on stories the real Mary Ellen told her children and is told from her point of view. The author has enhanced the story by adding feelings about her stepmother and loving grandmother left behind and enriched the account with details from her own research. While more polished than direct firsthand accounts, the book effectively conveys the dangers and physical difficulty of the journey from a child's point of view. The book is illustrated with a handful of black-and-white paintings that show highlights of the journey and define this particular family.

Wilder, Laura Ingalls. *Little House in the Big Woods.* Revised edition, illustrated by Garth Williams. Harper & Row, 1953.

————. *Little House on the Prairie.* Revised edition, illustrated by Garth Williams. Harper & Row, 1953.

————. *On the Banks of Plum Creek.* Revised edition, illustrated by Garth Williams. Harper & Row, 1953.

————. *By the Shores of Silver Lake.* Revised edition, illustrated by Garth Williams. Harper & Row, 1953.

————. *The Long Winter.* Revised edition, illustrated by Garth Williams. Harper & Row, 1953.

————. *Little Town on the Prairie.* Revised edition, illlustrated by Garth Williams. Harper & Row, 1953.

————. *These Happy Golden Years.* Revised edition, illustrated by Garth Williams. Harper & Row, 1953.

————. *The First Four Years*. Illustrated by Garth Williams. Harper & Row, 1971.

Source of Material: Author's childhood memories.

Locations: Wisconsin; Kansas; Minnesota; and Dakota Territories.

Dates: 1870 to 1889.

Grade: 4 to 8 (varies as the series progresses).

This series is it—the grandmother of them all—a near-perfect combination of memory, clean prose, and illustrations that combine historic accuracy with full character definition. Originally published during the 1930s and reissued in 1953 as a uniform series illustrated by Garth Williams, these books tell the story of Laura Ingalls's childhood and her family's travels from Wisconsin through Kansas, Minnesota, and finally into the Dakota Territory where she met and married Almanzo Wilder. The last volume, *The First Four Years,* traces the early years of her marriage before she moved for the last time to Missouri. Laura's wandering childhood and her vivid recall of daily events combine to paint a picture of the full range of the pioneer experience. She watches her father build houses, dig wells, and plant crops while her mother prepares meals over campfires and iron stoves. There is much adversity: one house has to be abandoned because it is built on disputed territory; grasshoppers devour a much-needed crop; scarlet fever leaves her older sister blind; and the family nearly starves one blizzard-filled winter. However, they are a loving family and find joy in simple things: Pa's fiddle, the good food her mother cooks from minimal ingredients, and the sense of peace in each new dwelling when Pa puts up the handcarved bracket and Ma brings out the china shepherdess, indicating that they are once again "home."

The books are notable for their character development and precise descriptions of each aspect of pioneer life. Neighbors are portrayed in short but vivid descriptions, reflecting Laura's impressions. Child readers share her delight with Mr. Edward's bouyant generosity and her antipathy toward Nellie Oleson. While Ma and Pa are somewhat idealized, their personalities come through, particularly their love for each other and a shared strength that sustains the family. Above all, Laura is honest about her own feelings; the wicked ones that boil up inside her as well as the joyful ones that make her eyes shine. This honesty and the simplicity of the prose invite young readers in and make this series universally loved.

Garth Williams's illustrations are the result of 10 years of research in which he followed the path of the Ingalls family and learned about all aspects of their life, including how the houses looked, how household tools and utensils were used, and the changing landscape. The black-and-white drawings throughout the series are not only historically correct, but express great empathy for the characters, the range of the physical experience, and the quiet joys the Ingalls found as a family. The drawings connect seamlessly with the text, providing visual reinforcement for each aspect of the stories.

Williams, David. *Grandma Essie's Covered Wagon.* Illustrated by Wiktor Sadowski. Alfred A. Knopf, 1993.

Source of Material: The author spent a week capturing his grandmother's memories, which he then shaped and arranged for this book.

Location: Missouri; Kansas; Oklahoma.

Dates: Early 1900s.

Grade: 2 to 6.

This picture book recalls the wanderings of a family as they move from place to place, seeking a better life. As the book begins, Essie is one of six children living in a two-room log cabin in Missouri. Their father, who works as a hired man, dreams of something more. He saves his money and moves the family west to raise wheat in Kansas. They travel in an improvised but comfortable covered wagon and are kept cheerful at night by sister Stella's mandolin. The new farm has an orchard and a red two-story house so big "we thought it was a castle." There are fierce winds, new animals, friends at the schoolhouse, a happy Christmas with handmade toys, and a new baby born to her sister Opal. But the next summer brings a disastrous drought, and Papa has to sell the farm. They move on, and after a brief sojourn with Mama's folks in Oklahoma, they try their luck in the Oklahoma oil fields. There are no houses available, so they camp in a tent in the workers' shantytown. Papa and the men work all day, and Stella plays her mandolin on the streets, helping the Salvation Army raise money for orphanages. She plans to marry a Salvation Army captain, but the cold air has made her ill, and though the family prays for her, holds her hand, and tells her stories, nothing makes her better. After Stella's death, Essie goes to work as a waitress, carrying trays of food with shaking hands and bringing home tips. After a year they have saved enough to move again, back to Missouri and a new farm—not as nice as the place in Kansas, but a real home once again. Papa breaks up the old covered wagon, turning it into furniture, and Essie's wandering days are over.

The story is illustrated with full-color paintings, primarily in shades of golden tan, gray, and blue. Double-page spreads effectively show the empty sweep of the plains, and single pages show the more intimate scenes of family and community life. All seem rather distant, and the family are generally seen as stiff, rather generic figures, though Essie can be recognized by her fair, straight hair. Though well researched, the paintings are impressionistic rather than detailed and give the sense of events seen through the eye of memory rather than specific, immediate reality. This is a good example of the kind of memoir that can be collected from older family members who vividly remember events from their childhood.

Wisler, G. Clifton. *Jericho's Journey.* Lodestar Books, 1993.

Source of Material: Diary of John English Deatherage, great-great-grandfather of a family friend, combined with other research.

Locations: Tennessee to Texas.

Date: 1852.

Grade: 5 to 7.

Pa has been talking about Texas as long as 12-year-old Jericho can remember, feeding his dreams with letters from Uncle Dan who joined the fight against Mexico as a teenager and stayed to farm the rich, black prairie lands. Though Grandpa Fitch warns against the move, Pa worries about a future for his four sons, and when Uncle Dan finds a farm for sale, decides to give Texas a try. They are joined by Eli, a 20-year-old who is returning to Texas and agrees to guide them and share expenses. Because they must harvest and sell their last crop, the journey begins in October, a bad time to travel, as frequent storms and winter are on the way. Pa and Ma and sister Jane Mary ride in the wagon and older brother Jake rides Pa's mare, but Jericho and his younger brothers Josh and Jordy walk alongside with Sandy the dog. At night all the boys bed down on the ground, wrapped in blankets and huddled together for warmth. The journey begins easily, but soon the rains come and the boys spend days slogging through the mud and nights shivering under wet blankets. As they travel west, they are forced to pay increasingly higher tolls for roads that are often little more than tracks through the wilderness. However, some settlers are kind, letting them shelter in barns or houses. On the road, they meet fellow Texas-bound travelers, and they take turns helping to pull each other out of the mud. The hardest parts for Jericho are the bridges, high rickety contraptions that terrify him and brother Jordy. He begins to think he is a coward, until he risks his life saving his dog from an oncoming train.

As they travel, the boys have various adventures: hunting, exploring a cave, and swapping tales with fellow travelers. They find an abandoned fiddle, which Jericho teaches himself to play. They reach Texas by November but are caught in a snowstorm that literally freezes Jordy's feet together and forces them back to the nearest town and generous shelter. They continue on through snow and mud, helped by settlers who recall their own days on the trail and share their warm houses. They finally make it, finding a house with four rooms, two fireplaces, a coop full of chickens, a sty with three pigs, a small barn, and a corral. There are beds with straw mattresses and a real table and chairs. As the story ends, Jericho feels "the wonderful sense of belonging that came with a journey's end—and a new home."

SPECIAL PROJECTS AND ENRICHMENT ACTIVITIES

The projects included in this chapter are designed to give students hands-on experience with a variety of the tasks and skills employed by pioneer families in their daily life. Using basic tools and the materials at hand, these resourceful men and women built simple homes and gradually added comfort and simple decoration. For the most part, the activities in this section would be those done by pioneer children as they learned these skills from their parents.

Pioneer Crafts

Caney, Steven. *Steven Caney's Kids' America.* Workman Publishing, 1978. **Grade:** 3 to Adult.

This book is a treasure trove of information and projects on all aspects of American life from past to present. Though organized by subject, not dates, pioneer crafts and projects can be found throughout the book.

D'Amato, Jane, and Alex D'Amato. *Colonial Crafts For You To Make.* Julian Messner, 1975. **Grade:** 5 to Adult.

The combination of clear instructions and easily read diagrams makes this a rich and accessible resource for making replicas of a wide variety of pioneer crafts, including furnishing a model room, weaving, quilting, toys, and decorative crafts.

Hoople, Cheryl G. *Heritage Sampler: A Book of Colonial Arts & Crafts.* Pictures and diagrams by Richard Cuffari. Dial Press, 1975. **Grade:** 5 to Adult.

This attractive book gives both historic background and clear instructions for a wide variety of household crafts, including simple cooking, sewing, weaving, candlemaking, and toymaking. The decorative crafts include embroidery, paper cutting, and holiday decorations.

Quilts and Quilt Making

The patchwork or pieced quilt was born from two facts of frontier life: fabrics of all kinds were expensive and scarce, and pioneer women needed to keep their families warm. These creative, tireless women saved scraps of fabric, then cut them into geometric shapes and sewed them together in a variety of striking patterns. The decorative top was stitched to a plain backing with a layer of fill in between, and the end result was a warm and beautiful bed cover. Many of these quilts are cherished family heirlooms, and enthusiastic quilters continue to create striking and beautiful designs for their homes.

ABC Quilts. *Kids Making Quilts for Kids: A Young Person's Guide to Having Fun While Helping Others and Learning About AIDS and Substance Abuse.* Quilt Digest Press, 1992. **Grade:** 4 to 8.

Bogen Constance. *A Beginner's Book of Patchwork, Appliqué, and Quilting.* Dodd, Mead & Co., 1974. **Grade:** 5 to Adult.

Ratner, Marilyn. *Plenty of Patches: An Introduction to Patchwork, Quilting and Appliqué.* Illustrated by Chris Conover. Thomas Y. Crowell, 1978. **Grade:** 5 to Adult.

Each of the books listed above gives an introduction to quilting and basic techniques. Starting with the instructions for a simple nine-patch square, they also show how to create appliqué patterns and special stitches and discuss a number of possible projects for novice quilters.

ACTIVITIES

1. Because making and collecting quilts continues to be popular, it is easy to find pictures of quilt patterns in books and magazines. Collect pictures of some of your favorites and look at them carefully. Can you see how the patterns work together and how they have been assembled? Using graph paper, design a quilt pattern of your own. Keep in mind the kinds of patterns you have found you like, the colors used, and the way contrast is used to create pattern. To see how the finished quilt would look, cut the pieces of the pattern from printed paper. Remember, you will want to use small patterns or stripes—wrapping paper or small-scale wallpaper patterns work well for this. Experiment with different combinations of pattern and color. When you are happy with the result, glue the pieces down and then create a border for your finished "quilt."

2. Quilts were usually sewn one block at a time, and the blocks were combined to create a variety of finished patterns. Young girls learned to sew by joining the patches for simple block patterns such as "nine-patch" or "simplicity." Select a simple pattern and try sewing a block yourself, following the directions in the books listed above or any other book on basic quilting. You can use the finished block to make a pillow or decorative simple bag or shirt. As a class project, you could join everyone's patches together to make one large quilt. You might want to complete the quilt and donate it to ABC Quilts, an organization that distributes small quilts to babies and children born with the AIDS virus or birth defects caused by alcohol and drugs. *Kids Making Quilts for Kids*, listed above, tells about this project and gives ideas for simple quilts.

Quilts Reflect the Life Around You

Paul, Ann Whitford. *Eight Hands Round: A Patchwork Alphabet.* Illustrated by Jeanette Winter. HarperCollins, 1991. **Grade:** 3 to 6.

In *Eight Hands Round,* Ann Paul has created an alphabet book showing both a variety of patchwork patterns and the ways the patterns were related to daily life. The shapes and patterns pioneer women cut and assembled would remind them of something in their own life or something they had seen, and they would name the pattern for that thing. Some names describe the shape of the finished pattern, such as Star of Bethlehem, Sunburst, Tumbling Blocks, or Mariner's Compass. Some tell about the life of the people: Delectable Mountains, Straight Furrow, Kansas Troubles, Log Cabin. Some, like Wild Geese Flying or Sun Flower, evoke the natural world of field and forest.

ACTIVITIES

1. As you learn about quilts, write down some of the pattern names and see how the same pattern can look using different fabrics and colors. Sometimes the same pattern will have several names. Copy some favorite patterns along with their names.
2. Design a quilt that represents something in your life. Like pioneer quilters, you can find inspiration in buildings, streets, signs, or the motion of your daily activities. Create a name for your quilt pattern, and explain what the name means to you.

Quilts Tell Stories

Bolton, Janet. *My Grandmother's Patchwork Quilt.* Doubleday, 1993/1994. **Grade:** K to 2.

Coerr, Eleanor. *The Josefina Story Quilt.* Pictures by Bruce Degen. Harper & Row, 1986. **Grade:** 1 to 3.

Lyons, Mary E. *Stitching Stars: The Story Quilts of Harriet Powers.* Charles Scribner's Sons, 1993. **Grade:** 5 to Adult.

Turner, Ann. *Sewing Quilts.* Illustrated by Thomas B. Allen. Macmillan, 1994. **Grade:** 1 to 3.

Each of the books above is about the ways quilts can be used to tell stories. *My Grandmother's Patchwork Quilt* shows how appliquéd pictures recall the grandmother's childhood on a farm, while the patches in *The Josefina Story Quilt* were sewn in a covered wagon as the family traveled west. *Sewing Quilts* shows a frontier mother and her daughters using quilts to capture memories.

Robbing Peter to Pay Paul

Swing in the Center

Old Maid's Puzzle

Octagonal Star

Nine Patch

Drunkard's Path

Hen and Chickens

Odd Fellow's Cross

Goose Tracks

Flying Geese

Pierced Star

Log Cabin

SAMPLE OF QUILT PATTERNS

FIGURE 1

Stitching Stars tells how Harriet Powers, a woman born into slavery and a life of hard times, used her skills as a needle woman with an artist's vision to create two extraordinary story quilts.

Appliqué quilts are created by sewing small pieces of fabric to a larger background. In each of the books listed above, appliqué was used to create a story quilt. The quiltmaker used the technique to make simple pictures that tell a story. Sometimes the fabrics used are a part of the story of memories that inspired the quilt. Appliqué is also often used to make friendship quilts—quilts in which each person makes a block designed to commemorate a special memory or favorite thing. All the blocks are then sewn into one quilt and given as a gift on a special occasion. An example of a friendship quilt is the AIDS memorial quilt, in which the friends and family of a person who has died of AIDS create a large quilt block commemorating that person's life. The finished quilt is used to educate people about AIDS and its impact on individuals.

ACTIVITY

Make a quilt block about your life or the life of a family member. You can use fabrics that remind you of a person or event, or you can create designs that picture a favorite thing. You can combine these quilt blocks into a single friendship quilt or make them into a pillow or wall hanging. Design or create an entire story quilt around a specific story or theme. Remember you can use printed or plain fabrics. What story are you telling in the quilt? How do the individual pictures or characters fit into that story? Write about your quilt and the story it tells.

Pioneer Games and Toys

Schnacke, Dick. *American Folk Toys: 85 American Folk Toys and How to Make Them.* Putnam, 1973. **Grade: 5 to Adult.**

Children on the frontier had few opportunities to visit stores, and their parents had little cash to buy manufactured goods. For this reason, the few toys that pioneer children had were made at home from materials that could easily be obtained. Parents made toys for little children, but older children leaned to sew and whittle and often made toys for themselves. These homemade toys were precious possessions and are vividly described in many pioneers' memoirs. The directions to make many of these simple toys have been assembled in Dick Schnacke's book, *American Folk Toys,* which is especially strong in showing a variety of wooden toys.

ACTIVITIES

1. In pioneer homes, dolls were made from whatever materials were available—scraps of fabric, natural materials, and carved bits of wood. A favorite material was corn, and almost every part of this common crop was used to make some kind of doll. The cornstalk and corncobs made

the bodies of dolls and animals, the husks could be tied and folded in a variety of ways, and the silk was used for hair. Most books on pioneer crafts include directions for corn husk crafts. Cornstalks and husks can be found in farmer's markets in the fall, and the husks are available year-round in craft supply stores and selected grocery stores. See how many different kinds of dolls and animals you can make from corn. For directions, see *Heritage Sampler* (see p. 42), pp. 107–111, or *American Folk Toys*, pp. 130–141.

2. Rag dolls can be made from remnants of fabrics and stockings. The style and degree of difficulty is infinitely varied, and directions can be found in a number of sources. Choosing a style that best suits your sewing skills, make a fabric doll and dress it in simple, frontier-style clothing. Directions for a very simple doll can be found in *Heritage Sampler* (see p. 42), pp. 101–103, and rag and sock dolls in *American Folk Toys*, pp. 142–147.

3. Charming and often surprising dolls can be made with apples. The apple is peeled and carved with exaggerated features, then left to dry. Wrinkles occur naturally, and the dried head can be attached to a wire body and dressed to match the character. For directions, see *Heritage Sampler* (see p. 42), pp.103–107, or *American Folk Toys*, pp. 136–137. Other natural materials that can be used for doll's heads are gourds and nuts.

4. Another popular material for toys was wood, which was carved to make a variety of dolls and whirligigs. Sometimes carved wood was used for the heads of cloth dolls, but bodies could also be carved of wood. A skilled woodcarver could even make hinged joints and moveable arms and legs. These dolls were then clothed from scraps of material. Simple wooden dolls can be made from old-fashioned, one-piece clothespins, especially those with rounded tops, for heads. If you can't find this kind in your local hardware store, try craft supply stores which have both the clothespins and directions for using them in craft projects. Directions to make these dolls can also be found in *American Folk Toys*, pp. 148–151.

Frontier Cooking

Frontier life presented a special challenge to cooks. During the actual trip to a new home, pioneers were restricted to the foods they could carry with them and whatever game could be shot enroute. The account of these journeys describes an assortment of menus cooked over campfires fueled with buffalo chips using carefully rationed supplies. Upon arrival, the campfires were replaced by fireplaces and later iron cookstoves. Each improvement added both convenience and new possibilities to the family menu, though many kinds of foods continued to be scarce and too expensive for frontier families. Still, pioneer women were masters of improvisation, and many family favorites were the result of either clever substitution or a new use of garden bounty.

Luchetti, Cathy. *Home on the Range: A Culinary History of the American West.* Villard/Random, 1993. **Grade:** 6 to Adult.

Though written at an adult level, this book is visually rich and filled with fascinating details, including diary entries, letters, and recipes. There are photos on almost every page showing the full range of cooking conditions, from buffalo chip campfires to elaborate iron stoves.

Perl, Lila. *Hunter's Stew and Hangtown Fry: What Pioneer America Ate and Why.* Pictures by Richard Cuffari/Seabury Press, 1977. **Grade:** 5 to 9.

This is an historic survey showing how pioneers from all over the world adapted to the conditions of a variety of frontiers. Though a few recipes are included with each chapter, this is primarily a region-by-region survey of the conditions pioneers found, the immigrant groups involved, and how they adapted and learned from each other to survive.

Walker, Barbara M. *The Little House Cookbook: Frontier Foods from Laura Ingalls Wilder's Classic Stories.* Illustrations by Garth Williams. Harper & Row, 1979. **Grade:** 5 to 9.

As the title suggests, the recipes were inspired by the vivid descriptions of food and eating found in the *Little House* series. Walker describes the food as it was used in that time and gives updated recipes that can be cooked in today's kitchen. The book also gives additional insight into the lives of the Ingalls family and the very real struggle for food that dominated much of their lives.

ACTIVITIES

1. Using the books listed above and other local history sources, learn about the problems of finding and storing food while traveling in the wilderness or living far from stores and having little cash to spend. What kinds of foods are common in pioneer recipes? Why do you think these foods were so popular? Imagine you are a pioneer, and plan meals for one week using only these foods.
2. Use Luchetti's *Home on the Range* and other sources with photos or drawings of pioneer kitchens. How are these kitchens different from those used today? Compare kitchen size, equipment, and the amount of work necessary to prepare a meal in a frontier kitchen with modern food preparation methods.

┌─ **ACTIVITIES cont'd.** ─────────────────────────────────────┐

3. Find as many descriptions as you can of the ways meals were prepared, who helped prepare them, and what foods were eaten. List all the ways in which modern food preparation differs from the way it was in pioneer days.

4. Using the books listed above, try to make some of the simple foods that pioneer children prepared. Some easy choices would be butter, johnnycakes, parched corn, and popcorn. Are there any other favorites you would like to try?

5. When pioneers got together to build a house for a neighbor or for some other work party, all the women brought food to be shared. Plan a pioneer feast where everyone brings a different dish. Use the cookbooks above or one from the history of your home town. Remember, the food must be something pioneer cooks prepared. Compile the recipes you used into a recipe book to be shared.

└──┘

Making Things for the Home and Community

Because very little could be taken to a new home and the settlers were miles from stores, they made many of the things they needed. They built plain furniture using simple hand tools, turned home-grown wool and linen into beautiful woven rugs and coverlets, and made household tools from iron and simple tin. They were master recyclers—fat was saved for soap and candles, scraps of precious cloth became quilts, and bits of paper became decoration, adding touches of beauty to their simple homes.

Maginley, C. J. *Models of America's Past and How to Make Them.* Illustrated by Elizabeth D. McKee. Harcourt Brace & World, 1969. **Grade: 6 to Adult.**

Parish, Peggy. *Let's Be Early Settlers With Daniel Boone.* Drawings by Arnold Lobel. Harper & Row, 1967. **Grade: 3 to 6.**

While Maginley's book is aimed at the experienced model maker, the furnishings are simple and the designs easily adapted to children in the upper grades. The Parish book, while less complete, is specifically designed for children.

┌─ **ACTIVITIES** ───┐

1. Do research on the kinds of homes pioneers built in different regions and the ways they were furnished. What furniture did pioneers bring with them, and what things did they make themselves? As a group or indi-

ACTIVITIES cont'd.

vidual project, try making minature versions of this simple pioneer furniture and use them to furnish a model room. The two books listed above and *Colonial Crafts For You To Make* (see p. 42) show how to make models of pioneer houses and their furnishings. *Log Cabin in the Woods* (see p. 30) and *Little House on the Prairie* (see p. 38), listed in the Recommended Reading for this chapter, also have detailed descriptions of a father making simple tables, benches, and beds. Before you start, decide on the period of history in which to place your room, as well as the geographic setting. It would be particularly interesting to re-create the home of a pioneer family in your own community or region. Some of these early homes may have been preserved as museums, which you could visit as part of your research.

2. Candles were important, as they were the sole source of light in many pioneer homes. Early settlers made candles by hanging string wicks from poles and dipping them repeatedly into warm tallow, building the candle layer by layer. When they owned candle molds, they merely hung the wick in the molds and filled each hole with warm tallow. This process can be duplicated using tin cans or other containers as molds. For directions, see *Steven Caney's Kids' America* (see p. 42), pp. 48–50, or *Heritage Sampler* (see p. 42), pp. 54–59.

3. Paper was another thing that was scarce, expensive, and never wasted. Paper was hoarded and used to create different decorations for the home. The art ranged from simple paper chains and borders to elaborate landscapes, flower bouquets, and baskets of fruit. Such paper cuttings are used today as wall decorations, pictures, and cards. Directions are found in books on paper cutting and in *Heritage Sampler* (see p. 42), pp. 73–79.

4. The most popular form of paper cutting was silhouette art, which was the specialty of traveling shademakers, or shadowmakers. Families could also make silhouettes themselves, and shadowmaking was a popular hobby and a way to make portraits of friends and family. Directions for making a silhouette portrait are found in *Steven Caney's Kids' America* (see p. 42), pp. 228–230, and *Heritage Sampler* (see p. 42), pp. 69–71.

5. Decoratively patterned papers, such as wallpaper and illustrations, were used to cover and line boxes. They were also glued inside clear glass vases to give the impression of fine painting. Directions for these kinds of decoupage projects are found in *Colonial Crafts for You To Make* (see p. 42), pp. 58–60.

Adams, Patricia, and Jean Marzollo. *The Helping Hands Handbook: A Guide-book for Kids Who Want to Help People, Animals, and the World We Live In.* Random House, 1992. **Grade:** 4 to 8.

Hoose, Philip. *It's Our World, Too! Stories of Young People Who are Making a Difference.* Little, Brown & Company, 1993. **Grade:** 5 to 8.

The two books listed above are about the ways young people have organized to make a difference in their communities. *It's Our World, Too!* discusses the contributions of both individuals and groups and includes a handbook on how to organize a group and use effective tools for change. *The Helping Hands Handbook* describes over a hundred projects that kids have organized to help their communities.

ACTIVITY

Think about ways you and your friends can work together to make a job easier or to improve your school or community. As a group, plan such a project, listing your goals, how working together will help achieve the goals, and how the project will improve your community. Is it something your group could do unassisted, or would you need the help of adults? How could you plan and promote such a project?

CHAPTER
· · · · · · · · ·

The Other Frontier Story:
The Changing World of
Native Americans

While the pioneers moved west and struggled to establish farms and homesteads, Native American families helplessly watched their entire lives and culture change. Because Native Americans had no written language with which to document their lives, the record of this change is limited. There are, however, a few memoirs, collected by sympathetic historians, that describe individuals and how their lives were changed. No record of the frontier would be complete without these stories and the picture they give us of loving families and a rich culture that was rapidly being swept away by the pioneers' expansion into their lands.

RECOMMENDED READING

Broker, Ignatia. *Night Flying Woman: An Ojibway Narrative.* Illustrated by Steven Premo. Minnesota Historical Society Press, 1983.

Source of Material: This is the story the author's grandmother told of the life of her grandmother.

Location: Minnesota.

Date: 1867 to 1930s.

Grade: 6 to Adult.

Broker recounts the life of her great-great-grandmother, Night Flying Woman, or Oona as she was called, and the enormous changes that came to the Ojibway during her lifetime. Born into a loving family, the child Oona becomes part of the traditional Ojibway cycle of life in which the people move from camp to camp, gathering and storing their traditional food and planting the crops that will sustain them through the long winter. When word comes of white strangers and their demands for furs and land, Oona's family joins others in a retreat deeper into the forest. It is here that Oona realizes she has "the gift of sight" and that her dreams predict a troubled future. She foresees many of the coming changes as her small tribe is finally forced to confront the demand that all Ojibway relocate and remain within White Earth Reservation.

After this forced move, the group decides not to join the larger, established village but to locate where they can continue their traditional life style of gathering wild rice, hunting, and making maple sugar. This decision protects them from the sickness and hunger of the larger village. However, when the authorities demand that all children attend school, Oona's mother decides the only way to survive is to learn the white man's ways and accept those that seem wise. Under her leadership, the men go to work in the lumber mills to earn timber for permanent homes, the children go to school, and Oona's mother works for the Indian agent's wife in order to learn new skills. The group struggles to maintain as much of their traditional life as possible, but customs continue to erode and are gradually discarded. Many of the old ways die with Oona's grandparents and parents, but she carries them in memory and teaches her sons and grandchildren the Ojibway traditions as the forests diminish, the animals retreat, and an entire way of life is swept away.

Despite an idealization of traditional ways and Oona herself, this book gives a detailed portrait of the Ojibway and the ways Native American cultures developed whole life cycles around the lands in which they lived. One also learns of the great emotional conflict engendered by the loss of these lands and the traditions the people sustained.

Eastman, Charles. *Indian Boyhood.* Fawcett, 1972.

Source of Material: Author's childhood memories.

Locations: Minnesota and Canada.

Date: 1858 to 1873.

Grade: 6 to Adult.

This first-person account was written by the adult, university-educated Charles Eastman, looking back to his youth and his life as a Sioux. His mother died soon after his birth, and he was left in the care of his grandmother, a singular woman who was to shape all the years of his youth. Ohiysea (Charles's Sioux name) was four years old when members of his tribe rose up against the white settlers, and his earliest memories are of the tribe's flight into Canada, where they are isolated from contact with the white world. Because his father and brothers have been captured and presumably executed, Ohiysea and his grandmother live with his uncle. Guided in the ways of the warrior by his uncle and the ways of the Great Mystery by his grandmother, he prepares to become a hunter and warrior who will avenge the death of his father. Sioux children learn by mimicking their elders, and the daily games of young boys include feats with bow and arrow as well as foot and pony races, wrestling, swimming, sham fights, and imitation of all the habits and rituals of their fathers and uncles. These games become more important as young boys gradually learn the skills of hunting, woodcraft, and survival amidst hunger, cold, and enemy raids.

Ohiysea is spiritually guided by his grandmother, who encourages understanding of his animal brothers and the relationship of all things to the Great Mystery. This spiritual training is exacting and serious. One compelling chapter tells how he is asked to sacrifice a beloved dog as his first offering to the Great Mystery. The combination of grief and dignity this young boy displays tells a great deal about the commitment of his family to the ways of their ancestors. Another part of this spiritual training is found in the tales of the elders, to which he listens avidly, learning the history and legends of his tribe. Ritual ceremonies, feasts, and the exhilaration of the first hunt are vividly recalled.

As Ohiysea approaches manhood and prepares to join the ranks of warriors, his father returns. During his years of imprisonment, Ohiysea's father becomes a Christian and decides that life on the reservation means physical and moral degradation. Renouncing all government assistance, he establishes a homestead and decides to try the white man's way of living. He wants his youngest son to learn these new ways and become educated. Wearing unfamiliar clothing, Ohiysea reluctantly joins his father, though, as he says, "I felt as if I were dead and traveling to the Spirit Land; for now all my old ideas were to give place to new ones, and my life was to be entirely different from that of the past." The book ends with this journey, which would change his life forever.

Though Eastman occasionally uses the word *savage* to describe his early life, the book disputes all the white world's misconceptions about his people. Eastman repeatedly points out the democratic nature of tribal structures, the discipline required, and the people's generosity toward one another. His is a loving portrait of the physical and mental abilities required for survival and the spiritual values that shaped his childhood world.

Linderman, Frank B. *Pretty-Shield: Medicine Woman of the Crows.* Illustrated by Herbert Morton Stoops. John Day Co., 1972 (1972 reprint of the 1932 ed., which has the title *Red Mother*).

Source of Material: Pretty-Shield told her story to Frank Linderman, herself, through an interpreter using sign language.

Location: Montana.

Date: Mid-1850s to 1930s, when Frank Linderman collected these memoirs.

Grade: 6 to Adult.

This book covers not only the life of Pretty-Shield, an elderly Crow woman, but the process Linderman used in gathering the stories. What emerges is a vital, life-loving woman who has seen her entire culture irrevocably changed and virtually lost. Through her conversation she paints a vivid portrait of Plains Indian life; the survival techniques; the constant warfare; and the mystical power of dreams, myth, and medicine to protect and cure. The memories are collected in roughly chronological order, starting with Pretty-Shield's childhood. She tells how she tried to be like her mother and aunt, carrying her doll on her back and setting up her own little teepee—racing to beat the adults at this task. She tells of childhood pranks and elaborate games, a beloved doll and ball that were nearly lost in a Lakota attack, and the time she borrowed a baby and nearly lost it. This was a life of movement and danger as the Plains tribes followed the buffalo and made war on each other, stole horses, counted coups, and killed each other in quick raids. She also gives detailed descriptions of women's life and work: how food was gathered and preserved, the way lodges were set up and used, the care of infants, and the treatment of children.

Many of the stories are about the connection between people and the animals, connections often made in visions and dreams. Such animals became good medicine and were protected and cherished. Stories with elements of magic and myth show the prevalence and power of these beliefs. The book concludes with her memories of Custer and the Battle of Little Big Horn (her husband had been with Custer as a scout against the traditional Crow enemies and witnessed the final battle). She describes the changes in her life since the loss of the buffalo and confinement to the reservation, but eschews bitterness, looking instead to the grandchildren she is raising and what life will hold for them.

This is a rich portrait, sympathetically conveyed, with a strong sense of this woman's character, her love of mischief, and the force of her will. The book is lightly illustrated with six black-and-white line drawings at chapter heads. Each drawing shows an aspect of Crow life with generalized but realistic pictures of daily life, reinforcing the tone of the text without adding additional detail.

Standing Bear, Luther. *My Indian Boyhood.* University of Nebraska Press, 1988. Originally published by Houghton Mifflin, 1931.

    Source of Material: Author's childhood memories.

    Location: Western Plains.

    Dates: 1870s to 1880s.

    Grade: 5 to 8.

Though there are some personal anecdotes and memories in this book, the author's intent was that "the hearts of the white boys and girls who read these pages will be made kinder toward little Indian boys and girls." Like Charles Eastman, Luther Standing Bear spent much of his adult life in the white world and sought to counteract the prejudices he encountered by writing about the life he had known as a child.

The first chapter relates the history of the Sioux, and the subsequent chapters describe, in detail, family life and the skills the Sioux used to create their rich and complex culture. He tells how hunters used their understanding of and respect for the natural world to help them hunt, and how the Indians learned the value of plants, trees, and herbs. He describes the games he played as a boy, and how they trained him as a hunter. There are detailed descriptions of the ways animal skins were prepared and used, clothing made and decorated, foods cooked, and various household implements made and used. He details the ritual involved in capturing and killing an eagle, the meaning of feathers as ornament, and other marks of achievement and respect. In the last chapter, he tells of his first buffalo hunt and the joy and pride he shared with this family when he came home in triumph with food for his family.

A handful of realistic and detailed engravings show both the events of the story and details of daily life. Though idealized and short on individual personalities, this is a detailed portrait of Sioux life, written by a man who experienced it and saw it swept away.

Stroud, Virginia A. *Doesn't Fall Off His Horse.* Dial, 1994.

Source of Material: Story told to author/artist by her adoptive Kiowa grandfather.

Location: Oklahoma Territory.

Date: 1890s.

Grade: 2 to 5.

Young Saygee knows that if she is patient, Great-Grandfather will tell her a story from a life filled with adventure and change. This time he shows her a long scar on his neck and tells her how he got his Indian name, Doesn't Fall Off His Horse. First he describes the Indian custom of counting coup, which was like a serious game of tag: a warrior approaches the enemy and tries to shame him by entering his village at night, touching him in battle, or stealing his horses. After hearing elder warriors brag of the coup they have made, Great-Grandfather and a group of boys decide to try to steal ponies from the Comanches who are camped nearby. A friend wakes him in the night, and he and the other boys sneak away, quietly riding their ponies. They approach the enemy herd with stealth and caution and cut the horses' hobbles before they are spotted and escape with Comanche warriors in close pursuit. Great-

Grandfather is hit by a Comanche bullet and not only stays on his horse but holds on to the ropes of two other ponies taken in the raid. Though he is badly hurt, the medicine woman treats him with a prickly pear leaf and he survives. When he is well enough to sit up, the tribal leaders chastise the boys for their bad judgment in raiding alone but show their respect for Grandfather's first coup by naming him Doesn't Fall Off His Horse.

Virginia Stroud is a well-known artist, and her brilliantly colored paintings add life and drama to the story. She combines meticulous details of Plains Indian life and customs with a contemporary color sense featuring lavender, blue-greens, and pinks. Other than Saygee and her great-grandfather, none of the characters are individually defined. Though the action of the story is vividly rendered, all the boys have similar faces and hair and are distinguished only by their colorful clothing. Simple outlines and flat fields of color and pattern are used for the animals, people, and lodgings, while the surrounding landscape is more loosely and casually painted. This serves to focus the action of the story, while the careful detailing gives the reader additional information. The combination of an adventurous story and dramatic illustrations makes this an attractive introduction to the life of the Plains Indians.

Valla, Lawrence Jonathan. *Tales of a Pueblo Boy.* Sunstone Press, 1993.

Source of Material: Author's childhood memories.

Locations: Jemez and Acoma Pueblos.

Date: 1920s.

Grade: 4 to 8.

Though some details place this story in the early part of this century, the traditions and cultures described are little changed by modern life. As a two-year-old, Rabbit and his older sister are left with their grandparents, two uncles, and an aunt, while their parents go to work in the city. Though he admires his uncles and enjoys the meals his grandmother prepares, Grandfather is the most important to young Rabbit. Working at his grandfather's side he learns to plant and care for crops, where to take the cattle for grazing, and the importance of traditions. Some chapters are devoted to Rabbit's participation in the daily activities that ensure food and survival: hunting pack rats, hoeing corn, camping out to gather pine nuts, and trapping birds in the fields. It is clear that every possible source of food is needed and that providing food for Grandmother is a source of pride for young Rabbit. Rabbit admires his young uncles, who teach him traditional dances and provide other role models. Though described with love and respect, none of the characters are shown as distinct individuals except Rabbit, who has flashes of mischief and finds great joy in hunting with his cousins.

Three memorable chapters give accurate descriptions of the dances and rituals of the Pueblo village. Described are fear and fun of the day when the katchinas come to the village bearing gifts for good children and switches for naughty ones and a Fiesta Day of food and trading when Rabbit earns enough money for *two* hamburgers (at a nickle each). He is selected to lead the young Antelope dancers on Christmas and spends the day alternately running through the village and dancing on drum cue. Valla describes in detail the preparations, the costumes worn by the dancers, and the excitement and pleasure of these special days.

The book is illustrated with numerous small, pencil sketches that, though awkwardly done, are an accurate and lively portrayal of the moments described.

Wahanee, as told to Gilbert L. Wilson. *Wahanee: An Indian Girl's Story.* Illustrated by Frederick N. Wilson. University of Nebraska Press, 1981.

Source of Material: Wahanee's story was written by Gilbert L. Wilson, a field collector for the American Museum of Natural History who visited the Hidatsas every summer for 12 years. Gilbert Wilson was assisted by his brother Frederick, who did the engravings that illustrate this book. This material was first published in 1921.

Location: North Dakota, a village overlooking the Missouri River.

Dates: 1839 to 1920.

Grade: 5 to Adult.

Wahanee was born in a time of great change for the Hidatsa people. Two years before her birth a disastrous smallpox epidemic wiped out over half the Hidatsa population and up to seven-eighths of their Mandan neighbors. Feeling the combined weight of this loss and the hostile Sioux, the remnants of these tribes moved from their traditional villages and built the Like a Fishhook village on a terrace overlooking the Missouri River. Wahanee's mother was one of four sisters married to her father, a common practice among the Plains tribes, and Wahanee was taught to call all of them "my mothers." When her mother died, she was raised in her father's lodge by these aunts and her grandmother, Turtle.

The book presents an intimate look into the daily lives and activities of Hidatsa women and children. Wahanee gives a child's view of life of the earth lodge, the housekeeping routine, the food preparation, and the way women clear the land and the crops they grow. There are chapters on childhood games, training dogs to work, pulling a travois, and the pride children feel as they are taught to work and become part of adult society. There is a supplement for young readers on how to make an Indian camp, including construction techniques to duplicate a lodge, a fireplace, cooking utensils, and the evergreen booths women erected in the cornfields. It also shows how to parch corn and includes recipes for Native American cooking. Wahanee describes her own transition to womanhood, her marriage, and the birth of her first child during one of their annual moves. The last chapter, "After Fifty Years," finds the elderly Wahanee looking back: her son, who attended a white man's school, lives in a house with a chimney, and his wife cooks on a stove. The old ways are gone forever.

This book clearly shows the love, concern, and strong sense of honor that was basic to Hidatsa culture. Although the writing is clear, concise, and nonsentimental, little sense of individuality is given to the characters. One senses that it would be difficult for Wahanee to speak of any beloved adult with anything but a rather distant respect. Only Turtle, Wahanee's elderly and formidable grandmother, comes across as an individual. However, the detail is fascinating, and Wahanee is a sympathetic person.

The book is enhanced by the small but detailed engravings that appear on nearly every page. Drawn by the author's brother, they not only illustrate specific events or activities, but give a great deal of additional detail: the various views of the earth lodges' interiors, the enclosed beds, the cooking and eating utensils, and the clothing. These engravings, combined with the sections on construction techniques, give a complete portrait of this culture.

SPECIAL PROJECTS AND ENRICHMENT ACTIVITIES
Learn About Your Neighbors

Waldman, Carl. *Encyclopedia of Native American Tribes*. Illustrated by Molly Braun. Facts on File, 1988. **Grade: 5 to Adult.**

Wolfson, Evelyn. *From Abenaki to Zuni: A Dictionary of Native American Tribes*. Illustrated by William Sauts Bock. Walker, 1988. **Grade: 4 to 8.**

Each of these books gives a brief overview of the history, lifestyle, and customs of the major Native American tribes in North America. Waldman's book emphasizes history, while Wolfson's gives a concise view of the basic lifestyle and customs of both tribes and culture areas.

ACTIVITIES

1. Using these books and other general surveys, find out which Native American tribes originated in your part of the country. What are the names of these tribes? Do they still live in your area, or were they moved to reservations in another part of the country? Pick one of these tribes and use these and other sources to learn as much as you can about these people. How did the tribe live before white settlers arrived? What has their history been? How do they live now? Is there a local museum you

SAMPLE DIORAMA OF A NATIVE AMERICAN TRIBE. THIS EXAMPLE SHOWS SIOUX TRIBAL LIFE.

FIGURE 2

ACTIVITIES cont'd.

can visit for more information about Native Americans in your region? If so, try to visit. Often, museum displays provide clear visual pictures and a lot of information on the way people lived in the past.

2. Use what you have learned to write an illustrated research paper or create a diorama showing the original life of this tribe. Describe or show all aspects of their life and culture, including housing, clothing, household objects, and gathering and preparing food. What did the children do, and how were they taught tasks and customs? Include as many details as possible.

3. Do additional research on the myths and legends of Native Americans from your region. As you read, you will notice that many legends feature animals as characters. Do any of these animals still live in your area? Write and illustrate one of these legends. Perhaps your group can collect your legends in a book to be shared.

Customs and Cultures

Goodchild, Peter. *The Spark in the Stone: Skills and Projects from the Native American Tradition.* Chicago Review Press, 1991. **Grade:** 6 to Adult.

Hunt, W. Ben. *Golden Book of Indian Crafts and Lore.* Golden Press, 1954. **Grade:** 5 to Adult.

————. *Indiancraft*. Bruce Publishing Co., Milwaukee, 1942. **Grade:** 6 to Adult.

Mason, Bernard S. *The Book of Indian-Crafts and Costumes*. Drawings by Frederick Kock. Ronald Press Co., 1946.

Smith-Baranzini, Marlene and Howard Egger-Bovet. *USKids History: Book of the American Indians* (Brown Paper School). Illustrated by T. Taylor Bruce. Little, Brown & Co., 1993. **Grade:** 5 to 8.

White, Jon Manchip. *Everyday Life of the North American Indian*. Holmes & Meier, 1979. **Grade:** 5 to Adult.

While each of these books takes a different approach, they can be combined to create a rich mixture of information and hands-on experiences. White's book discusses the everyday life of a number of tribal cultures, while Goodchild emphasizes the skills that provided housing, clothing, food, and medicine. Though he describes the methods used and includes some diagrams, many of the projects will be beyond the skills of most children. The approach in *USKids History: Book of the American Indians* is that of an anthology combining information on specific subjects, excerpts from first-person accounts, and a variety of projects and games with brief but useful diagrams and directions. Though the books by Hunt and Mason are too dated in some of their references to be unilaterally recommended, they are among the best sources for clear, well-illustrated directions on a variety of crafts, games, and customs. They are particularly strong on all the details of creating elaborate ceremonial objects and dance costumes. If you plan extensive projects on Native American cultures, it would be worthwhile to search out these books using your local library's interlibrary loan service.

Games and Toys

Baldwin, Gordon C. *Games of the American Indian*. W. W. Norton, 1969. **Grade:** 5 to Adult.

Hofsinde, Robert. *Indian Games and Crafts*. William Morrow & Co., 1957. **Grade:** 4 to 8.

Lavine, Sigmund A. *The Games Indians Played*. Dodd, Mead & Co., 1978. **Grade:** 5 to Adult.

In these books, both Baldwin and Lavine discuss the kinds of games played by Native Americans, showing the popularity of both games of chance and games of skill. While Hofsinde's approach is less scholarly, he gives clear directions for 14 different toys and games. Games of chance and skill were played by all ages, but like pioneer children, Native American children had few toys and spent much of their time helping adults gather and prepare food. Many of the games they played were imitations of things they saw adults do. Native American girls carried dolls and made small teepees which they took down and carried just like the large ones. Boys made small hunting weapons with which they hunted small animals for food. They also went fishing and had races and contests to test the skills they would need as warriors. All tribes played various handgames in which small objects or counters were passed around and hidden. Both Baldwin and Lavine describe a variety of these games.

ACTIVITY

Make an Indian doll using the materials that were available to Native Americans, such as corncobs, wood, or scraps of leather. There are descriptions and pictures of several kinds of dolls in *Games of the American Indian*, pp. 18–27. Make the doll's clothing like that of a doll belonging to a real Native American from a specific tribe. Make the clothes look as accurate as possible.

Yue, David, and **Charlotte Yue.** *The Tipi: A Center of Native American Life.* Alfred A. Knopf, 1984. **Grade:** 4 to 8.

The book listed above describes in detail all the elements of a tipi, its structure, its furnishing, and its intimate connection with a whole pattern of living. It gives all the steps in making and setting up a tipi, directions which will help you make a miniature tipi or even a toy tipi, such as those used by Native American children.

ACTIVITIES

1. You can use your miniature tipi to demonstrate how tipis were designed and how they were taken down and quickly reassembled. You can find directions for making a simple kid-sized play tipi in *USKids History: Book of the American Indians*, p. 62.
2. Bullroarers or whizzers are flat pieces of wood suspended on a string that, when whirled in the air, give a roaring or whirring sound. All tribes west of the Mississippi knew these ancient noisemakers, which were used in ceremonies by Southwest Indians and as children's toys elsewhere. Thin strips of wood are beveled and given a variety of simple shapes before being hung on a length of string. Try making a bullroarer and experimenting with the different sounds it can make. Compare the sounds made by different shapes. Simple directions can be found in *USKids*

┌───┐

ACTIVITIES cont'd.

History: Book of the American Indians, p. 10, and *Indian Games and Crafts,* pp. 59–65.

3. Other simple toys were used in games of skill involving tossing, catching, and aiming. There are directions for both making the equipment and playing several such games in Hofsinde's *Indian Games and Crafts,* including corncob darts, toss balls, snow snakes, double ball and stick games, and toss and catch games. In *USKids History: Book of the American Indians* you will find directions for making the equipment and rules for playing a ring-and-pin game on p. 56 and a hoop-and-pole game on p. 82. Directions for making a more elaborate hoop requiring more skill can be found in *Indiancraft,* p. 93. Try playing some of these games. How are they the same, and how are they different from the games you play?

4. All the tribes played and continue to play different versions of guessing games and games of chance. One of the most popular is the handgame in which objects are swiftly passed from hand to hand while other players guess where it is. *USKids History: Book of the American Indians* has a description of the game and a modern version on p. 27, as well as directions for playing an Iroquois bowl game on p. 84. A Crow bowl game and Plains Indian guessing game are described in the first two chapters of *Indian Games and Crafts.*

└───┘

Foods and Cooking

In addition to hunting and fishing, Native Americans gathered hundreds of different plants for food. Moving through the seasons, they systematically harvested berries, fruits, nuts, grains, roots, greens, and a variety of herbs, preserving as many as they could through the cold of winter. Although many tribes continued the nomadic life of hunter-gatherers, Native Americans in the eastern United States, the Southwest, and a few other areas grew most of their food. Important crops were corn, beans, and squash, and in some places, sunflowers. They had also discovered the medicinal value of plants in their regions. Though they cooked them in their own way, Europeans quickly adopted many of these foods for themselves, and they are now used throughout the world. Though today most tribes use modern technology, many of them still prepare these foods in traditional ways, preserving an important part of this heritage.

Cox, Beverly, and Martin Jacobs. *Spirit of the Harvest: Native American Indian Cooking.* Stewart, Tabori & Chang, 1991. **Grade:** 8 to Adult.

Peters, Russell. *Clambake: A Wampanog Tradition.* Photographs by John Madama. Lerner, 1992. **Grade:** 4 to 8.

Regguinti, Gordon. *The Sacred Harvest: Ojibway Wild Rice Gathering.* Photographs by Dale Kakkak. Lerner, 1992. **Grade:** 4 to 8.

Wittstock, Laura Waterman. *Ininatig's Gift of Sugar: Traditional Native Sugarmaking.* Photographs by Dale Kakkak. Lerner, 1993. **Grade:** 4 to 8.

Though intended for adults, *Spirit of the Harvest* offers an excellent and unusually attractive overview of the ways Native Americans developed food sources and originated recipes to suit a wide variety of indigenous ingredients. Each chapter discusses the cultures of major tribal groups, their diets, their ceremonial use of food, and the historic dishes they developed. Each chapter also includes a map placing the tribes and their principal foods in a geographical context. The other three books describe the way a tribe gathers and prepares traditional food important to that group.

ACTIVITIES

1. Learn about the traditional foods of the Native Americans in your area. Are such foods still available and eaten today, or have the sources for these foods disappeared? Which of these food are now eaten by everyone? Are they prepared in the same way?
2. Using the books listed above or other books on Native American cooking, prepare a meal based entirely on food found and created by Native Americans. Collect your favorite recipes along with the information on the origin of the food in a book to be shared.

Ceremonies, Music, and Dance

Music and dance are of great importance in Native American culture and are used for social gatherings and religious ceremonies. Though popular culture would suggest a generic style, each region has distinct traditions and these cultures should be studied separately. It is also important to remember that many of these dances and the music and chants that accompany them are associated with ceremonies that are important and often sacred expressions of Native American culture.

Highwater, Jamake. *Ritual of the Wind: North American Indian Ceremonies, Music and Dance.* Methuen, Toronto, 1984. **Grade:** 5 to Adult.

ACTIVITIES

1. Learn about the dances of a Native American group. What kinds of dances were used? Were the dances religious or social, or both? Who performed these dances, and which dances were forbidden to other groups of people? How were the dancers chosen?

2. Are these dances still performed today? Are they performed in the same way and for the same reasons? Using the resource listed above, try to find music and other information for a specific dance.

3. Learn about the music of different Native American groups. What instruments were developed? How was the music used? For a list of recordings of music from various tribes and regions, see pp. 188–189 of *Ritual of the Wind*. You may find these or other recordings at the library. Listen to the music. What instruments are used? Is there singing? Who are the singers? How is this music different from European music? How does it make you feel?

4. One obvious trait of Native American music is that it is dominated by percussion instruments, used primarily to provide a rhythmic accompaniment to dances or chants. Drums provide the basic beat and are made by stretching rawhide over a variety of frames. Small hand drums are carried and played by a single drummer, while large dance drums can be played by a dozen drummers at once. *The Book of Indian-Crafts and Costumes* (see p. 61) has directions on making several types, combining modern materials and traditional techniques. The *USKids History: Book of the American Indians* (see p. 61) shows how to make a simple drum using a five-gallon tub on p. 21, a simple wooden clapper rattle on p. 31, and a morache on p. 56. Try making a variety of these instruments and experimenting with the way they sound alone and together. Can you duplicate some of the sounds you hear in the recordings of Native American music?

5. Much of the sound and rhythmn of Native American dance is provided by the dancers, who carry or wear a variety of rattles and bells. The commonest rattles are gourds, which have been dried with pebbles inside. Rattles can also be made from steer horn, birchbark disks, and tin cans. Native American dancers traditionally used rattles made from the shells of small box turtles, which they either carried or tied to their legs. Directions for making many of these rattles can be found on pp. 72–73 of *The Book of Indian-Crafts and Costumes* (see p. 61).

6. The other traditional noisemaker is a string of dancing bells that are worn about the ankles and waist. In the Jingle-dress dance, an ancient dance for women, the dress is decorated with rows of tin cones that produce a tinkling sound during the dance. Try dancing using some of

---

ACTIVITIES cont'd.

these instruments. Do you feel or dance differently when you can create your own rhythm and hear the way your body is moving?

Powwows

Ancona, George. *Powwow.* Harcourt, Brace Jovanovich, 1991. **Grade:** 4 to 8.

Crum, Robert. *Eagle Drum: On the Powwow Trail with a Young Grass Dancer.* Four Winds, 1944. **Grade:** 4 to 8.

Into the Circle: An Introduction to Oklahoma Powwows and Celebrations. Full Circle Communications. 1992. **Grade:** 6 to Adult.

Pow-Wow! Produced by Haskell Indian Jr. College/ Centron Films. Distributed by Coronet MTI Film and Video. 1980. **Grade:** 6 to Adult.

These two books are photo-essays describing the sights, sounds, color, and excitement of the Native American powwow. Ancona's book discusses powwows themselves, while Crum's book is centered on the experience of one young dancer. In many parts of the country, Native Americans gather for powwows, which are celebrations of Native American culture. As the books listed above clearly show, one of the features of powwows is the dance competition, in which different groups of dancers wearing elaborate costumes perform traditional dances. If a powwow is held near your home, try to attend. Anyone is welcome, and it is a wonderful opportunity to hear traditional music, see wonderful dancing, and eat a variety of delicious foods.

If you are unable to find a powwow in your area, perhaps you would enjoy seeing a videotape of a powwow. Some that you might enjoy are listed above.

ACTIVITY

After you have visited a powwow or watched one on video, think of ways to show how the experience felt to you. Perhaps you might want to write a poem using some of the rhythmn and excitement of the music and dance. Perhaps you might want to draw a picture or make a design showing some of the color of the costume and movement of the dancers.

CHAPTER 4
·········

Growing Up in the Country

T he American continent is spacious and varied in its topography, but the children who grew up in small towns or farms shared a number of common experiences. Whether the children lived on an island in Maine, in the Appalachian mountains, or on a midwestern farm, they were often isolated, seeing only their families for days or weeks at a time. However, boredom does not seem to be part of this experience. Children were expected to help with the myriad of tasks necessary to keep families fed and comfortable far from towns. During their free time, they improvised a variety of entertainments. Jumping into straw piles and swimming in any available body of water seem to have been favorites across the country. They also found pleasure in a variety of handmade toys, often made on the spot by the children themselves.

One-room schools became social centers and provided an opportunity for games as well as learning, and farm families created opportunities to get together whenever possible. Threshing day was an exciting occasion, combining a day's hard work with a lot of good food and visiting with neighbors. Each family took turns hosting the threshing machine, its crew, and the neighbors who came to help. Community picnics, church socials, and box suppers were important events and are featured in many of these stories.

Despite the hard work, these families shared a deep and abiding love of the land and an awareness of their region's particular beauty. Detailed descriptions of landscape and seasonal change are featured in many of these books. The picture books mentioned in this chapter include the work of several notable artists. There are stunning paintings of rolling green hills, dramatic prairie skies, and empty southwestern deserts. This was, and is, the power that held families to the land, despite the uncertainty of each new year.

RECOMMENDED READING

Arrington, Frances. *Stella's Bull.* Illustrated by Aileen Arrington. Houghton
  Mifflin Co., 1994.

  Source of Material: Childhood memories of author's mother.

  Location: Not specifically told.

  Date: 1930s.

  Grade: 2 to 6.

Mary Wilson has never actually seen Stella's bull, but rumors of his fierce
anger are enough to feed her imagination and keep her well away from the
woods where he lives. Then Addison Fitzpatrick throws her new spelling book
over the fence and into Stella's pasture. Though she knows she'll be in trouble
at school, Mary just can't go over that fence and retrieve the book. As her fear
grows, she even mistakes a wandering cow for the bull, and her terrified
retreat earns her the scorn of her schoolmates. One stormy afternoon she
builds up enough courage to return to the field, where she finds the book
outside the fence and the bull inside, not 10 feet away. She spends long
minutes watching this source of her fear as it quietly grazes then drifts off into
the woods. Then she goes home knowing she'll remember Stella's bull, even
when she grows up.

   This quiet story is illustrated with colored pencil drawings featuring a
simply dressed girl with straight brown hair and bangs framing her solemn
face. It shows a rural setting of simple white frame houses and country roads.
Also featured are the rich greens of woods and fields and the intense blue of a
clear summer sky. There is no doubt about the intensity of Mary's fear, but the
Depression era, in which this story takes place, was a time when private fears
were faced and dealt with a minimum of fuss.

Baylor, Bryd. *The Best Town in the World.* Pictures by Ronald Himler. Charles
  Scribner's Sons, 1982.

  Source of Material: Memories of George Baylor.

  Location: Texas.

  Date: 1890s.

  Grade: 2 to 6.

This book is one man's memories of a small Texas town, a place he remembers
as the best town in the world. This town had everything that was important to
a young boy: caves to explore, hills covered with wildflowers, blackberries,
and an ice-cold creek for wading and swimming. The dogs were smart, and
the adults were gentle, generous, and good cooks. The adults also knew about
time, weather, and the building of everything from barns to toys. While this

loving account gently acknowledges that the teller's childhood memories are idealized, it also shares his profound pleasure in remembering and the basic truth behind his stories.

Ronald Himler's watercolor paintings echo the softened reality of the memory. Full-page paintings show boys playing, doing chores, and eating under the benevolent gaze of caring adults. The colors are soft and warm with tan, gold, and green landscapes topped by dramatically clouded skies. There are plenty of period details for viewers. A double-spread features a Fourth of July picnic, showing the entire community gathered around tables of food. Though consciously idealized, the pictures give an accurate view of country life at the turn of the century.

Boulton, Jane. *Only Opal: The Diary of a Young Girl.* Illustrations by Barbara Cooney. Philomel, 1994.

Source of Material: Opal Whiteley's diary was first published in 1920 by Atlantic Monthly Press and adapted by Jane Boulton in longer form as *Opal: The Journal of an Understanding Heart*, Tioga Publishing Co., 1988.

Location: Oregon.

Dates: 1905 to 1907.

Grade: 2 to 6.

This extraordinary book is excerpted from the diary kept by Opal Whiteley when she was five and six years old and just learning to print. Written with colored pencils on the backs of envelopes, the diary records the years immediately after Opal's parents "went to heaven" and she was sent to live with another family. The "mama where I live" is a demanding, difficult woman who keeps Opal busy with a variety of tasks. Still, Opal finds inspiration in the books her parents left, comfort in the beauty of the surrounding forest, and unexpected friendships and understanding.

As Opal does errands and explores the countryside, she meets a blind girl who shares her love of flowers and a sympathetic young housewife she calls Dear Love, who kisses her and gives her small gifts for her tame mouse, Felix Mendelssohn. She also befriends and names a mischievous crow (Lars Porsena), the family dog (Brave Horatius), a gentle calf (Elizabeth Barrett Browning), and a towering tree with an understanding soul (Michael Raphael). Her favorite thing is to "go explores," and in her private world, the flowers talk in shadows and the wind walks in the fields at night, pulling her out to listen. When the great tree Michael Raphael is cut down, only she hears its moans and sad sounds before it falls to the earth. As the book ends, the family (who lived in 19 different lumber camps) prepares to move, and Opal says goodbye to her friends. She is comforted by her belief that "Angel Mother" and "Angel Father" will always be with her because "guardian angels always know where to find you."

Barbara Cooney's color paintings feature a small child whose sweet face and earnest eyes betray little of the interior poetry that guides her. Most pictures show Opal as a solitary, dreamy child doing chores and errands or talking to her friends. Home is a simple frame cabin surrounded by the overwhelming presence and beauty of the forest. Mama is a foreboding background figure, and other adults are portrayed at a distance or from the back. This visual rendering perfectly matches the quiet, poetic quality of the text.

Carrier, Roch. *The Boxing Champion.* Illustrations by Sheldon Cohen; translated from the original French by Sheila Fishman. Tundra Books, 1991.

————. *A Happy New Year's Day.* Illustrations by Giles Pelletier. Tundra Books, 1991.

————. *The Hockey Sweater.* Illustrated by Sheldon Cohen; translated from the original French by Sheila Fishman. Tundra Books, 1984.

Source of Material: Author's childhood memories.

Location: Quebec, Canada.

Date: 1940s.

Grade: 3 to 6.

This series of picture books contains Carrier's wry, often comic, memories of his childhood in the French-Canadian village of Sainte-Justine. *The Boxing Champion* and *The Hockey Sweater* revolve around his ambition to excel as an athlete in the dominant sport of the season.

In *The Hockey Sweater*, Roch, like all his friends, spends the winter living only for hockey and idolizing the champion of the Montreal Canadiens, Maurice Richard. They all collect information on him, copy everything he does, and wear Montreal Canadien hockey sweaters bearing the famous number nine. Roch's sweater finally wears out, but when a new one arrives it bears the logo of the despised Toronto Maple Leafs. Forced by his practical mother to wear it anyway, he goes to play hockey and finds himself shut out by the coach/referee and sitting on the sidelines. When he loses his temper, he is sent off to church to ask God's forgiveness. There he fervently prays that God will send a million moths to eat the despised sweater.

In *The Boxing Champion*, spring is on the way and Roch knows his beloved hockey will be replaced by boxing in his neighbor's summer kitchen—and he will be defeated with a single punch every time. His friends are all larger and stronger, but this year he is determined to become a champion. He uses all his savings to order elastic "Miracle Muscle Builders" and a guidebook that urges him to "think like a champion." He spends weeks exercising and visualizing himself administering a knockout punch. When spring arrives, he eagerly climbs into the ring only to once again be knocked down with a single punch. But something is different. This time the prettiest girl in the class smiles at him and tosses him some wildflowers. It will be a wonderful spring after all.

Sheldon Cohen's illustrations perfectly capture the child's point of view. In the first book, the hockey sweater dominates the illustrations just as the sport and its hero dominated Roch's life. In all the books there is a wonderful mix of detailed reality and the child's point of view. The child who feels overwhelmed by larger, faster foes and the fantasies of success is well conveyed by these illustrations. Comic exaggeration makes the drama clear, but the illustrations also capture the period and setting of the story with dozens of amusing details.

A Happy New Year's Day differs from the other two books in both content and illustration style. In it, Carrier shares memories of the New Year's Day when he was four years old. His anticipation of the holidays starts to build in August, when he helps his grandmother make the traditional cherry wine, and continues through fall and winter, when the cars are replaced by horse-drawn sleighs. Christmas brings good food, a Christmas tree, and a crèche, but New Year's Day brings gifts, including a red locomotive! Though their grandparents' house is only 200 feet away, Father decides the day warrants a trip in his snowmobile—a car with runners and a rear propeller that sounds like thunder. They join their large extended family for prayers, feasting, drinking, more presents, and dancing. The simple joy of this memory is matched by brightly colored, primitive-style paintings that show in detail the countryside, busy town, and interiors filled with busy people. Although these paintings lack the intimacy and comic style of the other two books, they clearly convey the pleasure of these childhood memories.

Cross, Verda. *Great-Grandma Tells of Threshing Day.* Illustrated by Gail Owens. Albert Whitman & Co., 1992.

Source of Material: Author's childhood memories.

Location: Missouri.

Dates: Early 1900s.

Grade: 3 to 6.

Cross re-creates a child's-eye view of the threshing crews and neighbors who spent the day on her farm helping her father thresh his winter wheat. The excitement begins with an early morning trip to fetch the chunk of ice needed for cold drinks. Then the steam threshing machine arrives along with neighbors from all directions. The neighbor men arrive to help in the fields, and the neighbor women help prepare the noon feast. The children see the entire event as they carry cold drinks to the crews and help the women set up tables: the precision work of wagons carrying sheaves of grain to the thresher and bags of grain to the mill, and the bustle of women as they improvise tables from doors and prepare a huge meal. The whole neighborhood partakes in the meal; first the men, then the grandmothers and children, and lastly the women, who eat and laugh and visit for a long time. Afternoon brings return trips to the field, where the children watch the work, chase rabbits, and bring the men more lemonade and cookies. They help Mother fill mattresses with new straw, and as the sun sets, the work is finished. The neighbors return home, and the family starts the evening chores before sitting down to a meal of delicious leftovers. The next day the family will join the crew and help a neighbor with *his* wheat. As they go to sleep, the children decide that threshing day is the best day of the year.

The brightly colored, realistic illustrations match the vigor and descriptive quality of the writing. Many of the story's details are repeated in these illustrations, which show kitchen interiors, the entire threshing operation in several scenes, the sumptuous meal, and lively children. The brilliant colors give the book an immediacy and freshness, reflecting the author's lasting enthusiasm for the events of this special day.

Dewey, Jennifer Owings. *Cowgirl Dreams: A Western Childhood.* Boyd Mills Press, 1995.

Source of Material: Author's childhood memories.

Location: New Mexico.

Dates: 1950s.

Grade: 4 to 7.

In this book, the author/illustrator shares bittersweet memories of her childhood in New Mexico. Though her father was a successful architect, the family lived on a working ranch. Jennifer, unlike her older twin sisters was encouraged to ride and work outside with Bill, the ranch foreman, and his wife Edna. She avoids her sisters, especially Tasha, who is a tease and mean, preferring the friendship of Martha Salazar and Junior, a crippled boy who has been taken in by the Gonzoles family. She also has a pet pig, Jerome, who follows her everywhere but refuses to behave when she takes him to the community pet parade.

The book, which covers her life from ages 7 to 12, is episodic but shows a sensitive, compassionate child in tune with the beauty of the world around her. The vignettes also show the unique way three distinct cultures (Native American, Hispanic, and Anglo) coexist and interact in New Mexico. Jennifer shares her father's fascination with Hopi culture and religion but wants to become a Catholic like her friends. She and Martha are intrigued when their friend Miguel joins the Penitente Brotherhood and even more fascinated by the self-proclaimed witch who heals the wounds of his painful initiation ritual.

One of the more complex and difficult people in Jennifer's life is her father who alternates moments of generosity and courage with an angry racism she cannot comprehend. He is drinking when he gives orders to have her pig Jerome killed, and though he later tries to make amends by building her a tree house, she is afraid of him. It is her acknowledgment of that fear that ends the book.

The black-and-white sketches that head each chapter are a mixture of realistic portraits, drawings of favorite animals (there are three pictures of Jerome), and objects important to the story and unique to its locale. Though Jennifer's childhood was filled with the beauty and freedom of life on a ranch, the joy she felt was tempered by the poverty of her friends, encounters with tragedy, and her final realization of her father's dark, distant anger.

Ellison, Lucile Watkins. *Butter on Both Sides.* Illustrated by Judith Gwyn Brown. Charles Scribner's Sons, 1979.

Source of Material: Stories of the author's childhood initially written for a niece.

Location: Alabama, near the Tombigbee River.

Dates: Early 1900s.

Grade: 4 to 7.

This novel is built around three memorable times in the life of young Lucy and her close and devoted family: her teacher-farmer father, mother, two aunts, and six siblings, who range from the "Big Ones" away at school to Lucy and the other two "Little Ones." The story starts with the family preparing for a special trip up the Tombigbee River by steamer. On the day of departure, they visit with friends while awaiting the steamer, but the steamer is so late they finally give up and go home. They are disappointed, but the summer winds on and Lucy keeps herself busy with dolls, family pets, fishing for doodles in the sand, and reading. Then one day word comes that if they hurry, they can catch the steamer. Off the family goes, with practically no preparation, for two days of fun and adventure.

The next two sections involve Father's illness and the months of worry as he adheres to a strict diet but gradually becomes weaker and weaker. During this time it is Mother who takes them fishing and Brother who supervises gathering the cotton and cutting the sugar cane for cooking into molasses. Uncle Horace insists on taking Father to a specialist in New Orleans, and though the news is reassuring, the cure will take several months. Father returns in early summer, full of stories and gifts. But the gifts must wait because Sister has written with a wonderful idea. Father missed the last Christmas, Brother will be in Texas next Christmas, but they will all be together in July. Why not have Christmas then? So the preparations begin to share a Christmas where the tree is trimmed with roses and the food is a mixture of Fourth of July and Christmas: ice cream and water melon, oyster stew and Christmas cake. It is, as Daddy says, "like having Mother's good hot yeast bread with butter on both sides."

The events described in this book are simple but rich in the details of daily life. There are mouth-watering descriptions of cooking and meals, though, as in the Laura Ingalls Wilder books, it is clear each meal takes much coordinated preparation. There are also clear descriptions of processes such as ironing fancy clothes with an iron heated on a wood stove, food storage, and cane sugar cooking, as well as the traditional taffy pulls and games that accompanied it. The characterizations, though somewhat idealized, are realistic and much as a child would remember them. This is an unusually rich portrait of the life of a southern farm family with interesting details about steamboat travel and life in the logging camps. The simple black-and-white drawings scattered throughout add some details but are not essential to the story.

Garza, Carmen Lomas, as told to Harriet Rohmer. *Family Pictures.* Paintings by Carmen Lomas Garza. Children's Book Press, 1990.

Source of Material: "The pictures in this book are all painted from memories of growing up in Kingsville, Texas, near the border with Mexico." (Note in book.)

Location: Kingsville, Texas.

Dates: Late 1950s.

Grade: 3 to 6.

The author/illustrator conveys the book's events by pairing concise text with a series of paintings based on family stories. These include community events, fairs, birthday parties, and a fundraiser, as well as family memories: grandma killing chickens, a trip to the beach, and the whole family making tamales or eating watermelon on the porch. Though the illustrations are the main focus, the low-key text helps the reader enter into the emotions surrounding the events.

Carmen Lomas Garza is one of the major Mexican-American artists in this country, and the paintings, which are the core of the book, show the range of her talent. The style is naive yet strongly representational. This is a particular family living in a particular place. As you look, you begin to recognize specific family members and you get a clear picture of a large and loving family who enjoys being together. You also get a strong sense of Mexican-American community life. Several of the depictions display elements of Mexican culture: a Los Posadas procession, picking Nopal cactus to eat, a visiting healer, and piñatas at the birthday party. The colorful paintings also show interesting specific details of the interior of the family's house. This is resonant picture of the artist's family and the particularly emotional way she remembers her childhood.

Hall, Donald. *The Man Who Lived Alone.* Illustrated by Mary Azarian. David Godine, 1984.

Source of Material: Based on the life of a relative of the author.

Location: New England.

Dates: Illustrations indicate early in the 20th century.

Grade: 3 to 6.

In simple yet poetic language Donald Hall describes an eccentric but kind-hearted man, from childhood to old age. His father is stingy, lazy, and mean, and he is unhappy until his father's house burns down and he is sent to live with cousins Ezra and Rachel. They and their daughter, Nannie, welcome him, and he flourishes and learns to be a good carpenter and handyman. His father takes him away when he is 12, but he runs away at 14 and spends the next six years traveling all over the United States. Once he is old enough to do as he chooses, he returns to his cousin and builds a cabin nearby. He likes living alone and helping Ezra and Rachel and Nannie and her husband, who now run the farm. His life settles into a pattern of gardening, hunting, and doing odd jobs for cash. He fills his house with an odd assortment of rusty nails, deer pelts, newspapers, old clocks, and wasps' nests, and he befriends an owl and an intelligent mule. He is eccentric and independent but helpful to Nannie and her grandchildren and great-grandchildren, who come to play in the playhouse he made for Nannie long ago. In the end he mostly stays alone in his camp, remembering the past and letting his beard grow ever longer.

This affectionate portrait is illustrated with black-and-white woodcut prints that match the quiet text to perfection. They are filled with small details that clearly show the time and place and the New England setting. Though the pictures convey the eccentricity of the man's crowded cabin and growing beard, they also show his kindness and the real joy of his life.

Hendershot, Judith. *In Coal Country.* Illustrated by Thomas B. Allen. Alfred A. Knopf, 1987.

Source of Material: The author has drawn from her parents' and her own memories of growing up in Willow Grove.

Location: Willow Grove, Ohio.

Dates: 1930s.

Grade: 2 to 6.

This book describes childhood in an Ohio coal-mining community during the 1930s: the economic struggle, harsh conditions, and environmental hazards of mining balanced by the daily joys of childhood. Though the text is brief, it gives a precise view of the life of a miner's child. The father works all night, bathes in a galvanized metal tub, and goes to sleep as the children leave for school. Mama also works hard planting a garden, canning vegetables, preparing meals, and scrubbing clothes in water hauled from the creek. But she always has spring flowers on the table. Seventy-five children live in the row of company houses, and the author recounts memories of games, swimming near a clear waterfall, roasting potatoes over a fire, and sledding in the snow. There are also the harsh realities of mining life, foul smelling smoke that peels the paint from the houses, soot that covers everything, black water in the creek, and gob piles that burn for days.

The richly realized illustrations more than reinforce the text. They give it an emotional resonance that draws the reader in. The paintings are pastel on canvas, which gives a blurred sense to the documentary detail of the pictures. While rich, the colors are grayed and subdued, indicating both the grime that permeated the valley and the fact that these are events from the past. Like the text, the illustrations switch from matter-of-fact details, such as the trains that hauled coal day and night, to moments of family intimacy.

Hendershot, Judith. *Up the Tracks to Grandma's.* Illustrated by Thomas B. Allen. Alfred A. Knopf, 1993.

Source of Material: Author's childhood memories.

Location: Neffs, Ohio.

Dates: 1940s.

Grade: 2 to 5.

Whenever she visits Grandma, the narrator walks the railroad tracks from town to the deep hollow called Echo Stretch. There she helps Grandma catch a chicken for the soup pot and hoe and weed the garden. She stands an anxious watch as Grandma goes deep into a mountain tunnel to get coal for the cookstove. They share the good soup, and Grandma shows her how to make daisy wreaths like they did in the old country. When Aunt Katy breaks her leg, Grandma goes to help, and the little girl comes every day to feed Grandma's chickens and tend her garden. She picks bouquets of flowers, but the kitchen is quiet and she misses her grandmother. After Aunt Katy recovers, Grandma comes back, puts on her apron, admires the tomato patch, and makes a pot of chicken soup.

This quiet story is enriched and enhanced by Thomas Allen's richly colored pastel drawings. There are wonderful full-page portraits of Grandma holding an apronful of daisies and wearing large overalls and a miner's hat. There are many scenes of Grandma and the narrator working together in perfect harmony. The overall tone is soft; the lush greens and golds of an

Appalachian valley dominate, punctuated by reds and pinks and the lavender of Grandma's best polka-dotted dress.

Houston, Gloria. *Littlejim*. Illustrations by Thomas B. Allen. Philomel, 1990.

> **Source of Material:** Stories from the author's family.
>
> **Location:** Appalachian region.
>
> **Date:** Approximately 1918.
>
> **Grade:** 4 to 7.

However hard he tries, 12-year-old Littlejim cannot seem to win the approval of his father, Bigjim, who excels as a timberman and hunter and finds his son's interest in books and writing "unmanly." Littlejim tries to fit into his father's world, learning to plow, driving the team to town, and working at his uncle's timber mill on Saturdays, but somehow his father can only conclude that Littlejim is "not much of a man." Though his father forbids him to waste time on such "tomfoolery," his mother encourages him to enter an essay contest on what it means to be an American. The winner's essay is to be printed in the *Kansas City Star*, and Littlejim hopes that when Bigjim sees his words in print he will finally be proud of him. He thinks about the essay topic over the months in which he sees his best friend's father killed in a milling accident; travels to a nearby town; and continues with his life at home. He talks to adults, listens and writes, and turns his thoughts into an essay that wins the local contest and is sent on to the finals. However, he must now risk Bigjim's wrath by reading his essay at the Fourth of July celebration. Just as his finishes reading, he is informed that his essay has won the competition and is printed on the *Star's* front page. Littlejim finally hears from his father the words of approval he has longed for.

Layered through this story of father and son are vivid descriptions of early 20th-century Appalachian mountain culture and its variety of accents, the generosity of neighbors, and the importance of families. A handful of black-and-white pencil sketches illustrate major points of the story but don't add a lot of specific detail. This is a brief and personal portrait of a boy growing up in a rich culture at a time of great change in America.

Houston, Gloria. *My Great-Aunt Arizona*. Illustrated by Susan Condie Lamb. HarperCollins, 1992.

> **Source of Material:** Author's memories of her great-aunt and teacher.
>
> **Location:** Appalachian region.
>
> **Dates:** 1880s to 1950s.
>
> **Grade:** 2 to 6.

This is Houston's tribute to the great-aunt who taught several generations of children in her 57 years as a schoolteacher in the Blue Ridge Mountains.

Arizona is born in a log cabin and named by her older brother, who had earlier gone west. She is a tall, long-legged girl with braided hair; long, full dresses; white aprons; high-button shoes; and many petticoats. She loves to grow flowers, read, sing, and dance. These things do not change as she grows up and attends the local one-room school with her little brother. Her education is briefly interrupted by her mother's death, but she continues to read and dream of faraway places. Arizona is finally able to go away to school but later decides to return home and teach in the one-room school she and her brother attended. She marries the carpenter who helped build a new, larger school, but she continues to teach, bringing her baby to school. She still wears the long, full dresses, white aprons, and high-button shoes of her girlhood. Flowers grow in every window of Arizona's classroom. She has given up her own dreams of travel, but tells her students that while she has traveled only in her mind, they will one day visit these places themselves. She died on her 93rd birthday, but as Houston says, ". . . my great-aunt Arizona travels with me and those of us whose lives she touched . . . She goes with us in our minds."

This tribute is saved from solemnity by the bright and cheerful illustrations. The lush green of Appalachia is punctuated by colorful autumn leaves and flowers. Though Arizona's style never really changes, the artist uses the changing clothing styles of the schoolchildren to show the passage of time. Although the boys wear overalls throughout the story, the girls' sunbonnets and full skirts give way to increasingly simple, shorter dresses. While most illustrations are realistic depictions of the time and place, some contain an almost comic exaggeration to show Arizona's energy and humor. This is an affectionate portrait in both word and illustration.

Howard, Ellen. *The Cellar.* Illustrated by Patricia Mulvihill. Atheneum, 1992.

————. *The Chickenhouse House.* Illustrated by Nancy Oleksa. Atheneum, 1991.

————. *Edith Herself.* Illustrated by Ronald Himler. Atheneum, 1987.

————. *Sister.* Atheneum, 1990.

Source of Material: Family stories told by author's grandmother and great-aunt and recorded in her aunt's "memory book" when she was 90 years old.

Location: Hancock County, Illinois.

Dates: Late 1800s.

Grade: 2 to 5 and 6 to 8 [see annotation].

These four titles trace the lives of three sisters as their parents establish a farm on the prairie and the family grows. In *The Chickenhouse House,* eldest daughter Alena finds it strange to live in the small house meant for chickens, especially after living in Grandfather's big house. But winter is coming and there is no time to build a big house, and she gradually becomes used to the chicken house, the sounds of the family at night, and the smell of cooking in the morning. As the crops grow, so does a new house: Papa builds a cellar, and friends and neighbors help frame the walls. A carpenter builds the winding stairs, and Mother hangs wallpaper. As threshing time approaches, they move into a new house that seems big, bare, and empty to Alena. She tries to go back to the chickenhouse house, but it's empty and cold now and she realizes that she will get used to the new house just as she did the chickenhouse house.

In *The Cellar*, the family has expanded and the story features a younger sister, Faith, who struggles to prove that she is old enough to help her mother and Alena. Her brother William and Alena try to help, but brother Fritz constantly teases her and calls her a baby. After one particularly bad day Faith volunteers to go by herself into the dark cellar and bring up a basket of apples. It takes all her courage to go outside into the wind, open the heavy, slanted door, and carry her lamp down the steep stairs. The cellar is stocked with summer goods: jars of preserved fruits and pickles, stacks of vegetables, and big wooden barrels packed with apples. She has just filled the backet with sweet apples when Fritz slams the cellar door, causing her to drop and break the kerosene lantern. Her anger at him carries her through the dark, up the stairs, past the now frightened Fritz, and back to her family where she proudly presents an apple to her father.

The Chickenhouse House and *The Cellar* are short books intended for younger readers, but *Sister* and *Edith Herself* are serious works, meant for mature readers. In *Sister*, 14-year-old Alena is looking forward to eighth grade though she knows her father wants her to stay home and help Mother, especially as another baby is due soon. The year starts out well, the new teacher is Johnny Malcolm, who keeps the big boys in order and encourages Alena to think about scholarships and college. Then there is an unforgettable night: father has gone away for several days, and the baby comes early with only Alena to help. When the baby dies a few days later, Mother's mind and spirit seem to go as well, and she sits staring into space, unable to recognize anything. Alena leaves school and takes over, trying to do her mother's work and ignore the hollow place at the center of the family. Then Alena encounters a crisis that causes her to need her mother so badly that she manages to break through Mother's grief and bring her back to the family. But it's too late to go back to school—her family still needs her, and part of her dreams will be sacrificed to that need.

Edith Herself tells of the family's youngest child in the year following the death of her mother. The others can carry on the farm but decide to send Edith to live with her older sister Alena, whose child, Vernon, is about her age. At first life is difficult: Vernon teases, Alena's husband John is strict and often cold, and John's mother seems to dislike Edith. To make matters worse, John is the schoolmaster, and he insists that Edith go to school, even though she has begun to have "fits" in which she blacks out and falls to the floor. Alena fears the stigma and teasing Edith will encounter, but John insists and when an attack occurs, Edith finds she has friends who are willing to defend her, including Vernon. She tells Alena, "I have to go to school!" and finds to her surprise that she no longer wants to return to the farm; she wants to stay with her new family, be Vernon's friend, and help Alena with her new baby.

The Chickenhouse House and The Cellar are illustrated with black-and-white drawings that depict the story and give a sense of historic context, though the emphasis is on the children and their emotions.

Krupinski, Loretta. *Celia's Island Journal.* Written by Celia Thaxter; adapted and illustrated by Loretta Krupinski. Little, Brown & Co., 1992.

Source of Material: Adaptation of *Among the Isles of Shoals* by Celia Thaxter.

Location: Isles of Shoals, Maine; New Hampshire.

Dates: 1839 to 1846.

Grade: 2 to 6.

This picture book was adapted from Celia Thaxter's account of her childhood on White Island during the years her father kept the lighthouse there. Starting with the family's arrival in 1839 and continuing until 1846, the entries tell of the beauty of the island in all its changing seasons. They also tell of the isolation, especially in winter, when storms confine Celia and her younger brother to the stone house and long covered walk leading it to the lighthouse. Luckily their parents have provided flowering plants, singing birds, toys, and books from which Father teaches them. Celia's journal tells of daily life, her love of the island, and the hours she spends watching its changing wildlife.

The realistic but muted illustrations reinforce the text's mood of quiet beauty. The right-hand side of each page shows the family's life in the neat, cheerful house; Celia exploring the island with her little brother or alone, quietly observing or writing in her journal. The left-hand side contains the text, framed by isolated pictures of the plants and animals Celia details in her journal. The time period is shown in details such as clothing, household furnishings, and toys. During the course of the book Celia's brother grows from baby to a vigorous playmate and fellow explorer, and Celia gradually evolves into the young lady pictured on the last page. This book records in both text and illustrations a unique childhood that was rich and fulfilling despite its isolation.

Kurelek, William. *A Prairie Boy's Summer.* Houghton Mifflin, 1975.

———. *A Prairie Boy's Winter.* Houghton Mifflin, 1973.

Source of Material: Artist/author's childhood memories.

Location: Canadian plains of Manitoba.

Dates: 1930s.

Grade: 3 to 6.

Each of these books features a full-color painting on the right-hand page and a detailed explanation of the event on the left. Though the paintings dominate the books, the text that explains them is vivid and surprisingly honest. The stories are told from William's point of view. Though William admits he is not as quick or strong as other boys his age, the pictures emphasize the importance of games in his school. Fully one-third of the pictures show children playing: fox and geese; a fierce hockey quarrel; long-distance skating; snowball battles; softball; the school field-day competition; swimming; and shooting with homemade bows and arrows (the one sport at which William excelled). Included in these books are details of life on a dairy farm: plowing, cultivating, and harvesting; and the daily tasks of feeding, watering, and milking the livestock. William makes it clear that he finds much of this work tedious, but he also relates moments of joy, such as briefly holding a baby killdeer or skiing behind the empty hayrack sled. There is little in either the pictures or the text about William's family or the the nature of their homelife. Together, the two books give a clear but somewhat distant picture of the life of a farmboy on the Canadian plains.

Kurelek's painting are the main feature of these books. They show an obvious love for the endless Canadian prairie with its flat horizon and varying patterns of sky. This sense of space dominates all but the interior scenes, and it makes people's activities seem small by comparison. The paintings are richly detailed and beautifully colored, showing the full range of the seasons. Against this background are shown the details of William's life mixed with the yearly tasks of a prairie farm boy.

MacLachlan, Patricia. *Three Names.* Pictures by Alexander Pertzoff. HarperCollins, 1991.

Source of Material: Stories from the author's family.

Location: Midwestern prairie.

Date: Early 1900s.

Grade: 2 to 5.

Great-Grandfather tells of the days "a hundred years ago" when he attended a one-room school on the prairie, accompanied by the family dog, "Three Names." It is too far to walk, so they go by wagon. His sister Lily drives because she is the eldest, and they pick up three other children on the way. The small white schoolhouse has a barn for the student's horses as well as two outhouses and a storm cellar. All grades share one room and help each other.

George, the oldest student, teaches Great-Grandfather long division, and Great-Grandfather teaches Matty the alphabet. Three Names likes school: he barks at the animals they pass on the drive, sits near the stove as they study, and shares lunchtime meals and games. In the winter they travel by sleigh, and sometimes Mr. Beckett, the teacher, roasts potatoes in the stove. There is a holiday party at the school with food and punch and singing. When Martha plays her fiddle, Three Names howls at the rafters. Then spring comes, the snow melts, the slough fills with water, and Three Names jumps from the wagon to scare the migrating birds. All too soon, spring turns to summer, and on the last day of school, there is a special celebration because George is graduating. Though summer is fine with long warm days, Great-Grandfather and Three Names find they both miss school.

The illustrations combine skillful drawing with the spontaneity of water-color to create the feeling of barren prairie, long distances, and isolated dwellings. The landscape is almost impressionistic and dominates the illustra-tions, but some period details are included, e.g., the houses, the wagons and farm tools, and the children's clothing. Muted shades of sepia, olive green, and blue seem just right for this low-key story of the past.

McLerran, Alice. *Roxaboxen.* Illustrated by Barbara Cooney. Lothrup, Lee & Shepard, 1991.

Source of Material: Based on a childhood manuscript by the author's mother and the gathered memories and maps of Roxaboxen's former inhab-itants.

Location: Yuma, Arizona.

Dates: 1920s.

Grade: 2 to 5.

This lovely picture book celebrates the ability of children to create a separate kingdom for themselves, using the simplest materials. In Yuma, Arizona, a group of children living near a rocky hill turn it into a private place they call Roxaboxen. Stones are moved to outline streets and houses. Wooden boxes become shelves, tables, and store counters, where smooth black stones are used for money. Anything round becomes the steering wheel of a car to be raced around the roads (but not too fast or you go to jail), and any kind of long stick with a harness becomes a galloping horse. Marian is the mayor (of course), but it is Frances who moves to a side street and builds a house outlined in desert glass—a house of jewels. There are wars with ocotillo swords in which the boy bandits raid the girl scouts and they chase each other to the safety of their forts. In the winter when the weather is bad and the children are busy, no one goes to Roxaboxen for weeks at a time. It doesn't matter. Roxaboxen is always there, waiting for spring when the ocotillo blossoms are filled with honey and the children return to build and play.

The years go by, the seasons change, and the friends grow up and move away, but even that is not the end, because none of them ever forgets Roxaboxen and their children grow up hearing stories of that place. More than 50 years later, Frances goes back and Roxaboxen is still there, the stone borders outlining streets and houses, and in the place where she built her house of jewels, the desert glass still glows.

For this book, Barbara Cooney uses the ambers, rose, magenta, and blue of the desert landscape. She has captured the varying moods of a desert day, particularly the magic hours of the long twilight when the sun has set but the light lingers in a golden glow. Beyond Roxaboxen stretches the desert—as limitless as the children's imagination. The story has a universal quality that defies time, but the simple bungalows in the first picture and the children's clothing suggest an earlier, simpler time when children were less distracted from the world of pure imagination.

Moody, Ralph. *Little Britches: Father and I Were Ranchers.* Illustrated by Edward Shenton. Norton, 1950.

————. *Man of the Family.* Illustrated by Tran Marwicke. Norton, 1962.

Source of Material: Author's childhood memories.

Location: Colorado.

Dates: 1906 to 1913.

Grade: 6 to Adult.

Ralph Moody is eight years old when his parents buy a ranch in Colorado, hoping the change of air will cure his father's tuberculosis. The house is shabby and broken, and because they are at the end of the ditch, there is very little water, but they are determined to succeed. Though they encounter terrible storms and several accidents, Father is good with his hands, everyone is willing to work, and their neighbors are sympathetic and helpful. As Father struggles to grow crops on dry land, train reluctant horses, and create a real ranch, Ralph finds work herding a neighbor's cows and helping neighbors with the harvest. In the process he learns to ride well enough to be offered a job on a large ranch, where he spends a glorious summer with real cowboys. Under the guidance of his hero, a cowboy named Hi, he learns to train a horse well enough to win the local trick riding contest. But the ranch is not doing well that summer, the fights over water have begun again, and Father is not only in danger, he can't get enough water to sustain the ranch. Their neighbors offer to help them, but Father feels the family must face reality. They sell the ranch and move into town where Father finds work building houses and doing odd jobs. Then, when things seem to be going well, he contracts pneumonia and dies 10 days later—leaving 11-year-old Ralph to be the man of the family.

The second book, *Man of the Family*, tell of the family's struggle to survive through a variety of odd jobs and other enterprises. Ralph is sure he can get a job on a ranch, but Mother is determined to keep the children in school. She and daughter Grace begin a cookery route, selling homecooked food to women in the town. They then switch to a specialized laundry business. Ralph picks up work helping cattlemen drive their herds through town and hauling railroad ties. All the children pick fruit in summer, and Ralph earns extra cash as a jockey in match races at the local fairground. He spends another summer as a cowboy and can't imagine any other life, but his friend Hi tells him the cowboy's day is coming to an end and that Ralph should learn a trade. While he considers this, an old secret is disclosed, and Mother decides to leave the area rather than betray an old friend. They leave in the middle of the night with no opportunity to say good-bye to all their friends and the life they had come to love.

Full-page and small insert illustrations are scattered throughout the text. The black-and-white paintings capture the action of major events and give a sense of both the location and the time period.

Morris, Linda Lowe. *Morning Milking.* Illustrated by David DeRan. Picture Book Studio, 1991.

Source of Material: Author's childhood memories.

Location: Maryland.

Dates: 1950s.

Grade: 2 to 6.

This book simply and poetically traces the events of a single winter morning on a dairy farm as seen through the eyes of a young girl. It is dark when her father's alarm wakes her, but she loves the morning milking so she joins him, walking to the huge old barn in the clear still morning under a starlit sky. There they go through the familiar cow-feeding routines: first the silage and meal and then the hay from the bales in the loft. She takes a minute to talk to cow number 28, who is a calm and gentle listener. She gives the cat and her kittens a treat and helps her father, working down the rows "with a rhythm like a dance we have practiced many times." Sometimes, as they work, her father tells her stories about growing up on the farm and his parents and grandparents who came before. As they finish and head toward the house and breakfast, her father begins a story about a favorite horse. She wishes she could stop time and hold everything forever, and for a moment she is sad. Then she realizes that the stories her father and mother tell are a way of stopping time. "They took the things they loved and turned them into stories."

The clarity of the writing is matched by the simple watercolors that face each page of text. Though the father's and daughter's faces are never seen, other things are shown in specific detail: a shiny toaster and mug of coffee; sleepy cows; and a pair of gray-striped kittens. There is a wonderful sense of the scale and space within the barn and the stillness outside. The paintings' gray and sepia tones match perfectly the quiet yet poetic quality of the text.

Naylor, Phyllis Reynolds, and Lura Schield Reynolds. *Maudie in the Middle.* Illustrated by Judith Gwyn Brown. Atheneum, 1988.

Source of Material: Based on the childhood of co-author, Lura Schield Reynolds.

Location: Iowa.

Date: 1908.

Grade: 4 to 7.

Maudie, who falls right in the middle of the seven children in her family, thinks the middle is the worst place of all. The older three are allowed to do all sorts of things she can't because she's still too young, and the younger ones get special privileges and much of the attention Maudie longs for. Perhaps lovely Aunt Sylvie will choose Maudie for her godchild. She's not sure how one becomes a godchild, but she's sure it has to do with being good, so Maudie tries to be good. She helps her mother with the endless chores around the house and farm, tends her baby sister Violet, and even helps drive the horses during haying. But there are just too many ways to get into trouble. She is impulsive and quick tempered, always doing things she later regrets. Once she talks her brothers into a game so dangerous that Father spanks them all.

It's easier to be good at school. Maudie's the only third-grader in the one-room school, and Miss Richardson always seems to know just what she's thinking. There are also plenty of happy times at home: anticipating the yearly order from Sears, Roebuck; their first automobile; the box social where she recites three verses perfectly; and the first week of vacation when it seems all she does is play.

When Aunt Sylvie announces she is getting married and moving to another state, Maudie's dreams of their special life together abruptly end. She enjoys the fun and parties of the wedding, but she misses Aunt Sylvie and wonders if she'll ever be good enough to be special. She and her siblings are tested when Mother and Father are called away by a dying relative. The children are left in the care of Joe and Clare, the two eldest children. Guided by their helpful minister's wife, they manage quite well at first but soon grow weary of the daily chores and the cold of December. As the days drag on, they make plans for Christmas and wonder when Mother and Father will come home. Violet becomes sick, and Maudie is the one who takes care of her, holding and rocking her through long days and nights. As she holds her baby sister, Maudie learns what it is like to be needed and what for her is the true path to goodness. Then Mother and Father return and she hears the words she's been waiting for all her life: "Oh, Maudie, I missed you so!"

This is very much Maudie's story, and her character dominates the story. Though Maudie longs for her mother's attention, the reader soon realizes what Maudie already knows: the amount of work required to maintain a farm and raise seven children is simply overwhelming, and Mother works constantly. Father and Joe work equally hard in the fields, and it is this partnership of labor that provides the security for the family. Attractive black-and-white drawings at the chapter heads give added visual information but are not essential to the story. The story offers a keen insight into the life of a middle child as well as a clear picture of Iowa farm life, particularly that of the women and children.

Nickens, Bessie. *Walking the Log: Memories of a Southern Childhood.* Rizzoli, 1994.

Source of Material: Artist/author's childhood memories.

Locations: Louisiana, Arkansas, and Texas.

Dates: 1910s.

Grade: 3 to 6.

Though she has been painting since she was seven years old, Bessie Nickens began to paint full-time after her retirement. The paintings and text in this book recreate her childhood in the rural American South. Her African-American parents were migrant workers, and the family moved frequently as they sought work in the sawmills, oil fields, and cotton patches of the South. Though she makes it clear that their homes were frequently shacks and the family had few possessions or clothing, she found beauty in the world around her and support from a loving family.

While the text describes the details of poverty, the paintings emphasize remembered happiness and the beauty of her rural surroundings. The paintings show children picking wildflowers, roaming barefoot through a densely wooded swamp, and calling doodlebugs out of the sand. Other paintings show children playing hide-and-seek, jumping rope, swinging, and playing snap-the-whip. These are balanced by sections detailing the hard work this family faced: her mother washing clothes in an outdoor boiler and ironing with a heavy flat iron, the children carrying water, and the entire family picking cotton. Her paintings tend to be somewhat flat with inconsistent scale and perspective, but they are richly colored and filled with detail. The clean, minimally furnished interiors show many aspects of daily life and often feature her mother. Together the paintings and text give a view of life in the rural South early in this century.

O'Kelley, Mattie Lou. *Circus*. Atlantic Monthly Press and Joy Street Books, 1986.

————. *From the Hills of Georgia: An Autobiography in Paintings*. Little, Brown & Co., 1983.

————. *Moving to Town*. Little, Brown & Co. 1991.

Source of Material: Childhood memories of the artist/author.

Location: Maysville, Georgia.

Dates: Early 1900s.

Grade: 3 to 6.

The works of primitive painter Mattie Lou O'Kelley have been referred to as memory paintings, a particularly apt description. Using vivid color, pattern, and a sense of scale related more to perception than reality, she recalls in minute detail her childhood on a farm in Georgia. Her paintings have been collated to create three children's books. *From the Hills of Georgia* is an autobiographic work, showing events from her birth to age 15, when she is shown at a party in her "beau-catching outfit." Each painting reveals a separate memory: the birth of a brother, a tormenting turkey, picnics at the church, and parties at home. The paintings are loaded with details; in interior scenes, the sizes of rooms are dramatically increased to squeeze in all the people and their various activities. Such arbitrary shifts in scale can be disconcerting to those expecting a more conventional form of reality, but when considering a picture in which Papa kills hogs that look bigger than the horses, it helps to remember that that's probably how they looked to young Mattie. The paintings are decorative—filled with color and pattern; and dramatic—filled with stories and events. Though the text helps, there are many unexplained details in each painting, leaving much room for reader participation and imagination.

Though the above book is autobiographical and scattered, the text of the other two focuses on specific events. *Circus* describes the afternoon the family leaves school and the farm to go to the circus in a nearby town. Traveling by horse-drawn surrey, they encounter a thunderstorm and a flooded river. They then visit a couple of stores in town and arrive just in time for the circus parade. They follow the parade to the circus grounds and encounter a merry-go-round and a variety of sideshows. The show starts, and from the front row, the family sees each amazing act. They return home at night and are so sleepy that Papa does their chores "just this once." Though the paintings of the circus scenes have a sense of continuity, other paintings seem to have been arranged randomly. Many contain mysterious elements that are never fully explained: the ghostly "boogers" in the farmyard, a devil figure dangling over the covered bridge, and the shortcut through the graveyard. However, the individual pictures are filled with action, and the circus scenes are a delight.

Moving to Town centers around the family's brief attempt to live in the nearby city. They pack their household into three wagons and travel through valleys and steep hills to the city. The city scenes are very much from a child's point of view, with fantastic, almost surreal architecture side-by-side with store signs naively advertising "Lady Things" and "Men and Boy Things." Accompanied by their faithful black-and-white dogs, the two children, Mattie and Johnnie, take in all the sights of the city: the zoo, the movies, a mysterious underground shopping center, and a large school. A sister takes them to a restaurant, but the food is "not nearly as good as Mama's," so Mattie saves it for the dogs. Though they enjoy their stay in the city, they are all happy when Papa decides to move them home for Christmas. The neighbors are there to help them move in for a grand Christmas celebration complete with a huge tree.

The stories are slim, but the paintings used to create them are filled with action and a child's sense of adventure. The landscapes with their rolling hills, patterned trees, and crisp farmhouses show a strong sense of design and color. The interiors and other party scenes are bursting with people, all busily occupied. Young readers will be kept busy interpreting these scenes and entering Mattie Lou O'Kelley's world of memory.

Peck, Robert Newton. *A Day No Pigs Would Die.* Alfred A. Knopf, 1972.

Source of Material: Author's childhood memories.

Location: Vermont.

Dates: 1930s.

Grade: 6 to Adult.

When the boy, Rob Peck, saves a neighbor's cow and is mauled in the process, the grateful neighbor gives him a newborn pig, which Rob names Pinky. The pig becomes a devoted follower, a prize winner, and a good listener as Rob goes through a 13th year filled with learning and tragedy. His family are Plain Folk, followers of the *Book of Shaker*. Although his father, Haven Peck, can neither read nor cipher, his commitment to and love of the earth he stubbornly farms are deep. But times are hard and crops not reliable, so Haven earns his living killing pigs for another farmer, and the family struggles to survive each winter.

As Haven senses his impending death, he tries to show Rob—who will replace him as the man of the family—the importance of his guiding values, as well as the importance of the education that young Rob will need. When it becomes clear that Pinky is not the brood sow they hoped for, Rob and his father together do what is "needful": they slaughter the pig for winter food. As

Rob kisses his father's bloody hands in forgiveness, he accepts the burdens his father's death will place on him. When his father dies the following spring, Rob again does what is needful: he tells the neighbors, digs a grave, and speaks plain words over his father as he is buried in the ground that meant so much to him.

Despite the tragic ending, this book is filled with humor and a great love for both the Vermont countryside and the people who live there. Essentially, this is a book about the values held by one man and the way those values shaped his life, his relationships, and his work habits. It is also about the grace he gave his youngest child and only son.

Peck, Robert Newton. *Soup.* Illustrated by Charles C. Gehm. Alfred A. Knopf, 1974.

————. *Soup and Me.* Illustrated by Charles Lilly. Alfred A. Knopf, 1975.

————. *Soup for President.* Illustrated by Ted Lewin. Alfred A. Knopf, 1978. (and others in this continuing series.)

Source of Material: Author's childhood memories.

Location: Vermont.

Dates: Late 1930s.

Grade: 3 to 7.

This series features two boys growing up in a small Vermont town. Peck recreates all the adventures of a small town childhood: school; bullies (male and female); games; dares; and physical challenges such as whipping apples or rolling down the hill inside (or astride) an out-of-control barrel. The nature of Rob's friendship with the energetic and inventive Soup leads to frequent encounters with adult authority. The theme is that of a friendship delicately balanced among dominance, mischief, and unexpected acts of gallantry. Throughout the series, Peck perfectly captures remembered conversations and mixes reality, fantasy, lots of humor, and the mercurial emotions of childhood and early adolescence.

The series is illustrated with realistic black-and-white drawings, approximately one per chapter. Though the choice of illustrator varies from book to book, the style is similar, and all the illustrations accurately depict the small town setting, the clothing, and the physical reality of the life of these two boys.

Pelloski, Anne. *First Farm in the Valley: Anna's Story.* Pictures by Wendy Watson. Philomel, 1982.

————. *Stairstep Farm: Anna Rose's Story.* Pictures by Wendy Watson. Philomel, 1981.

———. *Willow Wind Farm: Betsy's Story*. Pictures by Wendy Watson. Philomel, 1981.

———. *Winding Valley Farm: Annie's Story*. Pictures by Wendy Watson. Philomel, 1981.

Source of Material: Based on personal and family memories tracing four generations of Anne Pelloski's own Polish-American family.

Location: Wisconsin.

Dates: 1960s, 1930s, 1900s, 1870s.

Grade: 3 to 7.

Starting with her niece Betsy's life in the 1960s and moving backward through her own life and that of her mother and grandmother, Pelloski re-creates the childhood activities and games of four generations of farm children in Wisconsin. Like true family stories, the books are episodic, each chapter relating a single event. Some are funny, some ordinary, and some tragic. All are seen through the eyes of children, so the sadness of the death of a grandfather is mixed with memories of games played in the dark while adults prayed and sang in the house. Throughout the series, the descriptions of games and other children's activities are clear enough to guide a novice.

In *First Farm in the Valley*, the family members and their immediate neighbors speak only Polish, and many holidays are celebrated as they were in the old country. For example, Christmas treats are brought by Gvozdki, young men wearing sheepskin masks, and at Easter, children play the game of Dyngus, in which they try to get the beautifully colored eggs from each other. These families are also part of the New World. There is a wonderful description of an 1876 Fourth of July celebration with a procession of evergreen-decorated farm wagons parading through a town that is also decorated with tall evergreen branches. As the series continues, English gradually replaces Polish in the homes, though some customs and foods remain in the family tradition.

All four stories describe farming households in which everyone works and large families in which older children take care of younger ones. At times they seem unrealistically cheerful about it all, even the seven-mile walks to school that are featured in *Winding Valley Farm*. While some of the adventures include children's misbehavior and repentence, most disputes and sadness are glossed over. The details of daily life are precise, with a clear picture of farm life and the lives of immigrant families in transition. However, the characters tend to be less defined and the narrative less compelling than other books dealing with farm life. Without names, it is sometimes difficult to distinguish family members, and when the large number of cousins is added, it is downright confusing.

At each chapter head and intermittent points in the books are black-and-white drawings of sturdy children busy at a variety of tasks. As in the text, the children in these drawings tend to be generic, but the backgrounds are detailed and will help urban children visualize life in a crowded farm household. The covers feature colored pictures showing all the children in each family and some aspect of their lives.

Polacco, Patricia. *The Bee Tree.* Philomel, 1993.

———. *Meteor!* Dodd, Mead & Co., 1987.

———. *Some Birthday!* Simon & Schuster, 1991.

———. *Thundercake.* Philomel, 1990.

———. *My Rotten Redheaded Older Brother.* Simon and Schuster, 1994.

Source of Material: Author's childhood memories and other family stories.

Location: Michigan.

Dates: Vary from turn of the century through late 1940s.

Grade: 1 to 5.

Despite the different publishers, these books can be considered a series in that they all spring from a common source: family stories from Polacco's childhood in rural Michigan. Her first picture book, *Meteor,* is based on an actual event. It tells, with comic exaggeration, the reaction of friends and neighbors when a meteor crashes into her grandparents' backyard. News of the event grows with each telling, and the growing number of sightseers creates an instant carnival complete with a band, a hot air balloon, scientists, and a Chautaqua Circus performance. Everyone who touches the meteor feels unusually lucky and special, "REALLY SPECIAL!" (Ms. Polacco still has a piece of the meteor which she shows to children when she tells this story.)

The child character in *The Bee Tree* is Mary Ellen Polacco's mother, and this picture book re-creates a chase across the countryside to find a bee tree. Mary Ellen's Grampa traps several bees in a jar, and the chase begins as they follow first one then another back to the hive. As they run through the countryside, they are joined by a growing number of neighbors and curious goats and geese. The successful hunt concludes with a party back at the house featuring baking powder biscuits, fresh brewed tea, and, "of course, the honey!" Then Grampa takes Mary Ellen inside and quietly shows her a lesson he learned from his father—that knowledge and learning are sweet but must be pursued.

In *Thunder Cake,* the author shares memories of her maternal grandmother, including how she helped young Patricia overcome her fear of thunderstorms. As a thunderstorm approaches, growing louder and more threatening, her grandmother keeps her busy gathering the ingredients for a "thunder cake." This process involves gathering eggs, milking the cow, going into the woods to the dry shed for flour and sugar, and picking strawberries and tomatoes. As they work, they count out the time between the lightning and thunder, judging the distance of the storm. By the time the storm arrives, they have completed the cake, and Patricia has learned she is braver than she ever realized. This book includes a recipe for a "thunder cake," complete with the secret ingredient.

Some Birthday! recalls a birthday celebration from the summers Polacco spent with her father and Gramma in Williamston, Michigan. Though it's Patricia's birthday and she has dropped hints, no one pays any attention and the day proceeds as usual: Dad goes to work, comes home, reads the paper, and starts watching TV. Suddenly he decides this is the perfect night to photograph the legendary Monster at Clay Pit Bottoms. Accompanied by Patricia's brother Rich and cousin Billy, they set off with camera, smelly cheese bait, flashlights, hot dogs, buns, and marshmallows. They pitch a blanket tent, build a fire, and eat while telling stories of the monster. They begin to hear noises, so Dad goes off to investigate, and when they hear a howl and loud *kerplash*, the children run straight home. The monster turns out to be a floating log, and dogs fighting over the cheese, and the splash was Dad, who fell into the water. When Gramma finally stops laughing, she brings out a whipped cream cake with a rubber monster and candles on top. The singing and presents that follow are the fitting conclusion to what has been some birthday!

In *My Rotten Redheaded Older Brother,* Polacco recalls the frustration of always being four years younger and never being able to beat her brother at anything. He teases her into endless, hopeless competitions, enjoying her anger and his triumph. One night, she wishes on a shooting star to beat him just once, and the next day she not only beats him, she also discovers how much he cares about her. The illustrations for this book combine Polacco's exaggerated physical gestures with realistic and affectionate portraits of her family. As usual, the farm animals join in comic appreciation of Patricia's dilemma. The end papers are a collection of real photos of Patricia and her brother taken through their childhood.

Though the illustrations vary somewhat from book to book, they all share the same dynamic design and joyous energy. Many of these stories' bystanders are exaggerated to the point of comedy, but each are also individuals, affectionately portrayed. Everyone enters into the event, even the curious farm animals who tag along, observing every detail. Gramma's cat is a special source of delight, wonderfully observed and drawn with loving humor. The family's Russian heritage is shown in the clothing, brightly painted furniture, the tea somovar, and the icons that sit on special shelves. Polacco is particularly strong in page design. Her dynamic lines , strong colors, and white pages focus the action and keep the stories moving forward. Though based on layers of memory, there is little sentiment or nostalgia in these lively stories.

Rossiter, Phyllis. *Moxie.* Four Winds Press, 1990.

Source of Material: Based on the childhood memories of the author's husband.

Location: Cloud County, Kansas.

Date: 1934.

Grade: 5 to 8.

Drew Ralston knows it's bad luck to turn 13 on Friday the 13th, but he can't imagine how things could get worse than they already are. The country is locked in a depression, drought has once again destroyed any chance for a crop, and there's barely enough feed to keep the livestock alive. Drew's older brother Poke begs his father to give up the farm and try their luck in the city. But Granddad homesteaded this farm, and Drew loves it too much to give up without a fight. When he and his best friend Jay do their best to make Drew's birthday memorable, they get in trouble, as usual. Drew's bad luck continues when school is cut short by a blinding dust storm and it takes all his energy and self-control to find his way home and save his small herd of sheep. This small herd and Dad's promise to hold on until Drew's eighth-grade graduation in June are his only hope as the dust storms continue, family after family is forced off their land, and Drew unexpectedly buys a mule as a gesture of friendship. On the day he fights off a thieving hobo who has threatened Mom, he finds he has more courage than he realized, and eventually he sees his way to a last, desperate solution. On the day Jay's family is forced to leave their farm, Drew decides to sell his precious sheep, though he is not sure whether Dad will use the money to hang on or to leave. When a fire threatens to sweep everything away, Dad realizes how much the land means to him, and though they have lost the barn and precious hay, he decides to hang on as long as possible.

The novel's strengths are solid character development and a tangible sense of the times. Though this is Drew's story, all the characters are distinct. Mom fights bad luck with a litany of superstitions but can't get used to shabby clothes and the dust that creeps into everything. Dad takes refuge in silence and temper but really loves his sons. Laconic Poke sees more deeply than he lets on; he loves his family but cannot make himself love the farm. Drew's character is the most fully realized. Hard times have made him grow up in some ways, but he still can't curb the impulsive mischief that gets him in trouble at school.

The novel also gives readers a sense of the despair of hardworking people when even the elements have turned against them. It is a story filled with the individual triumphs and tragedies that sum up the times.

Rylant, Cynthia. *Appalachia: The Voices of Sleeping Birds.* Illustrated by Barry Moser. Harcourt Brace Jovanovich, 1991.

Source of Material: Author's and illustrator's childhoods in the region.

Location: Appalachia. Appalachian Region, Southern.

Dates: 1940s through 1960s.

Grade: 3 to Adult.

In words that capture the cadence of speech and the understated emotion of the Appalachian people, Rylant describes the region and its people. This is a book of near-poetry, filled with affection unmarred by nostalgia. Rylant takes the reader into the minds and hearts of people whose love for their mountains is stronger than ambition or the need to travel. Quickly dismissing the term *hillbillies,* she describes the variety of life, the joy of each season, the deeply felt religious beliefs, and the genuine affection manifested in casual hospitality with friends and quiet generosity to everyone.

The watercolor illustrations by Barry Moser are as inspired as the writing, matching its understated quality. The pictures are almost like snapshots from a family album. There are "good dogs," simple frame houses, a dresser cluttered with photos and knickknacks, a wood-burning stove with biscuits in the warming shelf, and wonderful portraits of a variety of people. Even if you have never been to Appalachia, this book will give you a clear picture of the place and the people.

Rylant, Cynthia. *The Relatives Came.* Illustrations by Stephen Gammell. Bradbury Press, 1985.

———. *Waiting to Waltz: A Childhood: Poems.* Drawings by Stephen Gammell. Bradbury Press, 1984.

———. *When I Was Young in the Mountains.* Illustrated by Diane Goode. E. P. Dutton, 1982.

Source of Material: Author's childhood memories.

Location: The Appalachian region of West Virginia.

Dates: Late 1950s and 1960s.

Grade: 2 to 6 (see page 130).

Though these three books were written at different times and are in different styles, they are all based on Rylant's childhood in Appalachia. *When I Was Young in the Mountains* describes her early childhood when she lived with her grandparents in a small house in the mountains. These are memories of special moments and good times: Grandmother's cornbread and hot okra; a muddy swimming hole; baths in tin tubs; church and baptisms; and the long black snake Grandmother killed with a hoe. Diane Goode's softly colored pencil drawings add a myriad of details to the text: a hanging kerosene lamp, an old-fashioned general store, the handpump outside the house, and the black cooking stove in the kitchen. Though realistically portrayed, this is a world where poverty is softened by loving, caring adults—and to this child, that is enough.

Waiting to Waltz is a collection of poems covering the next period of Rylant's life—the years she lived in a small town with her single mother. The simple, low-key blank verse explores the quiet longings and sudden perceptions of a girl edging toward adulthood. The voice is clear, with a distinct edge and no hint of nostalgia. Here are the moments that create reality: romance, religion, death, and the unexpected way people move in and out of your life. Stephen Gammell's soft pencil sketches have the same edge, and there is nothing pretty about them. This is a town of old buildings, weedy sidewalks, and worn-out pickup trucks. The poetry and images combine to create a portrait of a girl whose imagination and longings are growing beyond the confines of the town. By comparison, *When I Was Young in the Mountains* ends with a statement of contentment, but *Waiting to Waltz* is filled with adolescent longing.

In *The Relatives Came*, author and artist combine talents to create a loving description of the joyous mayhem of a visit by a large group of relatives. The book is structured almost like a piece of music. It starts with the quiet mystery of packing the car, departing before dawn, and the long trip through the hills. This quiet beginning gives way with a bang when the relatives arrive and builds into a crescendo of hugs, hugs, and more hugs with the hosting family. The initial excitement winds down with supper, quiet talk, and people bedding down all over the house. The relatives stay "for weeks and weeks," visiting, helping with the garden, and fixing things. Then early one morning they pack up and leave, once again driving into the night and leaving behind a house that, to the hosting family, suddenly feels too big and too quiet.

Gammell has illustrated this reunion with affectionate comic glee, starting with a multihued station wagon precariously piled with luggage. The picture of the arrival is filled with energy as the car hits the fence, the luggage explodes from the top, and three children leap from a swing to greet them. The hugging relatives come in a wonderful assortment of faces and bodies, all smiling and happy. Especially comic are the pictures of everyone sleeping on the floor, including a dog on his back with all four feet in the air. Gammell introduces to the story elements such as picture taking, a string band, and an uncle who insists on cutting the boys' hair. These affectionate caricatures match the warmth of the story to create an enduring memory.

Saunders, Susan. *Fish Fry.* Illustrated by S. D. Schindler. Viking Press, 1982.

Source of Material: Stories told by the author's Aunt Edith about her childhood.

Location: Chandler, Texas.

Dates: Early 1900s.

Grade: 2 to 5.

This picture book depicts young Edith at an all-day fish fry in the piney woods of east Texas. The story is a straightforward account of the day in which Edith helps her mother pack baskets of cookies, cakes, pies, pickles, and jams and load them in the wagon for the long drive to the river. Daddy and the other men have been there since dawn and the others arrive to find catfish hanging from all the tree branches—just as Edith's friend Eugene has predicted. Mama sets to work with her frying pan, and the children play until dinnertime. Each family has a large groundcloth, and they all share a dinner featuring fried catfish, hushpuppies, and a variety of side dishes and pickles. For dessert there are all those cookies, cakes, and pies, and watermelon cooled in the river. After the feast, Eugene promises to show Edith the biggest alligator in the river and accidentally pushes her into the river. He gets a spanking but they're all surprised when they come upon the biggest alligator anyone had ever seen this far up the river. There will be plenty to tell the folks in town about this fish fry.

   Much of the sense of the time and place is carried by the illustrations that fill most of each double-spread page. The first few illustrations are filled with details of the house, especially the kitchen with its assortment of gadgets and big black stove, as well as the wagons and harness. They travel through a green landscape of small farms and winding streams to a piney wood. The picture of the picnicking families enjoying the good food and each other shows clearly why this was a day to be remembered.

Shasha, Mark. *Night of the Moonjellies.* Simon & Schuster, 1992.

Source of Material: Story from the author's childhood.

Location: Connecticut.

Date: Unknown.

Grade:: 2 to 5.

The author/artist recalls the summer he was seven and the busy days he spent helping out at Gram's seaside food stand. Young Mark is exploring the beach one day when he finds something that feels like jelly, so he takes it to the stand to show Gram. She tells him he has found something special, but that it's a surprise for later. She gives him a kiss and they go to work welcoming the other workers and getting ready for the day. In addition to the usual fare,

Gram's stand serves the best lobster rolls in New England. Soon they are hard at work serving lines of people. After a brief pause in the afternoon, it's time to set up the popcorn machine for the evening rush. It's a busy, noisy night, but Gram hasn't forgotten her promise. As soon as they have cleaned up, she hands him a sweater and leads him down to the pier and a waiting boat. Tyler, a fisherman, serves them hot chocolate and takes them out to the dark sea. Gram holds up Mark's bag of beach treasures, and something sparkles inside. It's a moonjelly, and Tyler is taking them to the place where it belongs. Thousands of glowing moonjellies stretch along the sea in every direction, and Mark pours his out to join the others in the shimmering sea. At home as they share chamomile tea and melon, Gram puts his other sea treasures into a box with a note that says, "With love to Mark from Gram—night of the moonjellies."

Shasha uses richly colored oil pastels and the long horizontal space of the page to effectively illustrate his story. The rich blues of the early morning beach and harbor gradually merge into brighter colors and more dynamic lines as the stand opens and the rush begins, and the focus moves from Mark and Gram to the crowds at the stand. Later, the orange glow of sunset merges into an overhead view of the stand, its red and yellow umbrellas, and the surrounding cars and customers. After Mark and Gram clean up, they emerge from the darkened stand into a setting of soft moonlight and a glittering sea. The artist uses strong line, various points of view, and dynamic color to tell the story of a hard-working grandmother who still has time to create a special memory for her grandson.

Slawson, Michele Benoit. *Apple Picking Time.* Illustrated by Deborah Kogan Ray. Crown Publishers, 1994.

Source of Material: Author's childhood memories.

Location: Yakima Valley, Washington.

Dates: 1950s.

Grade: 2 to 5.

The author remembers her childhood in the Yakima Valley of Washington and an occasion when everyone took time from regular tasks, including school, to help pick the fruit before it spoiled. Leaving before dawn, they join friends and neighbors in the cold morning air of the orchard. This year Anna is bigger; the canvas bag is not so heavy and fits better, and she knows how to lean forward, leaving both hands free to twist and snap off the apples. Anna is determined to pick an entire bin of apples in a day, just like her parents and grandparents. All day a tractor moves back and forth, collecting the full bins of apples and punching a half-moon on the picker's tickets. At midday they picnic under a tree with their grandparents, and Papa leads Mama in an impromptu waltz; but when the work whistle blows, Anna is back up the ladder, picking in the hot afternoon sun. As the day winds down and the pickers begin to leave, Anna fills her bin, earning the precious half-moon stamp on *her* ticket.

The simple text is lushly enhanced by Ray's paintings, which set the story in the golden-green glow of autumn. Ruby has captured the early morning haze, fruit-laden trees, and dappled sunlight of an orchard. The reality of the situation is not sacrificed: the pickers are warm and smiling, but also apparent are the focused intensity of the work and body postures showing the fatigue of the pickers at day's end. Anna's pride clearly shows in her beaming face pictured above the rounded pile of deep red apples she has picked that day. Together, the text and pictures clearly portray a time when harvesting involved entire communities.

Smothers, Ethel Footman. *Down in the Piney Woods.* Alfred A. Knopf, 1992.

Source of Material: Based on incidents from author's childhood.

Location: Camilla, Georgia.

Dates: 1930s.

Grade: 5 to 8.

This is an intensely remembered and vividly written portrait of an African-American sharecropper's family in the backwoods section of Georgia. Though life is often difficult, 10-year-old Annie Rye loves being the oldest, so she is bitterly angry when her mother and father decide it's time for her three older half-sisters to live with them and become a real family. Through the period in which the girls grudgingly come to terms with this new life, they share household tasks, deal with the potential danger of an intensely prejudiced white neighbor, and pitch in to buy a baseball suit for Daddy. This common goal and the frustrations they meet in getting the money help them to finally become a family—a family who can cheer together when Daddy's pitching skills help his team win the game.

Written in first person and filled with colorful dialogue, this account recalls the particular joys of a rural childhood: waiting, pennies in hand, for the rolling store; making grass dolls; catching June bugs; and hunting opossums in the moonlight. Visits to grandparents are a special treat, with good food and stories. Though the family is large, the characters are distinctive, especially feisty Annie Rye. Although racial prejudice naturally makes life more difficult for this family, Daddy has a white boss who respects him and protects him when the Ku Klux Klan burns a cross in front of their house. Daddy is finally able to solve the problem by rescuing the child of his enemy, at the risk of his own life. In the end, Annie is reconciled with all her sisters, and they are truly a family.

Soto, Gary. *Living Up the Street: Narrative Recollections.* Strawberry Hill Press, 1985.

————. *A Summer Life.* University Press of New England, 1990.

Source of Material: Author's childhood memories.

Location: Fresno, California.

Dates: 1950s to 1960s.

Grade: 6 to Adult.

These two books deal with the same period of the author's life, often with the same events. *Living Up the Street* is written as direct narrative while *A Summer Life* strips events to a sensory essence, evoking the sights, scents, and sounds of life in a rural barrio. Soto makes tangible both the oppressive heat of California's Central Valley and the grit of Fresno's industrial side, a neighborhood where noisy factories and food processing plants coexisted with the homes of the poor.

Soto's father died when he was young, and his mother had to leave her three children alone for most of the day. Despite her rules and warnings, the children were often bored and improvised a variety of entertainments that were ingenious, but often dangerous. What emerges is a portrait of a child who was lonely, alienated from his stepfather, and increasingly aware of the limitations he faced as a poor Mexican-American. In one chapter, he vividly describes how his dreams of wealth become buried by the realities of summers spent picking grapes.

This bleak picture is balanced by his keen awareness of his environment. Though the language is careful, precise, and poetic, it serves to pull the reader into a world of heat, dust, and the uncertainty of poverty. While the essays and stories capture both the jagged edges and stultifying boredom of his childhood, Soto also captures simple pleasures: fruit from his grandfather's garden, the cooling spray of a garden hose, and the comfort of old tennis shoes. His world was small, but he explored it openly and deeply, savoring each success and dreaming of a better life. Soto's exact descriptions pull readers into a reality that is tangible and deeply felt.

Williams, Sherley Ann. *Working Cotton.* Illustrated by Carol Byard. Harcourt Brace Jovanovich, 1992.

Source of Material: Author's childhood experience.

Location: Fresno, California.

Date: Unknown.

Grade: 3 to 8.

This book is based on poems from the author's collection, *Peacock Poems,* published by Wesleyan Press in 1975. The spare text uses an African-American child's voice and point of view to capture the bleak reality of a day in a migrant worker's life. The day starts in the early morning cold with workers riding on buses and then clustering around a fire waiting for the sun to rise and burn off the fog. The family picks the cotton in rows: one for Papa, one for the two older sisters, and one for Mamma, Leanne, the baby, and the narrator, Shelan. Shelan is still too small to have her own sack but can help pile cotton for Mamma's sack. The rows stretch as far as the eye can see, but Daddy picks so smooth and fast that they have to fold his sack double to weigh it. There are other kids in the field, but everyone always moves on so you can't make friends. After a meagre lunch, the work continues. It is hot now, the children are tired, and it's a long time till night. As the sun sets, Daddy finds a cotton blossom. "Cotton flower this late in the year bound to bring us luck."

The understated quality of the text is balanced by the dynamics of the illustrations. Color is used to show the passage of time. The deep blue-grays of dawn contrast sharply with the yellow school buses, fire, and the thin crimson line of the rising sun. These colors merge into blue skies and golden fields speckled with fluffy cotton. The viewer is pulled in close to feel Daddy's power, the weight of the long bags, and the growing fatigue of the children. The pickers' brown faces contrast sharply with the white-blue sky, and the field's beauty contrasts with the tired, worried faces of the children who will work there until the sun sets and the bus comes to take them home.

SPECIAL PROJECTS AND ENRICHMENT ACTIVITIES

Even after the frontier became settled, many farm families remained isolated and children entertained themselves in imaginative ways. The activities in this section are centered around seasonal celebrations and creative play and are designed to give children direct experience with the kind o f activities rural children enjoyed. There are also activities which invite comparisons of the way authors and artists convey similar experiences. The final activities are designed to build awareness of the ways rural life and landscape are changing as cities expand.

PROJECT **Connections and Comparisons**

Though they are from different times and different places, *A Happy New Year's Day* (see p. 70), *Family Pictures* (see p. 74), *From the Hills of Georgia* (see p. 87), and *The Relatives Came* (see p. 94) all have detailed pictures and descriptions of families getting together on special occasions. Read the text of each and compare the detail in the pictures. How are these celebrations the same? How are they different? Think about your own family and the ways you celebrate together. Draw a detailed picture of a celebration in your family, and write about what is going on in the picture.

Up the Tracks to Grandma's (see p. 76), and *Night of the Moonjellies* (see p. 96) are picture books about visiting with and helping a grandmother. Each of these children has a special relationship with the grandmother. Think about the different things they do together and how they help each other. Write about these stories, discussing how they are the same and how they are different. How are these stories the same or different from your relationship with your own grandparents? Write about a special time with one of your grandparents.

Apple Picking Time (see p. 97) and *Working Cotton* (see p. 99) are both about families working together to harvest a crop, yet there are many differences in the two picture books and the stories they tell. Compare the ways these books are the same and the ways they are different. Think about the differences in both writing style and illustration, and write how these experiences are different.

The Best Town in the World (see p. 68) and *Appalachia: The Voices of Sleeping Birds* (see p. 94) are both tributes to a particular place. Though both describe the physical environment and the people who live there, the styles of writing and illustration are distinct. Think about how well these books describe these places. Write an essay describing a place you have heard about from your parents or grandparents or where you yourself have lived. Think of the details that will help the reader imagine this place in his or her mind. You might want to do this project with a friend, with one of you writing the text and the other illustrating it.

Both *The Man Who Lived Alone* (see p. 75) and *My Great-Aunt Arizona* (see p. 77) describe the life of a relative from childhood through death. As you read these picture books, think about the ways the authors and illlustrators tell about these two people. Think about the details they chose to describe these people and what was important to them. Can you imagine how these books would be if the illustration styles had been switched? How do the illustrations help you understand the characters? Think of a relative you know or have heard of and write about that person.

Objects From the Past

Jackson, Louisa A. *Grandpa had a Windmill, Grandma had a Churn.* Illustrated with photos by George Ancona. Parents Magazine Press, 1977. **Grade: K through 5.**

1897 Sears, Roebuck Catalog. (A facsimile of the *1897 Sears, Roebuck Catalog.*) Chelsea House, 1993. **Grade: 4 to Adult.**

Sears, Roebuck and Company. *The 1902 Edition of the Sears, Roebuck Catalog.* Bounty Books, 1969. **Grade:** 4 to Adult.

Sears, Roebuck and Company. *The 1908 Catalog, Number 117: The Great Price Maker.* Digest Books, 1971. **Grade:** 4 to Adult.

Seymour, John. *Forgotten Household Crafts: A Portrait of the Way We Once Lived.* Alfred A. Knopf, 1987. **Grade:** 5 to Adult.

In *Grandpa had a Windmill, Grandma had a Churn,* Jackson describes the variety of fascinating tools and objects found in a grandparent's farmhouse, including a windmill, whetstone, churn, and quilting frame. The facsimilies of Sears, Roebuck catalogs offer a fascinating view into the past, showing an endless array of objects and prices that never fail to surprise. *Forgotten Household Crafts* gives information on the ways many of these fascinating objects were used, showing the complexity of household management in the past.

ACTIVITIES

1. This exercise can be prepared in advance by a teacher or used as a research project by students. Look through old catalogs, like the Sears, Roebuck facsimiles listed above, or old magazines and newspapers and find pictures of a variety of household utensils. Look for unusual ones or ones whose appearance has greatly changed. Make copies of these pictures and mount them on cards. On the back of each card, explain what the object was called and how it was used. Mount the cards so the explanations are hidden, and let other students try to guess what the object was used for. Write down their guesses, then read the actual explanation from the back of the card. You could also try this using farm equipment and other tools from the past.
2. Look around your home and ask people in your family for interesting utensils or tools from the past. If possible, bring one of these utensils from home and demonstrate its use.
3. Visit a local history museum or antique shop that has a friendly owner. Look for old utensils and tools. Compare these household objects from the past with what you have in your home today. Can you guess what the objects are and how they were used? Do you use any of the same things today? Do they look the same? How are they different? Pick an opject and write an essay, telling about the object and answering these questions. Collect the essays for a class book on unusual objects from the past.

Seasons and Celebrations

People who depend on the land for food and shelter are very aware of the natural world, weather, and the importance of changing seasons. Many of the holidays we celebrate today were developed long ago in recognition of seasons and their importance to farmers and others who live in the country. The celebrations themselves feature food and decorations made from things in the natural world that pertain to a particular season. Many of the projects that follow are based on crafts that hearken back to pioneer days, and others are from the turn of the century. Still others are contemporary.

Beard, Lina, and Adelia B. Beard. *The American Girls Handy Book: How to Amuse Yourself and Others.* David R. Godine, 1987. (Reprint. Originally published: Charles Scribner's Sons, 1887.) **Grade:** 6 to Adult.

The Complete Book of Nature Crafts: How to Make Wreaths, Dried Flower Arrangements, Potpourris, Dolls, Baskets, Gifts, Decorative Accessories for the Home and Much More. Rodale Press, 1992. **Grade:** 6 to Adult.

Diehn, Gwen, and Tery Krautwurst. *Nature Crafts for Kids: 50 Fantastic Things to Make with Mother Nature's Help.* Sterling, 1992. **Grade:** 4 to 8.

Drake, Jane, and Ann Love. *The Kids' Summer Handbook.* Illustrated by Heather Collins. Ticknor & Fields, 1994. **Grade:** 4 to 8.

Mitchell, John, and the Massachusetts Audubon Society. *The Curious Naturalist.* Illustrated by Gordon Morrison. Prentice Hall, 1980. **Grade:** 4 to 8.

The American Girls Handy Book provides a peek into the past and the amusements and hobbies enjoyed by young ladies in the 1890s. Though the illustrations and tone of writing are from the past, many of the activities are surprisingly adaptable to our time. *Steven Caney's Kids' America* (see p. 42) mixes information about the past with various activities cleverly adapted for contemporary children. The last four books emphasize an awareness of the natural world and ways to understand and enjoy different environments and seasons. They also feature a wide variety of ideas that use natural materials to create playthings and objects for the home.

Welcoming Spring: A Look Back

After months of overcast days, bitter cold, and isolation, country children joyously welcomed spring. They eagerly sought young greens, which for many were the first fresh foods for several months. Many accounts tell of the particular joy found in the beauty of spring flowers that were gathered, preserved, and given as gifts on special occasions.

> **ACTIVITIES**
>
> 1. Knowing that each year brought months of cold, it was common to preserve the beauty of flowers in a variety of ways as a reminder of their fragrance and beauty. Fresh flowers and various herbs were usually dried by hanging them from their stems for several weeks in a dry place. *The American Girls Handy Book* describes how flowers were preserved in fine sand, dipped in wax, and crystallized. The dried flowers were used for winter bouquets, decorations, and a variety of sweet-smelling potpourris and sachets. Directions for drying flowers and suggestions for projects can be found in many nature craft books; *Nature Crafts for Kids* and *The Kids' Summer Handbook*, listed above, are but two possible sources.
> 2. Most flowers, including those too fragile to be dried using the method mentioned above, can be pressed flat to dry. You can press them between the pages of an old telephone book, sheets of newspaper, paper towels, or a catalog. Or, you can make a plant press like the one described in *Nature Crafts for Kids*, p. 186.

Lovejoy, Sharon. *Sunflower Houses: Garden Discoveries for Children of All Ages.* Interweave Press, 1991. **Grade:** 5 to Adult.

Pelloski, Anne. *Hidden Stories in Plants: Unusual and Easy-to-Tell Stories from Around the World Together with Creative Things To Do While Telling Them.* Illustrated by Lynn Sweat. Macmillan Publishing Co., 1990. **Grade:** 5 to Adult.

In addition to the more permanent craft of drying and preserving flowers, children around the world have spontaneously used flowers for dolls, wreaths, chains, and other kinds of decorations. Anne Pelloski has incorporated some of these activities into a book of stories, while *Sunflower Houses: Garden Discoveries for Children of All Ages* is centered around the joy children find in gardens. This book describes how to grow plant houses and create special children's gardens. Both books include clear directions for making flower toys and decorations such as dolls, chains, wreaths, garlands, necklaces, and bracelets. There are also directions in *Steven Caney's Kids' America* (see p. 42) on pp. 108–09.

> **ACTIVITIES**
>
> 1. Talk to older people in your family or community and ask them about making toys from flowers. Have them show you how they made them. Try making some of these flower objects yourself.

ACTIVITIES cont'd.

2. May Day celebrations were brought to this country by the colonial settlers, though the origins of the holiday go back to prehistory. Many May Day customs persisted well into this century, and you may enjoy some of the ways children in the past welcomed the spring. One charming New England custom popular through the turn of the century is described in *The American Girls Handy Book*. Small baskets, made of common household materials and filled with a handful of fresh flowers, were hung on the doorknobs of special friends. The giver would then knock and run away. Directions for three simple baskets can be found in *The American Girls Handy Book* on pp. 73–76. Immediately following those pages are directions for setting up a may pole and instructions for performing a may pole dance. You can learn more about the may pole and other May Day customs at the library. Perhaps your group would like to plan a May Day celebration and pole dance, using music from the colonial period.

Summer and Old-Fashioned Country Fairs

Emery, Carla. *Carla Emery's Old Fashioned Recipe Book: An Encyclopedia of Country Living.* Illustrated by Cindy Davis. Bantam Books, 1977. **Grade:** 6 to Adult.

Written as an aid for those who are neophytes at country living, the above encyclopedia describes in detail every aspect of living and surviving on a small homestead. Since Emery operates on the premise that most readers will not have electricity or labor-saving devices, these recipes are designed for those who will *really* be cooking the old-fashioned way. Several of the books discussed earlier in this chapter recall the joys of a summer fair, often held on the Fourth of July. People enjoyed getting together for a day of good food, games, and other entertainment. It was a needed break from the hard work of planting and harvesting crops.

ACTIVITIES

1. Plan your own country fair with old-fashioned food and games. When you plan the food for your country fair, try making all the dishes from scratch, as your grandparents might have done. Many of the recipes for preparing these foods the way they were prepared in the past can be found in Carla Emery's *Old Fashioned Recipe Book,* listed above. Some foods you might want to try are: homemade ice cream, made in a hand-

cranked ice-cream maker (pp. 332–333); fresh lemonade from hand-sqeezed lemons (p. 229); homemade ginger ale and root beer (pp. 442–447); hot corn on the cob (p. 159); bags of popcorn or homemade cracker jack (p. 84); and any home-baked items you want to try.

2. Before, during, and after the meal, the fair-goers kept busy with a variety of games and races. Remember you will need to plan activities for *all* ages; everyone should have a chance to participate. Look at the pictures in the books recommended in this chapter and talk to your grandparents, relatives, or older friends. Ask them to describe some of the games and races they remember from community fairs and picnics. You can also find lots of ideas in game and party books from the library.

3. *The American Girls Handy Book* (see p. 103) has directions on pp. 112–117 for several kinds of daylight fireworks to help celebrate your fair. They are fun to make, and because they are make from brightly colored paper, they are a good choice for a daytime fair or for any area that prohibits the use of fireworks.

4. A traditional part of many Fourth of July celebrations was and is a kid's parade, in which kids decorate and parade their bicyles, wagons, and doll carriages. If you want to include such a parade in your celebration, you might look at the decoration ideas in *Steven Caney's Kids' America* (see p. 42) on pp. 362–363.

Fall: Harvest Crafts of Yesterday and Today

Fall is a particularly beautiful time of year in the country, and as people harvested crops and gathered nuts from the woods, they saved parts of the harvest and gathered seeds and leaves from the surrounding countryside to make decorations for the approaching cold months of winter.

1. If you live near a field or wooded area, take a walk and gather some of nature's fall decorations to make a winter bouquet. Look for plants with graceful or unusual shapes and colors such as dried grasses, seed pods, unusual branches, and colorful fall leaves.

2. Fall is the time of year when gourds ripen. The gourds can be gathered and crafted into a variety of decorations and useful household objects. On pp. 476–477 of *Carla Emery's Old Fashioned Recipe Book* (see p. 105), Carla Emery tells how to prepare the gourds and lists the useful

---

ACTIVITIES cont'd.

objects that can be made from them. *The American Girls Handy Book* (see p. 103), pp. 210–213, describes decorative objects that were popular at the turn of the century. Try making some of these.

3. You can use corn husks, wheat stalks, and straw to make beautiful decorations for your home. Many of these objects were traditionally made in the fall and used later as winter holiday decorations. Directions for them are found in books on traditional holiday crafts. There are directions for corn husk flowers in *Nature Crafts for Kids* (see p. 103), pp. 104–105, and straw dolls and animals in *The Kids' Summer Handbook* (see p. 103), pp.190–191. Try making some of these decorations.

4. Halloween was a favorite holiday in the past, and though we continue to celebrate it today, many of the games and customs have changed. Children who lived in the country could not go door-to-door for trick or treat. However, many families planned parties with games, fortune-telling, and traditional fall treats such as popcorn, roasted nuts, and fresh apples. Talk to older relatives or another older person and read about how people used to celebrate Halloween. Use what you have learned to plan an old-fashioned party with your group.

Winter Holidays: Old-Fashioned Gifts and Treats

Hall, Donald. *Lucy's Christmas.* Illustrated by Mike McCurdy. Browndeer Press/Harcourt, Brace & Co., 1994. **Grade:** 2 to 5.

This picture book, based on the childhood memories of Hall's mother, describes a typical country Christmas celebration in the early 1900s. Such celebrations centered around the community church, where everyone gathered for a musical program and the Christmas presents were distributed from a single community tree. Lucy begins planning early, making small presents for her family and friends all through the fall. As Christmas gets closer, the children practice for the program, their mothers make costumes, and everyone gets busy making the last-minute presents. Lucy and her sister make paper chains to decorate the church and netted bags of popcorn for the tree. When the day arrives, they join their neighbors for the celebration, good food, and the exchange of simple gifts.

This book combines many of the features of a typical country celebration with a personal story filled with particular details: how simple gifts were made, how the house looked, and the growing anticipation of one little girl. McCurdy's colored scratchboard illustrations give additional visual detail and have a vigor and energy that saves this quiet memory from sentiment.

London, Jonathan. *The Sugaring-Off Party.* Paintings by Gilles Pelletier. Dutton, 1995. **Grade: 2 to 5.**

Combining his wife's childhood memories and the stories his sons hear from their Canadian grandmother, London describes a sugaring-off party held near Montreal. In this story, young Paul's grandmother tells him about the first sugaring-off party she attended, over 60 years ago. This annual event was a joyous celebration of spring, where family and neighbors gathered at Tante Loulou's sugar shack to feast and dance while the maple syrup boiled in long pans on a big wooden stove. The party culminates with the serving of "la tire," boiled down syrup poured into troughs of snow and eaten off a wooden paddle. The folk paintings of French-Canadian artist Gilles Pelletier match the text perfectly. Their color and the vigor of the figures express the joy and energy of this celebration, and the details of both landscape and interiors give a clear picture of the time.

ACTIVITIES

1. Decorate a Christmas tree using only the simple materials that would be available to a farm family. Some choices might include chains made of threaded popcorn and berries (especially red cranberries), chains made of links of cut paper, stars and simple figures made from corn husks or straw, and stars and snowflakes cut from scraps of colored paper.

2. You could make Christmas tree ornaments that could also be eaten as a holiday treat. Try making some gingerbread cookie ornaments in simple shapes such as stars, hearts, and gingerbread men. Other possibilities are popcorn balls and hard candies.

3. Candies and other treats were sometimes put into colorful paper cornucopias or small baskets and hung on the Christmas tree. These candies were generally homemade, and candy making was an important part of the holiday preparations. *Carla Emery's Old Fashioned Recipe Book* (see p. 105) has directions for candy making on pp. 257–260. You might want to get together with your group and have an old-fashioned taffy pulling party. It's a lot of fun, and the results are delicious!

4. As winter slowly turned to spring, children looked forward to gathering maple sugar. They made special candies out of the maple that was boiled down into syrup and sugar. If you live where there is snow, you can plan a sugar-on-snow party. Maple syrup is boiled until it is foamy and slightly thickened. When the warm syrup is poured onto smooth, clean snow, it becomes cold, waxy, and chewy. This has been a favorite treat since the colonial days.

The Changing Countryside

Ross, Pat. *Whatever Happened to the Baxter Place?* Illustrated by Roger Duvoisin. Pantheon Books, 1976. **Grade:** 3 to 5.

Surany, Anico. *The Covered Bridge.* Pictures by Leonard Everett Fisher. Holiday House, 1967. **Grade:** 2 to 6.

Turner, Ann. *Heron Street.* Paintings by Lisi Desimmi. Harper & Row, 1989. **Grade:** 1 to 4.

Whatever Happened to the Baxter Place? tells how a family farm is divided and changed as the city moves closer and the original families get older, and *Heron Street* shows the entire history of a marsh near the sea as people create a city and the animals move away. *The Covered Bridge* tells how the children of a small town convince the citizens to preserve an old covered bridge.

ACTIVITIES

1. Many of the cities we live in now were part of the country not long ago. Talk to some older people in your town or city. Ask if they remember how the city looked when they were younger. Ask them to describe, with as much detail as possible, the changes in the city or town that have occurred in their lifetime. Keep notes about what you have learned.

2. Do additional research in the library. Look at old maps, newspapers, and telephone books. What do they tell you about your community? Has it grown larger, or is it getting smaller? How has the landscape changed as people have moved and changed your community? Which would you choose, the open space and farms, or the new buildings that have replaced them?

3. As you read about your city or town as it was 50 or 100 years ago, look for descriptions of the common plants and animals of the countryside. Can any of them be found in the area today? Have any of the streams, ravines, or other landscape features changed or disappeared? How has the growth of your town affected the people, animals, and plants who live there? What has been lost, and what has been gained?

4. Think about all you have learned about the changes in your community. If you could go back in time and start the town over again, what would *you* do, and how would your town look today? You can show this with a map or pictures. Write about your planning process and explain your decisions.

CHAPTER 5

Growing Up in Cities and Suburbs

W
hile accounts of country life have a strong sense of physical place and nature, those of growing up in the city have more descriptions of people and social activities. Many of these families were crowded into small apartments, and the children spent much of their time playing on the streets. Their lives were dominated by families, friends, and neighbors, often with memorable personalities. In some of these books, several generations of a family share a household. Many of the books tell of neighborhoods where children moved freely from one household to another. These relationships, combined with daily visits from the street peddlers, gave children opportunities to interact with adults in a variety of ways.

The neighborhood was the center of social life. Adults held cellar parties, and children met on the street in groups to hang out and play games: jump rope and hop scotch for the girls, and a variety of ball games for the boys. Some books mention the dark side of city life: the crowded tenements, the air pollution and dirtied rivers, and the prejudice that divided cities into distinct sections. Yet in most of these stories, the excitement of city life and its wide range of things to do is combined with a feeling of security. This was a world that depended on generosity and cooperation, and the neighborhoods described in these books gave children a strong sense of belonging that began with extended families and moved to neighbors and the streets where they played.

RECOMMENDED READING

Bell, Bill. *Saxophone Boy*. Tundra Books, 1980.

Source of Material: Author/artist's childhood memories.

Location: Philadelphia, Pennsylvania.

Dates: 1930s.

Grade: 3 to Adult.

This book is dominated by full-page, colorful paintings that are enriched by the author's witty explanations of the action and characters. All the richness and visual texture of Bell's urban Philadelphia childhood are shown in the text and paintings: his crowded home; busy neighborhood streets; civic delights such as the zoo; local amusement parks; Wanamaker's at Christmas; and the Mummer's Parade on New Year's Day. His young life was focused on music and the saxophone he was given on his 10th birthday. He later fulfilled his childhood dreams by returning as a paid musician to scenes of his childhood, but his final return is as a self-taught painter. The paintings combine great rhythm and energy with a gentle, comic quality. All the details of loving memory are here. There is a tiny kitchen stuffed with appliances, furniture, cats, and people. Also depicted is a busy street of tiny row houses with everyone cleaning, painting, and polishing while a variety of peddlers sell or deliver goods. The red-brick architecture of old Philadelphia is shown, complete with elaborate cornices, bell towers, and a multitude of window styles. The people shown are uniformly chubby and cheerful. Though Bell's text discusses some serious issues, such as his mother's death and World War II, and one painting depicts racial segregation, the majority of the paintings show happy memories, unmarked by fear or anger. The precise detail and energy of the paintings give a light-hearted and loving view of city life in the 1930s, and the text describes the author's place in this urban world.

Cooney, Barbara. *Hattie and the Wild Waves.* Viking, 1990.

Source of Material: Based on the life of the author's mother.

Location: Brooklyn, New York.

Dates: Late 19th century.

Grade: 3 to 6.

The third child of a successful German immigrant, Hattie is a child of wealth and privilege who lives in a big red-brick house in Bushwick. Older sister Pfiffi plans to be a beautiful bride like Mama, and older brother Vollie plans to work with Papa in his business and make lots of money. But Hattie, who loves to make pictures of the moon, sky, and ocean, wants to be a painter. They share the house with Clara, the cook; Mary Wagner, the maid; Clara's daughter, Little Mouse; and a series of young girls who come to look after the children. On Sundays and holidays the house is filled with uncles, aunts, and cousins who gather around Mama's table to eat and gossip. After the meal, they go into the parlor where they admire a famous painting by Mama's father and listen to Mama play her beautiful rosewood piano. Though Hattie is obedient and quiet, she never quite fits into this life. Her hands are too small for the piano, she cannot do fine needlework, and she fidgets through the fittings for new clothes while Pfiffi preens in front of the mirror. She is happiest when the family moves to their summer house on the beach at Far Rockaway. She loves to sail on Papa's beautiful boat and walk along the beach, watching the waves. She fills the walls of her room with pictures and wishes the summer would never end. She is sad when she learns that Papa has bought a new summer house, as big as a castle far out on Long Island. Here they can ride, play tennis, and give parties, but Hattie misses the waves. Pfiffi marries amidst great ceremony, and Vollie becomes a businessman. Papa builds a hotel in Brooklyn and moves them to an apartment on the top floor with splendid views of the East River and New York City. As she settles into a life of shopping and concerts, Hattie ponders her future. Her friend, Little Mouse, has gone on to become a teacher, and now Hattie must make a decision. First she visits the Art Institute, then goes to Coney Island to walk along the beach and have her fortune told. Then she goes home and tells her parents she is going to be an artist.

Cooney's signature paintings recreate the brisk promise of the turn of the century, when success was more assured and life easy for those who had achieved it. The houses range from large and comfortable to truly palatial, but the luxury is balanced by glimpses of the utilitarian kitchen and Little Mouse, who is generally pictured in her role of servant and helper. The paintings also give detailed views of the richly furnished rooms, handsome yachts, and opulent public spaces that surround Hattie and her family. Cooney also subtly shows Hattie's discomfort with the role she is expected to assume and her courage in breaking away from this life of ease to become a real painter. This is an inside view of an American era and a visually detailed and deeply felt portrait of a girl who loved her family but also listened to her heart.

Flory, Jane. *It Was a Pretty Good Year.* Houghton Mifflin Co., 1977.

Source of Material: Stories of childhood told by a friend of the author.

Location: South Philadelphia.

Dates: Early 1900s.

Grade: 3 to 6.

Ten-year-old Barney loves his life on Reed Street. The sounds, the sights, and the smells of the street are all detailed in the first chapter. Here is a vivid word picture of a crowded South Philadelphia neighborhood where peddlers, businesses, and families mingle in joyous confusion. With two older brothers and lots of friends, Barney can always find something to do. Though money is scarce, an enterprising boy like Barney can fish it out of a grating with a stick and bubble gum or earn it by helping the baker make deliveries in the predawn hours. There are also odd jobs he can do around the neighborhood.

And there are adventures around every corner. Taking Papa's Saturday lunch through the Catherine Street section of town is a weekly adventure, requiring the ability to run without spilling the hot soup Mama has packed. The Italian boys who hang out there won't take Papa's lunch, but they will take marbles, knives, pennies, or anything else in a boy's pockets. Barney also specializes in injuries: he is kicked in the head by a pony, repeatedly scrapes his knuckles learning to ride a bicycle in the basement, and falls out of a tree in the middle of an important Fourth of July speech. An entire chapter is devoted to a typical summer expedition: swimming in a pond in the midst of the marshes and burning dumps that line the Delaware river. Though the pond is "a nameless puddle, thick and dark brown, more mud than water," every boy on Reed Street has learned to swim there. It is a not a place anyone's mother would approve of, but the boys return year after year to swim until the midday sun is overhead. That's when they pull off the leeches clinging to their bodies, share their lunches on the bank, and swim again.

This book is filled with the heady sights, sounds, and smells of the city experienced by a boy open to every possibility who sees everything as part of an adventure. Barney is the most clearly developed character, but there is also a strong sense of the family and Barney's particular friend, Charley. Flory makes no attempt to disguise the confusion, clutter, and basic poverty of the neighborhood, yet all the episodes have a pervasive sense of humor. This is an accurate portrait of the time and one child's adventures in the midst of the city.

Haskins, Francine. *I Remember 121.* Children's Book Press, 1991.

Source of Material: Author's childhood memories.

Location: Washington, D.C.

Dates: 1950 to 1956.

Grade: 1 to 4.

African-American artist Francine Haskins recalls her early life in the three-story brick house at 121 S Street in Washington, D.C. Her grandparents bought the house when they moved north, and her mother, aunts, and uncles all grew up in it. It remained a house filled with family and friends. She remembers many things about her years in the house: the birth of her brother, Aunt Winona fixing dinner, everyone eating together, train trips to Baltimore with Mama, and the songs Daddy made up just for her. She remembers dressing up at a friend's house, playing on the street, being chased by a neighbor's crazy dog, and the day she left school without permission and got in trouble with Mama. These recollections are enhanced by the vigorous, full-page illustrations in Haskins's unique style. The richly colored paintings of the family stand out against the sketchy crayon backgrounds and show house interiors and city streets. While the bodies and clothing are fairly realistic, the heads of all the people are large, featuring enormous eyes and open, smiling mouths. This gives the characters an unusual dynamism, as if all are talking or reacting at once. The combination of dynamic line, childhood, and deliberate distortion have created a strongly personal view of simple childhood memories.

Howard, Elizabeth Fitzgerald. *Aunt Flossie's Hats (And Crab Cakes Later)*. Paintings by James Ransome. Clarion, 1991.

Source of Material: Author's memories of her Aunt Flossie.

Location: Baltimore, Maryland.

Dates: Early 1900s to Present.

Grade: 2 to 5.

On Sunday afternoons, Sarah and Susan go to visit Great-Great-Aunt Flossie and her house that is crowded with all kinds of things: books and pictures and lamps and pillows. Most of all they love the boxes of hats! After tea and cookies, Aunt Flossie lets them look at the hats, and as they try them on, she tells the story of each one. A green woolly hat reminds her of a big fire that burned for days when she was just a girl; a hat with a red feather reminds her of the big parade at the end of the Great War; and her special straw hat reminds her of their favorite story because they were with her the day it blew into the water and was rescued by a dog. Of course that story reminds them all of the crab cakes they always have on Sundays, and both girls agree that "crab cakes taste best after stories . . . stories about Aunt Flossie's hats!"

James Ransome's richly colored oil paintings fill in many of the details and enrich this simple story. A tree-lined street, crowded with rows of narrow brownstone houses, shows the Baltimore setting. The comfortable house is crowded with the treasures of a lifetime, and shows the roots of this African-American family. All of the characters shown are African-American: the firemen racing to the fire, the returning soldiers and the parade that honors them, and even the boy with the dog that rescues the hat. The girls and their aunt are fully realized portraits of believable people, though the aunt seems more middle-aged than elderly. The house's warm colors and multiple patterns and clutter contrast with the stories' action. The action is characterized by deep blues and greens. This picture book captures the obvious affection and respect for an elderly relative and the stories she shares.

Howard, Elizabeth Fitzgerald. *Chita's Christmas Tree*. Illustrated by Floyd Cooper. Bradbury Press, 1989.

Source of Material: Childhood of author's cousin.

Location: Baltimore, Maryland.

Dates: Early 1900s.

Grade: K to 3.

The author's cousin, nicknamed Chita, was the only child of one of Baltimore's first African-American doctors, and this story describes her family's Christmas celebration. Though she often joins her father when he visits patients on Saturdays, this day is special because they are going into the deep, deep woods to find a Christmas tree. The carriage takes them through the city, where they stop for a treat of hot waffles, then out into the country and the woods. Though it's cold, Chita takes her time selecting a beautiful, graceful tree. Papa takes out his gold pocketknife and carves her name into the trunk of the tree so Santa Claus will know which tree she wants on Christmas Eve. Back home, she and Mama bake dozens of star-shaped cookies, and Chita makes a special one for Papa, a round cookie face with a raisin mustache. On Christmas Eve, the aunts, uncles, and cousins come for a special supper and dancing. Through it all, Chita wonders if Santa really can bring the right tree, but on Christmas morning it is there, twinkling, sparkling, and bright with shining balls. And there on the trunk is her name, "CHITA," just as Papa carved it.

Floyd Cooper's soft oil wash paintings show all the details of a city family's Christmas in the early 20th century. They depict the family's comfortable brick home, their carriage, and the horse's bell harness, all decorated with wreaths and garlands. All the illustrations are suffused in a golden glow accented by the red and green of Christmas. The details of the city and interiors clearly indicate the time period. This is the time of carriage travel, wood-burning stoves, and player pianos. The story and illustrations combine to show the traditions of this particular family and the city that is their home.

Jones, Adrienne. *A Matter of Spunk.* Harper & Row, 1983.

Source of Material: Author's childhood memories.

Location: Hollywood, California.

Dates: 1920s.

Grade: 6 to 9.

After their father leaves them, Margery and Blainey's mother decides to make a fresh start in the theosophical colony of Krotona, in the Hollywood hills. Their new home is an apartment in an exotic oriental palace with terraced gardens, pools of golden fish, and an elegant kiosk for meditation. As they explore the house and the hills beyond, they discover equally exotic neighbors: Mrs. Goldie, the kindly housekeeper who lives upstairs; a movie star, Genevieve Corday, who lives just across the courtyard; and Peter, a cheerful barefoot hermit who lives in the nearby hills. Though they are all homesick for Atlanta and Margery has nightmares about Daddy, Mother is determined to stay and encourages them through their first days at the theosophist School of the Open Gate. They gradually settle in and make friends, but for Margery (who tells this story), it is a time that tests her courage, as she confronts a bully at school and a Chinese houseboy whose broken English and intent are both misunderstood. While the girls are in school, Mother keeps busy, working in the society office and learning to run their printing machine. They make the best of it when their apartment is rented to someone else and they are moved into a separate, though less elegant, house, but Mother wishes for a place of their own.

Margery worries about their old neighbor, Genevieve Corday, who seems to be under the control of Alabad Arundi, an Eastern mystic who predicts the end of the world in two weeks and plans a special gathering of his followers in the hills. She much prefers Genevieve's other friend, a friendly doctor named Jim, and promises him she will accept Genevieve's invitation to join Arundi's group that night so she and Jim can protect her. With the help of Jim and a group of youthful helpers armed with fireworks, Arundi is exposed and Jim persuades Genevieve to give up being a movie star and become his wife. Then the colony puts a strange, ghost-ridden guest in their new home, and after a few weeks of broken dishes and walking spirits, Mother decides it is time to leave. They move out of the hills into an apartment, and the girls transfer to a public school where they discover that the School of the Open Gate has left them woefully behind in math skills. They gradually save enough money to buy a home of their own, and though the Depression brings hard times, they all are now strong and independent.

This novel gives a fascinating view of Hollywood and Los Angeles in the 1920s, especially the various spiritual movements that were popular at that time. The portrait of Los Angeles as a young and growing city with large stretches of farms and fields is of historic interest, but the novel's strongest element is the cast of vividly realized characters. Many are extraordinary, but seen through Margery's eyes, they all seem real. The most memorable is Mother, a genteel southern lady who broke through the traditions of the time to build a new life. Clearly, she is the source of the spunk that characterizes this loving trio.

Khalsa, Dayal Kaur. *Cowboy Dreams.* Clarkson N. Potter, 1990.

Source of Material: Author's childhood memories.

Location: Brooklyn, New York.

Dates: 1950s.

Grade: 2 to 5.

A city child yearns to be a cowboy and have a horse of her own, just like the Lone Ranger and the movie cowboy heroes she studies on Saturday afternoons. She begs her parents for a horse and buys raffle tickets to win one, planning how to convert the garage into a stable. In the meantime, she practices cowboy moves on her bicycle, the merry-go-round, the mechanical horse in front of Eli's store, and the real ponies Tony the Pony Man brings on visits to her block. When it becomes too cold for any of these, she builds herself a horse on the basement banister and spends hour after hour riding her banister horse and singing her favorite cowboy songs.

The words to these songs and the illustrations of the world of dreams that accompanied them fill the pages of this colorful picture book. Khalsa's vividly colored paintings show the reality of suburban life in the 1950s. They also show the trips to the city museums and toy stores that fed her dreams and that dream world of lush green valleys, cactus-studded deserts, and endless horizons.

Khalsa, Dayal Kaur. *Tales of a Gambling Grandma.* Clarkson N. Potter, 1986.

Source: Author's childhood memories.

Location: Brooklyn and Queens, New York.

Dates: 1950s.

Grade: 1 to 5.

The author/illustrator remembers the grandmother who shared her childhood home. Grandma had been born in Russia, but her only memory of the old country was a night attack by Cossacks and her family's escape across the ocean in a hay cart drawn by a tired white horse. At least that's how Grandma told the story. She had grown up in Brooklyn, married a plumber, and learned to play poker to make extra money. After her husband's death, she moved in with her daughter, caring for her granddaughter and enriching her life in numerous ways. They took trips to Coney Island and went to vaudeville shows, movies, and Chinese restaurants. Grandma gave advice: "Just in case the Cossacks come to Queens, learn to say 'da,' and always keep plenty of borscht in the refrigerator." And there was what she called, Laws of Life. "Don't worry. Sooner or later for every pot there's a lid." She shared her treasures, made bed tents when she was sick, gave her tiny sandwiches for lunch, and taught her to play cards. She also maintained her interest in gambling with weekly meetings of the Sunshine Ladies Card Club and annual trips to California where she played cards with her son and his friends. When the little girl was told her grandmother died, she went up to Grandma's room and looked once more at her drawer of treasures. "Then I opened her closet door and stepped inside. I closed the door behind me and hugged and smelled all my grandma's great big dresses."

The exaggerated perspective and flat coloring of Khalsa's paintings have a childlike quality, which is perfect for this book of memories. It is also rich in details of the time: curved metal lawn chairs, large plastic radios, cowboy boots and toy guns, and a bright yellow kitchen—a classic feature of the 1950s tract house. Grandma sits at the center of almost every picture, dominating the scene with her white hair and brightly colored dresses. It is easy to see her importance in the life of the little girl.

These memories are a collection of quietly told details that create a joyful portrait of the rich relationship between a little girl and a grandmother who never lost her sense of fun or appreciation for life's small treasures.

Levinson, Riki. *Dinnie Abbie Sister-r-r!* Illustrated by Helen Cogancherry. Bradbury Press, 1987.

Source of Material: Author's childhood memories.

Location: Bensonhurst and Brooklyn, New York.

Date: Unknown.

Grade: 3 to 5.

Five-year-old Jennie wishes she could be like Dinnie and Abbie, her two older brothers. They are bigger and faster; share a big, bouncy bed; and best of all, go to school, riding the El to get there. Still she shares their fun with Mama, swimming at the beach on summer mornings and dancing together in the rain. Then one morning Abbie doesn't want to get up, and he's so sick that Mama uses the phone *three* times—to call the doctor, Papa, and Aunt Dee. And because Dinnie is scared, he won't talk to Jennie or play with her, though he's supposed to take care of her while Mama takes care of Abbie. Abbie is sick a long time, and even when he gets better, he can't walk. Dinnie has to go to school alone, and Mr. Simon comes every day to help Abbie's legs get strong again. When Abbie finishes the exercises, he teaches Jennie to play checkers and cards. But when he is well enough to go back to school, Jennie is lonelier than ever. That winter they all use garbage can lids to slide on the snow, and Jennie finally gets her wish to ride on the El. The story ends with the joyous day when the boys let her join their stickball game and Jennie runs for Abbie so Dinnie can hit the winning home run.

This is a story of love and affection, with a mother who truly enjoys being with her children. Although much of the story deals with a serious illness, the emphasis is on the small details and genuine emotions that create a whole experience. This sense of reality is enhanced by the black-and-white drawings that show details of clothing, kitchens, a grocery store, and city streets. The family's affection is also conveyed, creating a quiet but satisfying portrait.

Lovelace, Maud Hart. *Betsy-Tacy.* Illustrated by Lois Lenski. Thomas Y. Crowell, 1940.

―――. *Betsy and Tacy Go Downtown.* Illustrated by Lois Lenski. Thomas Y. Crowell, 1943. (*And five others in this nine-volume series.*)

————. *Betsy and Tacy Go Over the Big Hill.* Illustrated by Lois Lenski. Thomas Y. Crowell, 1942.

————. *Betsy-Tacy and Tib.* Illustrated by Lois Lenski. Thomas Y. Crowell, 1941.

Source of Material: Author's childhood memories.

Location: Mankato, Minnesota.

Dates: 1890s through early 1900s.

Grade: Vary with age of the characters. Early books in the series can be read aloud to primary-level children; later books are more appropriate for middle grades.

Starting with Betsy's blossoming friendship with Tacy when they were both five years old, Lovelace has re-created her own happy childhood in Mankato, Minnesota. From the beginning, their friendship was based on mutual appreciation and a shared love of home, town, and the power of imaginative play. Though their early world was limited to their street, the hill beyond, and the route to school, Betsy and Tacy imagine what lies beyond. They enjoy the simple sheltered pleasures of an earlier time: a piano box playhouse, picnic suppers, playing with paper dolls, and dressing up. Babies are born: one lives, and one dies, and the girls find their own way to explain this mystery. By the end of the first book they are ready to expand their friendship to include Tib, a new girl in town.

As the adventure of these friends continues, the author records their mischief, their running feud with "bossy" older sisters, and their fascination with the new boy-king of Spain and royalty in general. Betsy takes the first steps toward becoming a writer, encouraged by her mother, who provides a special writing desk. Though the girls occasionally get into trouble, their parents are understanding, and neighbors, in this almost idyllic, small city, are generally amused by their pranks.

The tone of the stories changes somewhat in the later books when the family moves across town and Betsy and Tacy start high school. Betsy's world expands beyond her friendship with Tacy to include a whole group who meet regularly at the Ray home for music and fudge. Betsy begins dating and experimenting with different roles and versions of herself. Though for a time she is romantically sidetracked and distracted from her writing, she remains essentially the same open-hearted person. The series gives an idealized but satisfying view of one girl's life in a gentler and kinder time.

Lois Lenski's deceptively simple line drawings, prevalent throughout the series' early books, capture perfectly the nature of these stories. The three girls are distinctly defined, and their adventures are shown in lively but not overwhelming detail. The period setting is depicted in the clothing and background details: a hanging gas lamp, the pump on the kitchen sink, wood-burning kitchen stoves, selected bits of architecture, and other details which clearly place this series at the turn of the century.

McDonald, Megan. *The Potato Man.* Illustrated by Ted Lewin. Orchard Books, 1991.

———. *The Great Pumpkin Switch.* Illustrated by Ted Lewin. Orchard Books, 1992.

Source of Material: Stories from the author's parents.

Location: Unknown.

Dates: 1920s.

Grade: 2 to 5.

In these picture books, Grandpa tells of his youth and two encounters with one of the many peddlers who frequented his street. He is used to peddlers, but at the first sight of the Potato Man, with his lumpy face and missing eye, his sisters run away and Grandpa hides in the tool shed. Though Mama tells them there is nothing to be afraid of—he is just old Mr. Angelo who lost his eye in the Great War—bad luck seems to follow Grandpa whenever Mr. Angelo is around. When he steals some potatoes that have fallen from the wagon, Mama makes him peel potatoes for a week, and he is punished again for squeezing orange juice in his sister's hair. And it's the Potato Man's sudden call of "Abba-no-potata-man" that makes Grandpa break a neighbor's garage window. Then one snowy day, his dog Dukie brings him a bright red ball—it is a pomegranate from the Potato Man's wagon. When he tries to return it, the Potato Man winks, tells him to keep it, and wishes him a Merry Christmas.

The Great Pumpkin Switch takes place in the fall. Mama is making apple butter in a huge kettle in the backyard, and Grandpa's job is to stir it and drop in pennies so it won't stick. His sister Rosie is growing a pumpkin next to the steep steps leading to their house and hopes "Big Max" will be big enough to win her some patches for her "Sunflower Girls" quilt. The Potato Man stops to admire Rosie's pumpkin and warn them that a storm is on the way. He is right. The storm comes with thunder and lightning, and during the night, a tree falls across the front walk. While Grandpa clears it with his friend, they accidentally cut the pumpkin vine and the pumpkin rolls to the street and smashes. The Potato Man sells them a pumpkin on credit, and they tie it to the vine just before Rosie comes out. She lets out of scream of delight: Big Max has grown during the night, earning her all the patches she will need for her quilt. After a celebration of apple butter and hot chocolate, they pay the Potato Man with pennies scraped from the bottom of the apple butter kettle.

Ted Lewin's masterful watercolors add historic details and human reality to the rather basic text. The first picture shows the peddlers who frequented the neighborhood, including an ice man, a tinsmith, and an ice cream vendor whose cart is pulled by a goat. You get a close view of sparks flying from the knife sharpener's wheel and the organ grinder with his lovebird. The kitchen, tool shed, and city streets are filled with the small details that create an accurate view of the period. There are particularly fine portraits of the unnamed narrator—an energetic boy in knickers with a cap pulled halfway over his eyes and a face that reflects his emotions. Grandfather's memories are given power and precision by illustrations that pull the reader into the reality of the stories.

Mohr, Nicholasa. *Nilda.* Harper & Row, 1973.

Source of Material: Author's childhood memories.

Location: New York City.

Dates: 1941 to 1945.

Grade: 6 to 9.

Ten-year-old Nilda is the youngest child and only girl in her family. She lives in the New York neighborhood known as El Barrio, and though life is hard for her mother, Nilda feels at home in the familiar crowded streets. She has learned to ignore most of the prejudice against Puerto Ricans that she encounters at school and elsewhere and finds solace in making cutouts and drawings for the precious box of things she keeps under her bed.

Nilda's life revolves around her family: her four older brothers; her stepfather; her elderly, eccentric Aunt Delia; and most of all, her loving mother. Although she is vaguely aware of some problems, her youth protects her from many of the harsh realities of their life: older brother Jimmy's criminal connections and drug use; her stepfather's poor health; and the potential dangers of another brother's membership in a gang. She resents giving up her bedroom when Jimmy's pregnant girlfriend comes to live with them but adores the baby and misses them both when Jimmy comes to take them away.

Religion is an area of confusion for Nilda. Her socialist stepfather despises all religion while her mother finds comfort in the Catholic church as well as in spiritualism. She finds the services entertaining and enjoys the food at friend Benji's Pentecostal church, but his family is just too strict and religious for her. Then World War II comes and the family's life changes. Jimmy disappears into the world of crime and drugs and two of her brothers join the military. She has one glorious summer of beauty and friendship at a camp in the mountains, and though she is happy to return to her family, she misses the camp's space and beauty.

After months of illness, her stepfather dies and her mother also becomes ill. Before she dies she speaks to Nilda, imploring her to be careful and not have a bunch of babies and waste her life. She has loved all her children, but she has nothing to demonstrate who she was. She tells Nilda that she must not give up the special something that is hers alone. With her death the family is gone: Frankie will join the service; Aunt Delia, who has become steadily more impossible, will be sent to a home; and Nilda will leave the barrio and live with her aunt and uncle in the Bronx. There she will share a room with matching bedspreads and be like a sister to her cousin Claudia. As the story ends, she is sharing her precious drawings with her admiring cousin.

The characterization and sense of time and place are very strong in this work. Even minor characters such as Nelda's friend Benji are well defined. One clearly feels her stepfather's anger at the system and the way her mother wards off despair with a mixture of mysticism and faith. The war that opens an escape route for her brothers has little impact on Nilda's daily life. Though she participates in street rallies and buys war stamps when she can, she doesn't really understand the issues involved. Her life is centered on her neighborhood, her friends, and most of all, her family. Nicholasa Mohr is a well-known graphic artist, and her illustrations convey the mood and reinforce the essential character of this story.

Polacco, Patricia. *Chicken Sunday.* Philomel, 1992.

Source of Material: Author's childhood memories.

Location: Oakland, California.

Dates: Late 1950s.

Grade: 1 to 5.

To young Patricia, Stewart and Winston are more than neighbors. A solemn backyard ceremony has made them her brothers, and their gramma, Eula Mae Walker, has, for Patricia, taken the place of her own babushka, who died two years ago. Sometimes Patricia's mother lets her go to church with them so she can hear Miss Eula sing and join them afterward for a lunch of fried chicken. On the long walk home, they always stop to admire the hats in Mr. Kodinski's shop, and the children all know how Miss Eula longs for the Easter hat in the window. The children have been saving for weeks, but they still don't have enough money for the hat, so they ask Mr. Kodinski if they can earn the rest helping him in his shop. Unfortunately, just as they arrive at the shop, some boys throw eggs at his door and Mr. Kodinski thinks Patricia and the boys did it. Though they convince Miss Eula it was someone else, they don't know how to change Mr. Kodinski's mind. Then Patricia has an idea, and she and her mom show the boys how to decorate eggs the way they do in Russia, with hot wax and dye. They take a basket of the beautiful Pysanky eggs to Mr. Kodinski, who is delighted and invites them in for tea. He has no odd jobs for them but suggests they make more of the beautiful eggs and sell them in his shop. The eggs sell quickly. They finally have enough money for the hat, but Mr. Kodinski has guessed what they want and gives them the hat in a beautiful hatbox, already gift-wrapped for Miss Eula. "Tell her that I know you are very good children, such good children!" That Sunday in church Miss Eula looks beautiful in her hat, and the solo she sings is just for them.

Polacco has combined memories of her childhood and a strong sense of design to illustrate this tale of trust and acceptance. Though bodies and gestures are somewhat stylized, the portraits are drawn with loving accuracy. The interiors are equally faithful depictions of character. Miss Eula's house is filled with (actual) family photos and religious mementos, while Patricia's home reflects her Russian heritage. Though Miss Eula refers briefly to Mr. Kodinski's past, it is the illustrations that really tell his story: he is Jewish, religious, and a concentration camp survivor. Bold color and pattern silhouette the action against the white page, creating comfortable space for the text. This loving and low-key story shows how respect and understanding can cross barriers of both race and religion.

Rosenblum, Richard. *My Block.* Atheneum, 1988.

————. *Brooklyn Dodger Days.* Atheneum, 1991.

Source of Material: Author's childhood memories.

Location: Brooklyn, New York.

Dates: 1940s.

Grade: 2 to 5.

In *My Block,* as the boy sits on the steps of his house eating a tomato-and-lettuce sandwich, he thinks of the future and a job that would allow him to stay on his block forever. He thinks of all the adults who visit his street and imagines himself as an ice cream man, fruit man, or any of the others who make regular deliveries to the block. Of course, there are also the street bands, firemen, policemen, and the pony man who takes your picture. Like other books set in 1940s urban America, this story centers on the child's life on the street, the adults he meets there, and the games that were played. While the text details a series of peddlers and their uniqueness, the pictures show the games the children played. The paintings are defined by simple black lines and depict in accurate detail the peddlers and their horses and wagons. Also, each page features the groups of children playing a variety of games such as baseball, football, jump rope, marbles, stickball, hide-and-seek, and hopscotch. There are sleds in winter and homemade box scooters when it's warm. This book is as much a tribute to the scruffy kids in knickers and high-top sneakers as it is to the peddlers of another time.

Brooklyn Dodger Days is a partly fictionalized account of a visit to Ebbets Field in 1946, the heyday of the Brooklyn Dodgers. Buddy and all his friends are members of the Knot Hole Club, which is sponsored by the beloved Dodgers. On this day, the schools are closed so all club members can go to a free game. The whole gang goes: Elliot the Announcer; Marty the Hammer, a good first baseman but a New York Giants fan; Herby the Honker; Noodie Lippman, who is famous for his appetite; and of course, Buddy, the Handyman. They are prepared with mitts and boxes or bags filled with lunch and snacks. They take the train and join the army of fans headed toward Ebbets Field. Buddy loves everything about Ebbets Field: the green playing field and the billboards, the scoreboard, and the Dodgers Sym-phony, a small band formed by musical Dodgers fans. As the game proceeds and the score seesaws up and down, the boys finish their lunches and start buying hot dogs, peanuts, and sodas. A home run slams toward them and is caught by Marty the Hammer, the Giants fan. Buddy is consoled, however, by the Dodger's win, and he and the fans cheer all the way home.

The cartoon-style paintings capture the enthusiasm and energy of this special day with realism and humor. The boys' excitement carries them through the day and home. The excitement is shared by the hordes of youthful fans at the game and the adults they meet while coming home. There are plenty of details in these drawings that place this story in the past yet convey the timeless joy of the experience.

Smalls-Hectory, Irene. *Irene and the Big Fine Nickel.* Illustrated by Tyrone Geteer. Little, Brown & Co., 1991.

Source of Material: Author's childhood memories.

Location: Harlem district of New York City.

Dates: 1950s.

Grade: 2 to 6.

Irene wakes in the early morning of Harlem to the music of nearby radios and stereos and remembers that her godmother has taken the younger kids and left her alone with Mommy, who is still sleeping. As Irene washes, she remembers this is the day that Lulamae's mother, Miss Sally, makes banana pudding. She likes going to Miss Sally's house; with 13 kids there's always something going on. But Irene is too early; there's a plate of biscuits on the table, but no one's up but Li'l Brother. She shares a biscuit with him then goes out to the street where she meets Charlene. They play a hand game while the streets slowly come to life and the stores begin to open. When the girls start teasing each other, Charlene forgets the unwritten rule about calling names of people's mommas, so Irene goes upstairs and prepares herself to fight: braided hair can't be pulled and Vaseline stops scratching. When she returns, Charlene is gone, so she once again looks for Lulamae and Lulabelle to see if they are ready to play.

The girls climb in the park and dig out a box of dirt so they can plant the seeds Irene ordered from a comic book. Then they make a wonderful discovery: a nickle—a whole nickle—enough to buy a raisin biscuit from the bakery. As they sit on the curb ready to divide the bun, Charlene reappears. After a brief pause they decide to share with her. With a raisin bun, three best friends, and Miss Sally's banana pudding yet to come, "Irene was feeling seven and in heaven on this summer day in Harlem."

Through details such as the bathtubs in the kitchens and toilet rooms in the halls, the author shows the crowded living conditions and difficulty of life in 1950s Harlem. She also shows a tightly knit, caring community where doors are left unlocked and children feel happy and secure. Irene shares her nickle as freely as Miss Sally leaves biscuits on the table for anyone who comes in. The gentle tone of the story and period are reflected in the book's sketchy but realistic oil paintings. The early morning streets are empty and the apartments crisp and uncluttered, focusing attention on the children. Both the text and illustrations subtly refer to musicians and other African-American heroes of the time: Billie Holiday, James Brown, Marcus Garvey, and Sugar Ray Robinson. The richly colored, expressive paintings and the quietly detailed text create a clear picture of a special moment in this child's life.

Smucker, Anna Egan. *No Star Nights.* Paintings by Steve Johnson. Alfred A. Knopf, 1989.

Source of Material: Author's childhood memories.

Location: Weirton, West Virginia.

Dates: 1950s.

Grade: 3 to 6.

In the steel mill town of the author's youth it was impossible to see the stars at night because the red glow of the furnaces hid them. Instead, the sky is lit by a sudden orange light whenever molten steel is poured or hot slag dumped from the trains. Everyone's dad works at the mill, and when fathers work the night shift and the children are in school, days go by when they don't see each other at all. Still, there are special times when families go to see the Pittsburgh Pirates play and afterward drive past endless rows of smokestacks and through the hills to home. July is the best month because the mill workers get a vacation bonus and everyone looks forward to the Fourth of July parade with bands, fire engines, and floats of all kinds. ·

At the school across from the mill you have to squint your eyes when the wind blows because the air is filled with bits of graphite and some days it feels like the whole world is filled with smoke. The road to school goes right through part of the mill, and the children can look down at the mammoth furnaces on one side and the huge rollers on the other. One day two of the girls decide to climb the slag hill near their house. They avert a tragedy when they race to stop the driver from dumping a load of hot slag on their little sisters who have followed them up the slope. As they sit breathlessly at the top of the hill, the sky around them turns red and orange and gold as clouds of orange smoke swirl into the colors of the sunset. A coda on the last page tells readers that the slag hill is now covered with trees and grass. The mills have closed and most of the younger people have moved away to find work, but their children come back to visit and hear their grandparents' stories about "the days when all night long the sky glowed red."

Steve Johnson's richly colored, realistic oil paintings are a perfect accompaniment to the text of this picture book. There is a tangible, sometimes oppressive sense of smoke and haze, and many of the paintings are suffused with the golden glow described in the text. Family life is seen at a distance: through a window or from the back, and Dad is one of the army of men seen leaving the mill, lunchbox in hand. The mill is omnipresent, lying at the center of their lives; the paintings show its awful power. It is easy to see why the children imagined it as a huge beast, "always hungry, always needing to be fed." This presents a tangible, sensory view of life in the steel mill towns of the 1950s.

Stevenson, James. *When I Was Nine.* Greenwillow Books, 1986.

————. *Higher on the Door.* Greenwillow Books, 1987.

————. *Fun, No Fun.* Greenwillow Books, 1994.

Source of Material: Author's childhood memories.

Location: A suburb of New York City.

Dates: Late 1930s.

Grade: 1 to 5.

Author/illustrator James Stevenson remembers his childhood in a village outside New York City. *Higher on the Door* is textured with the details that were important to him: delivery men, neighbors, games, his bicycle, his dog, and the fears his older brother found so entertaining. While some items, such as the change boxes traveling across stores on wires, may need some explanation, *Fun, No Fun* shows that many of the feelings of childhood are universal. Part of the charm of the series is how this timelessness mixes with details of daily life in the 1930s: James's interest in radios, steam locomotives, and the handprinted neighborhood newspaper he creates with friends. This quiet life is broken by occasional trips to New York City that feature eating at the Automat, traveling to the top of the Empire State Building, and watching huge ocean liners sail away. In *When I Was Nine,* the family travels out West, and Stevenson recalls days of driving, roadside cabins, and a dude ranch in New Mexico complete with long hot rides into the mountains and a new cowboy hat.

Stevenson makes a departure from his detailed and linear illustration style in this autobiographical series. Though filled with life and motion, these watercolors are like gesture drawings, creating the essence of the experience without the particulars. The characters are uniformly faceless. However, Stevenson is such an accomplished draftsman that a few brushstrokes create the power of a steam engine, the emptiness of the Western desert, and, most often, the image of a boy throwing a baseball or skating or climbing trees, accompanied by a small, black dog. This shorthand style gives visual universality to one person's particular memories.

Taylor, Sydney. *All-of-a-Kind Family.* Illustrated by Helen John. Taylor Productions, Ltd., 1951, 1979.

————. *All-of-a-Kind Family Downtown.* Illustrated by Beth and Joe Krush. Follett Press, 1972.

————. *More All-of-a-Kind Family.* Illustrated by Mary Stevens. Follet Press, 1954.

————. *All-of-a-Kind Family Uptown.* Illustrated by Mary Stevens. Follett Press, 1958.

————. *Ella of All-of-a-Kind Family.* Illustrated by Gail Owens. E. P. Dutton, 1978.

Source of Material: Author's memories of her childhood and family.

Location: Lower East Side of New York City and the Bronx, New York.

Dates: 1912 to 1919.

Grade: 4 to 7.

This series begins in 1912 and continues through World War I. It traces the lives and fortunes of an immigrant Jewish family. The early books feature five sisters living in a crowded neighborhood on New York's Lower East Side. Though life is a struggle, there are pennies for special treats, weekly trips to the library for books, and special outings to Coney Island. Each of the books also features the observance of one or more Jewish holidays. Details of the holidays are provided, as is a wonderful portrait of Jewish life and culture. At the end of the first book, a long-awaited son is born and is the baby featured in later stories. As the girls grow, so does their circle of friends. Life gradually becomes easier, and the family moves uptown to the Bronx and a seven-room apartment with carpets and electric lights! The girls grow up and begin to attend evening parties, and Ella finds herself involved with Jules just as World War I takes him from her. When the war ends and he returns, she faces a difficult choice, one that will decide her entire future. This choice ends the series.

As in most family memoirs, serious problems alternate with amusing incidents and moments of love and happiness. On one hilarious occasion, the children eat someone else's supper in the wrong apartment. A more serious time finds the family holding a Seder while four of the children are ill with scarlet fever.

The generally positive nature of this series is tempered by realistic descriptions of life, especially in the chapters that describe the Lower East Side. There is a wonderful chapter devoted to the sight and smells of a shopping expedition on streets crowded with small shops and pushcart peddlers. When Mama and Ella go in search of their friend Guido, they encounter the worst of tenement slums and learn to appreciate the help settlement workers bring to the community. The house is dusted carefully and the girls are kept clean in starched white pinafores, but their father works long hours in a cold and dirty junk shop, bundling up rags and papers for resale. The author makes it clear that the Lower East Side was neither pretty nor clean, and life was often difficult. While the family is strong and close, each of the girls has moments of mischief, stubbornness, and temptation. This is a realistic portrait of a close family growing up in a city full of change and promise.

Thomasis, Antonio de. *The Montreal of My Childhood.* Tundra Books, 1994.
Source of Material: Author's childhood memories.
Location: Montreal, Canada.
Dates: 1940s.
Grade: 3 to 6.

In 24 richly detailed paintings supplemented by text, Antonio de Thomasis recalls his childhood spent in Montreal's back lanes with children who improvised games from sticks, string, and whatever else they could find or borrow. They collected ice chips, baked apples in hot roofing tar, and built scooters from orange crates and roller skates. One illustration, called "plans for posterity," gives directions for a scooter, "ticktack" line (guaranteed to drive a neighbor batty), and a Jughead hat made from an old fedora. De Thomas is also shows their favorite hangouts: the corner store, a soda shop with a nickel juke box, and the market where they competed to deliver groceries for tips. The electric streetcar is remembered as a glorious way to get around town, especially if you could sneak on without paying. It is not surprising that many memories are of the long cold winters when the underwear froze on the line and games included back lane hockey, skating, and making tunnels and forts in the snowbanks that lined the streets. His last picture shows the happiest time of all: coming home half-frozen to the warmth of a wood stove where a pot of soup simmered, waiting for supper.

There is a gritty reality to de Thomasis's sketchy, expressive paintings, which are centered on alleys, construction sites, and the streets of a crowded neighborhood. They show delivery men, street peddlers, and an occasional mother, but at the center of each painting are the children in vigorous pursuit of adventure and fun.

SPECIAL PROJECTS AND ENRICHMENT ACTIVITIES
Background Sources

These background sources give a general overview of architectural styles and the ways cities change over time. They provide information that can be used for all the activities which follow.

D'Alelio, Jane. *I Know That Building: Discovering Architecture with Activities and Games.* The Preservation Press, National Trust for Historic Preservation, 1989. **Grade:** 4 to 8.

Devlin, Harry. *What Kind of House is That?* Parents Magazine Press, 1969. **Grade:** 5 to Adult.

Gaughenbaugh, Michael, and Herbert Camburn. *Old House, New House: A Child's Exploration of American Architectural Styles.* Illustrated by Herbert Camburn. The Preservation Press, National Trust for Historic Preservation, 1993. **Grade:** 5 to Adult.

Weitzman, David. *My Backyard History Book.* Illustrated by James Robertson. Little, Brown & Co., 1975. **Grade:** 5 to Adult.

————. *Windmills, Bridges & Old Machines: Discovering Our Industrial Past.* Charles Scribner's Sons, 1982. **Grade:** 5 to Adult.

Much of the history of a city or town is found in old buildings and the way different parts of the city change. The books listed above will help students learn to look at the city from a historian's point of view and learn about life in the past by studying the buildings around them. *Steven Caney's Kids' America* (see p. 42) includes activities and information on both the history of architecture and the ways children amused themselves in the past. *I Know That Building* describes how different styles of American architecture developed, points out a variety of details, and is filled with hands-on activities. *What Kind of House is That?* has full-color paintings of a variety of houses and buildings and describes the history of specific architectural styles. *Old House New House* is centered around the restoration of a large old house and a child's exploration of the history of houses in America. The illustrations show, in detail, the ways family living has changed over the years. *My Backyard History Book* points out the ways history can be found in fragments of the past all over the community and suggests a number of activities for young historians. In *Windmills, Bridges & Old Machines*, Weitzman focuses on industrial buildings and their importance to the history of a community.

The Changing City

Von Tscharner, Renata, and Ronald Lee Fleming. *New Providence: A Changing Cityscape, 1910–1990.* Illustrations by Dennis Orloff. Harcourt Brace Jovanovich, 1927.

————. *New Providence: A Changing Cityscape, 1910–1990.* Illustrations by Dennis Orloff. This expansion of the previous title consists of seven posters and a 32-page teaching guide, giving background information about New Providence and suggested activities. It is available from Dale Seymour Publications, P.O. Box 1088, Palo Alto, CA 94303-0879. **Grade:** 4 to 8.

Wallner, Alexandra. *Since 1920.* Doubleday, 1992. **Grade:** 1 to 4.

These sources give visual examples of the ways a single street or neighborhood evolves over time. *New Providence* traces the evolution of an imaginary but typical American city, as it grows, modernizes, and rediscovers its own past. *Since 1920* tracks the changes in a single rural neighborhood as it becomes part of a city, suffers neglect, and finally is revitalized as part of an urban renewal project.

ACTIVITIES

1. Look for pictures of your city from the past. A good place to look is the public library, or you can contact your local history association for ideas. Resources to check in the library are old newspapers, local magazines, advertising brochures, and city reports. Copy as many pictures as you can of main streets or other areas you recognize. Whenever possible, write on the copies the date the picture was taken.

2. Compare the pictures you have found with the way the same streets look today. How many of the original buildings are still there? Do they look the same, or have they been remodeled or changed in some way? If you have pictures that were taken at different times, you may be able to tell when a building was replaced or remodeled. Some buildings may have been remodeled several times. Record when each change was made.

3. Draw a simple map of the streets you are investigating. Include all the buildings and lots that are there now. Look at pictures and see when and how things have changed. If there have been a lot of changes, you might want to keep track of them by using a time line for these streets. If you like to draw, you could do a series of drawings like those in *Since 1920* to show how these streets have changed.

ACTIVITIES cont'd.

4. As a group, discuss the changes in your city. Which changes do you think have improved the city? Have any of the changes had a bad effect on the neighborhood? How would the streets look if you could choose what to change and what to keep? Write about your ideal street and draw a plan of how it would look.

PROJECT   Looking at Buildings

Because building styles change just as fashions do, it is often possible to tell when a building was built by its style. Sometimes the style is changed or covered when a building is remodeled, but you can still find clues about the original design.

Look for old buildings or houses in your neighborhood or city. You might want to take pictures of some of the most interesting ones. On some buildings, the date they were built or the names of the first owner are carved into the stone over the main entrance or on the cornerstone. Using these and other clues, try to find out when these old buildings were built, who has used them, and what they are used for now. Don't forget to look in the library for pictures and other records of these buildings.

Many older buildings have beautiful decorations that are either carved into the stone or made of cast iron, wood, or tile. Look for these decorations and "collect" some of them by taking pictures or drawing sketches. If you can get permission from the buildings' owners, you can make a paper rubbing of some of the patterns or textures, especially those that are stone, iron, or tile. Directions for making a rubbing can be found in *Steven Caney's Kids' America* (see p. 42), p. 224, or *My Backyard History Book* (see p. 129), pp. 101–107.

Some of the buildings in your community are registered historic landmarks. Such buildings cannot be torn down nor can their appearance be changed if they are remodeled. Contact your local history group or historic preservation group for information on the registered landmarks in your community. Some of these are private homes and businesses and can be looked at only from the outside, but many are open to the public and tours can be arranged. Look at these buildings and see if you can tell why they were considered important enough to be saved.

Are there other buildings in your area that you think should be preserved? Make a list of the buildings you think are architecturally important or those you think are important to your community's history. Contact your local historic preservation society to learn about the procedures for designating a building as a registered landmark.

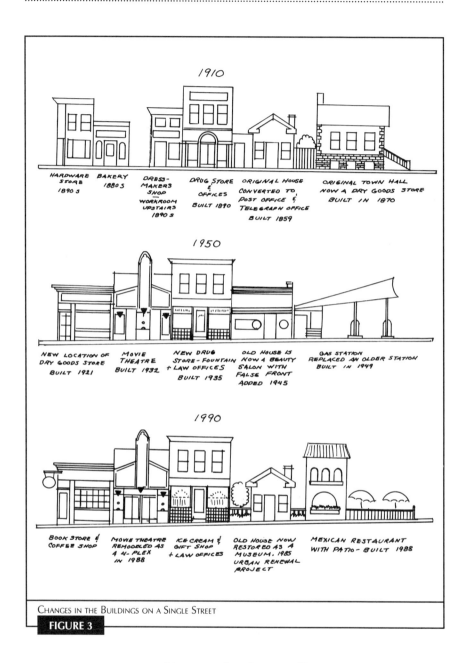

CHANGES IN THE BUILDINGS ON A SINGLE STREET

FIGURE 3

Signs and Other Stuff

Gladstone, M. J. *A Carrot for a Nose: The Form of Folk Sculpture on America's City Streets and Country Roads.* Charles Scribners's Sons, 1974. **Grade:** 5 to Adult.

In the book listed above, Gladstone points out the charm and artistry found in such familiar forms as weathervanes, pavement lids, gravestones, trade signs, and carousel figures.

ACTIVITIES

1. Look around your community for old and interesting signs. In the past, many trade signs and figures were made or painted by individual local artists. Of these, the most well known are the cigar store Indians, which stood outside stores all over America. Other signs were shaped like the products sold: shoes, fish, glasses, and keys. While some of these are in museums now, many can still be found on older buildings. Look for interesting neon signs, especially those that move; signs shaped like an object or symbol; large figures of men and animals, both handmade and manufactured; barbershop poles and other moving signs; and painted tin signs and clocks. Using a camera or a sketchbook, collect as many examples as you can. Remember to record the location of each item as well as any information you find on its origin and history.

2. Look around you community for sculpture and other kinds of art attached to buildings or decorating the streets. Look for large sculptured figures in buildings (often found near the top or over doorways), gargoyles (waterspouts shaped like monsters), weathervanes, fountains, decorative street lights, and various kinds of iron ornaments. Collect your discoveries by taking pictures or making sketches. Record the location of each piece of art as well as any information you can find about its origin and history.

3. Look for sculpture and other kinds of art in community locations such as parks, churches, graveyards, even your neighbors' front yards. Look for carousel figures; sculptures on memorials; gravestones and other graveyard figures; and folk creations, such as rock sculptures, whirligigs, and fancy scarecrows. Collect and record the location of these art works.

4. Combine in a book all the art your group has collected so that it can be shared with others outside your group. You could create a map and guide book that give some information about each object and tell where the art can be found. You could design a walking tour in which your group acts as docents. On your tour, instruct the tour group about the art and its history.

PROJECT   How Much Did Things Cost?

One of the most fascinating things in history is the way prices have changed over time. The concept of inflation can be easily demonstrated by tracking the prices of a few simple household items over a single generation.

Using old catalogs, magazines, and newspapers, collect both the pictures and the prices of some common items from the past. Track the changing size and price of some common items through several generations. Think of simple things like a spool of thread, needles and pins, soft drinks, a package of gum, a chocolate bar, or a milkshake.

Use the material from the activity above to make a game. Make cards for simple items including a picture, the size, the date, and all other information except the price. Put the price on the back of the card. The players must guess the price of the item that existed at the specific time period. They should look only at the picture, not the back of it. Most players will be amazed when they discover the correct answer.

Interview older people about prices from their childhoods. How much allowance did they get, or what did they do to earn money? Ask how they spent the money. How much did it cost to go to a movie, buy a candy bar or a toy, etc.

Toys

Schwartz. Marvin. F.A.O. Schwartz Toys Through the Years. Doubleday, 1975.
   Grade: 3 to Adult.

Using reproductions from catalogs and advertising, F.A.O. Schwartz Toys Through the Years looks at the toys children wished for and have played with since 1911. Unlike children who lived on farms or in small towns, children who lived in cities could see a variety of toys displayed in stores. When radio and television came along, children all over the country would hear and see advertisements for these toys, and some toys would become popular everywhere.

ACTIVITIES

1. Talk to your parents and grandparents about the toys they remember from when they were children. What were their favorite toys, and do they remember when or how they got them? Which toys were most popular when they were growing up? Some of the toys they played with are still sold today. Ask if they remember hula hoops, Barbie dolls, Slinkies, and Silly Putty.
2. Collect toy catalogs from a variety of sources; they are especially easy to find at Christmas. Look through the catalogs and/or go to a toy store with an adult. How many toys or games can you find that this adult remembers playing with as a child?
3. Using your library or other source, look at catalogs, magazines, or newspapers from the past that advertised toys. Which of these toys

ACTIVITIES cont'd.

would you choose? How are these toys the same, and how are they different from the ones children play with today?

Street Games

One of the most common memories of childhood is playing games with friends on the playground or after school. The books listed below talk about these games as well as the riddles, rhymes, and jokes children told each other. Though collected for adults, children will enjoy the books and will find many familiar games and jokes. They are also a useful tool for comparing the various names and rules for common children's games. Whether played in the past or present, many of these games have a set of important but unwritten rules about where they are played, what time of year they are played, and who plays which games. It is fascinating to discover how the games and taboos have changed over the years.

Bronner, Simon J. *American Children's Folklore.* August House, 1988. **Grade:** 6 to Adult.

Ferritti, Fred. *American Book of Sidewalk, Stoop, Dirt, Curb and Alley Games.* Workman, 1975. **Grade:** 6 to Adult.

———. *The Great American Marble Book.* Photographs by Jay Good. Workman, 1973. **Grade:** 6 to Adult.

Maguire, Jack. *Hopscotch, Hangman, Hot Potato, and Ha Ha Ha: A Rulebook of Children's Games.* Prentice Hall Press, 1990. **Grade:** 6 to Adult.

Vignola, Ray, and Dennis Vignola. *New York City Street Games: The Greatest Games Ever Played on Concrete.* MIG Communications, 1994. **Grade:** 6 to Adult.

ACTIVITIES

1. Interview an older person. Ask about the games they played on the school playground. How did they decide which games to play? Did they play different games at different times of the year? What were the rules? How were the teams chosen? Were they themselves good at the games? How are these games the same or different from those you play at school today?

2. Interview older people about the games they played *after* school. Where did they go to play these games? Who decided what to play? Were the teams chosen, or did everyone play? Where did they get the equipment they needed? What were the games called, and what were some of the rules?

3. Write down the names and rules for all the games of the past that you have learned about. If there are several versions of the rules, you can refer to the books listed above or decide as a group which rules you will use. Try playing some of these games with your friends. Maybe you could plan a special heritage game day in which parents and grandparents teach children favorite games from their childhood. Or you could write your own book of street games combining the games you play now with those of the past.

4. Sometimes there are special rhymes or chants that go with games. Some examples are: counting out rhymes to choose who's "It"; jump rope rhymes; and the chants that go with different hand-clapping games. Talk to older people and ask if they remember any of these kinds of rhymes. Write them down. Collect as many of them as you can, making sure you document the name of each person who told you a rhyme. A classroom collection of such rhymes could become a book.

Sports and Radio

Adorjan, Carol, and Yuri Rasosky. *WKID Easy Radio Plays.* Albert Whitman & Co., 1988. **Grade:** 3 to 6.

In the past, children got all their information about sports events from the radio or newspapers. If you read *In the Year of the Boar and Jackie Robinson* (see p. 12) or *The Hockey Sweater* (see p. 70) you can see that even though these children didn't actually see the game, they still got excited and involved with their favorite teams and players. They also listened faithfully to favorite radio dramas, especially the adventure and mystery shows.

1. Interview an adult about how it was to follow sports on the radio or in the newspaper instead of on television. Ask if they found that as enjoyable as watching sports on television. How is their favorite game the same, and how is it different?

ACTIVITIES cont'd.

2. Find some tapes of old radio shows. Look in the library or order by mail from a company such as *Radio Yesteryear*. Their address is: Box C, Sandy Hook, CT 06482. There are also regular broadcasts of old shows on some radio stations. As you listen, notice the way the stories are told all in sound and dialogue. Do you think the pictures you make in your head while listening are as exciting or scary as the ones you can see on television? How is the storytelling different?

3. Interview some older people about the radio shows they enjoyed as children. Did they enjoy the radio programs as much as they enjoy watching television? How do they think radio and television are the same, and how do they think they are different?

4. Find, adapt, or write your own radio play. The book listed above has four choices along with information about producing radio plays. If you write your own script, make sure the script includes all the information and sound effects you need to tell the story. Think about how you can produce different sounds. *Steven Caney's Kids' America* (see p. 42) gives script ideas and tells how to make a variety of sound effects on pp. 348–351. There are recordings of sound effects available in many libraries. Do you want to add music between scenes or to set the mood? Get together with friends and produce your show as a recording.

CHAPTER

Fear, Loss, and Courage: Families During World War II

Wars are great slashes across the fabric of history that often over-whelm and change the lives of adults. But unless a war is fought near them, children experience war on a different level; usually in small ways. The stories described in this chapter show that for many children, the impact of World War II was first felt in shortages. Adults struggled to create meals without butter, meat, or sugar, and children noticed the absence of candy and bubblegum. They were surrounded by victory slogans and encouraged to plant victory gardens and collect scrap metals. As the war went on, families began to change. Mothers went to work in factories, and fathers went off to fight. Children who had relatives and friends fighting in the war felt a great sense of loss, especially if their father was among them. Many of the accounts tell of the emptiness, and constant fear children felt watching movie newsreels and waiting for letters from the front. For some children the loss was absolute and unforgettable.

During World War II, the children who were among the most deeply affected were Japanese-Americans. Their secure lives were shattered by fears they could not understand. Fathers, who were the decision makers in the family, were taken away during the stressful weeks when families prepared to be sent to internment camps in unknown locations; camp life eroded family structure; and older siblings were asked to make decisions that further divided families. Many of the adults were embittered by the experience, and even the most resilient children had to re-create a sense of identity when they returned to the outside world. These children created their own understanding of the war and what it meant in their lives—an understanding they share in the following books.

RECOMMENDED READING

Hall, Donald. *The Farm Summer 1942.* Illustrated by Barry Moser. Dial Books for Young Readers, 1994.

Source of Material: Author's childhood memories.

Location: New Hampshire.

Date: 1942.

Grade: 2 to 6.

In 1942, Peter's father is on a destroyer somewhere in the Pacific and his mother has been asked to spend the summer in New York to work on a secret war project, so Peter spends the summer on his grandparent's New Hampshire farm. Peter and his mother fly from San Francisco to New York on a DC-3 airliner—coast to coast in only 16 hours! A streamliner takes them to Boston, and a steam locomotive takes Peter to New Hampshire, where his grandfather meets him in a buggy pulled by a white horse named Lady Ghost. That night Peter sleeps in the feather bed his father slept in, under a quilt his great-grandmother made out of scraps from her mother's dresses. The next morning he is introduced to the cows and chickens, and he helps his grandfather with the haying, wearing his father's old hat to keep the dust off his head. He also wears the hat when they listen to the war news each night on the radio. Peter meets his cousins (all older than he) when they go to church and spends half a day with a girl named Emily, who is the only other nine-year-old for miles around.

As the summer moves on, Peter settles into a routine of milking and haying, listening to his grandfather's stories, eating Grandmother's gingersnaps, and riding to church behind Lady Ghost. He doesn't want the New Hampshire summer to end, but he misses his mother and his friends and he wants the war to be over. The day before he takes the train back to Boston, they do all the usual things he has come to love. That night all the relatives come with ice cream, cake, and a patchwork quilt to remind him of New Hampshire. Everyone sings his favorite hymn, "Life is Like a Mountain Railroad." He says good-bye to the cows and chickens, hangs his straw hat on the peg in the toolshed, and flies back across the country with his mother. They arrive home to a surprise: his father has come home for a whole week's leave!

In this book, Hall combines a wartime setting with his memories of summer visits to his grandparents. Peter's joy in being on the farm with his grandparents is always tempered by his fears about his father. This fear is conveyed in the pictures of him sitting by the radio next to his grandmother, and the tension in their bodies as they listen to news about the war. The illustrations reflect Peter's sense of living in two worlds: first, he is pictured peering through the window of a DC-3, and this is followed by a moonlight view of his arrival at the farm via horse and buggy. The watercolor paintings by Barry Moser echo the spare, poetic style of the writing and give a strong sense of place and time. This is a portrait of real people. It captures the grandfather's humor, the grandmother's quiet support, and Peter's utter contentment on the farm. Combined with detailed paintings of the barns, animals, and architecture, the book creates a loving picture of life on a small New England farm 50 years ago.

Herman, Charlotte. *A Summer on Thirteenth Street.* Dutton, 1991.

Source of Material: Author's childhood memories.

Location: Chicago.

Date: Summer of 1944.

Grade: 4 to 7.

Eleven-year-old Shirley Cohen is looking forward to another blissful summer of hanging out with best friend Morton Kaminsky and their other friends and drinking malteds at Zelnick's drugstore. When she finds out that Manny Zelnick, on whom she has a crush, has joined the army, she decides it's time to do something to help with the war effort. Maybe she can help stop the war before Manny can be shipped overseas. She persuades Morton and a few of their friends to start a victory club. Their first project is a victory garden, which they dig in a small strip of hard city soil near their apartment house, using the seeds Shirley ordered from a comic book. They also collect jars of chicken fat, though they're not quite sure what to do with them, and Shirley and Morton begin to spy on a neighbor, Otto, who has a German accent and seems very mysterious.

   The rest of Shirley's life continues as usual: she takes care of Stinky, an ugly and very pregnant stray cat she and Morton adopted; she puts up with her older brother Irving, who alternates teasing with comic routines; and she visits with an assortment of friends and neighbors. Then the summer begins to change for her. One morning she finds Stinky's newborn kittens dead, and the next day word comes that Manny Zelnick has died from the shots the army gave him. In her despair and anger, she and Morton find themselves accusing and hurting Otto. Shirley doesn't know what to do, but Otto quietly helps her see both his pain and his forgiveness.

   This novel captures the variety of personalities and the texture of city life in the mid-1940s. There are well-integrated references to popular radio shows, favorite childhood treats, and the atmosphere of the war effort and the upcoming election. Shirley, who stands between the enthusiasms of childhood and the longings of adolescence, is the most developed character. Her relationship with Morton is believable, but one senses that this, too, could change. The families and neighbors are vividly described but are relatively two-dimensional characters in a story whose focus is Shirley, her life, and her feelings.

Hest, Amy. *Love You Soldier.* Four Winds Press, 1991.

Source of Material: Author's childhood memories combined with a friend's story.

Location: New York City.

Date: Early1940's.

Grade: 3 to 6.

In a short 47 pages, Hest gives a resonant account of one family's love, loss, and recovery from the war. The story begins as Katie's father is leaving for the war. She has made him a picture, working late into the night on this message of love, but saying good-bye is hard. As the weeks become months, they send pictures and letters back and forth, but Katie misses her father and she hears her mother crying at night. Mother works long hours at the hospital, and Katie settles into a routine of school, afternoons at the library, and quiet evenings when she does her homework and Mother knits. Then Mother's best friend Louise comes to visit. Her husband is also in the war. She is expecting a baby and is lonely. It is decided that Louise will stay with them and have her baby in the city. Now there are three of them, and in the evenings, Mother and Louise tell stories by the hour. April brings a surprise blizzard, and as Katie and Louise wait for Mother, Louise goes into labor. Katie tries to hail a cab, but because of the huge snow drifts, there are none to be found. There is no choice: they walk the four long blocks to the hospital, where Louise gives birth to Rosie. Now Louise and Rosie share Katie's room, and after school, Katie takes Rosie for long walks and helps take care of her.

Then comes the worst day ever, with a telegram and the news that Katie's father has died in the war. Mother reads and rereads all his letters, and together they look at the old family photos that tell over and over the story of their happiness as a family. Katie has Rosie to comfort her, as well as Mrs. Leitstein, who lives downstairs and is teaching her to cook. Rosie is two years old when her father comes home and takes Louise and Rosie back to Massachusetts. A few weeks later, Louise's brother Sam visits them. He's sorry about Katie's father, grateful to be home, and planning a new start in life. Mother begins writing letters again: to Louise and Rosie, and to Sam, who has settled on a ranch in Texas. At first Katie refuses to answer Sam's letters, but she finally relents, sending him a picture of a girl in new blue jeans and shiny city shoes. She and her mother will love Daddy always. Forever. But they are ready to make a new start—with Sam.

Houston, Gloria. *But No Candy.* Illustrated by Lloyd Bloom. Putnam/ Philomel, 1992.

Source of Material: Author's childhood memories.

Location: North Carolina.

Date: Early 1940s.

Grade: 2 to 6.

Five-year-old Lee's favorite part of the day is the afternoon. If she has been good, she is allowed to take a nickle and choose a treat from the curved glass showcase in her father's big general store. Her favorite treat is a Hershey chocolate bar, and her favorite place to eat it is her secret hiding place in a hickory tree, where she peels off the paper and eats the candy one square at a time. Every night neighbors come to the store to sit around the stove and listen to the news on Daddy's big brown radio. Lee knows everyone is worried, but the war seems far away until Uncle Ted joins the army and she sees Mama cry.

As the days pass, there are fewer and fewer boxes of candy in the showcase, and one day the shelves are bare. Daddy says all the sugar is going to make candy for soldiers like Uncle Ted. Lee decides she doesn't like the war and even being big enough to help Daddy collect ration stamps from his customers doesn't change her mind. Daddy trades a box of nails for a box of Valentine candy for Mama, and she shares it with Lee and her brother, one piece a day.

As Lee gets older, she begins to understand that Uncle Ted could be one of the soldiers she sees in the movie newsreels. She helps with the war effort and wonders if the war will ever be over and if they'll ever have candy again. They celebrate when the war ends in Europe and wait for Uncle Ted to come home. The day the war in the Pacific is won, Uncle Ted returns with a special gift: a Hershey bar! Lee climbs into her special tree, unwraps the bar, and starts to eat it, but something has changed. The candy bar can wait; right now she wants to be with her family and Uncle Ted.

Lloyd Bloom's vigorous oil paintings are realistic but show only the most basic elements of the story. The colors are generally muted, though stronger colors are introduced in the clothing. The figures have sturdy bodies and strong features defined by strong light and shadow. The clothing is simple and the backgrounds are minimal and—except for the views of the store—not specific for time and place. The somewhat crude illustrations match the basic honesty of a story in which a child has to learn for herself that war means more than the loss of candy.

Houston, Jeanne Wakatsuki, and James D. Houston. *Farewell to Manzanar.* Houghton Mifflin, 1973; Bantam Books, 1974.

Source of Material: Based on the author's recollections and shared memories of family and friends.

Locations: San Pedro, Owens Valley, and San Jose, California.

Dates: December 7, 1941 to November, 1945. Jeanne's story continues through her high school years and into the mid-1950s.

Grade: 6 to Adult.

Jeanne Wakatsuki is seven years old and the youngest in a large, extended Japanese-American family when the Japanese bomb Pearl Harbor. Her father, a fisherman with a boat and radio, is taken away almost immediately, and within months, the entire family is uprooted from their home and sent to live at the Manzanar internment camp in the Owens Valley of California. They arrive in April, settling into hastily constructed, drafty barracks-type buildings where they suffer from cold, dust, lack of privacy, and almost inedible food. As the months pass, they build a semblance of a life. Jeanne's older brothers patch cracks and improve the living quarters, their mother finds a job as a dietician, and Jeanne and her younger brothers join in a variety of activities until schools are organized. In September her father returns, dramatically changed by months of imprisonment. A dynamic, domineering man who always did everything with a flourish is now bitter and a heavy drinker. This adds a new dimension of misery to the family's crowded life.

This book gives a bittersweet portrait of the community created by the Japanese internees who keep busy organizing clubs, improving their living quarters, and planting gardens. However, the lack of privacy, the communal dining hall eating, and the endless debates over divisive political issues gradually take a toll on this large, close-knit family—though affection and loyalty remain. As opportunities arise to leave the camp, the older children leave and the family shrinks. Jeanne's mother grows in many ways, but her dynamic, patriarchal father is broken by the experience and leaves the camp too old and bitter to reinvent himself. Jeanne herself is profoundly changed and spends the rest of her childhood and teens trying to erase every quality that makes her seem foreign. Hiding a deep-seated anger, she calmly accepts all the slights of postwar society: the assumption that she can't speak English, the exclusion from Girl Scouts, and her teachers' obvious hesitation to allow her to take a leadership role among her classmates. The book ends with the adult Jeanne returning to Manzanar with her husband and children and remembering her last days there.

This is a moving and disturbing account of the Japanese internment, the underlying racism that allowed it to happen, and the profound change it made in the life of one little girl.

Ray, Deborah Kogan. *My Daddy Was a Soldier: A World War II Story.* Holiday House, 1990.

Source of Material: Author's childhood memories.

Location: Philadelphia, Pennsylvania.

Dates: December 1941 to December 1945.

Grade: 2 to 5.

After the Japanese attack Pearl Harbor, Jeannie and her parents listen to the radio reports, but she feels safe until one by one the men on their street leave to fight in the war. She tries to be brave when Daddy leaves, but when she kisses him good-bye, she cries and cries and can't wait for his letters. Mama takes a job at the naval yard, and even though Jeannie joins other children at a neighbor's house after school, she still gets "the lonelies" waiting for Mama to come home. The war has caused food shortages, and even with rationing, most of the stores run out before the family shops on Saturday. So Mama makes do with Spam, canned vegetables, and fruit. They plant a victory garden in a narrow strip of dirt, and each day Jeannie waters it and pulls the weeds. Maybe Daddy will be home in time to eat some of the tomatoes. But he writes that he won't be home soon and will instead board a ship to fight the Japanese in the Pacific.

That summer the women on the street talk about the war news and the letters from husbands and sons while the children play "Kill the Enemy" around the parked cars. The news, the letters, and the blackouts make the war seem close, and Jeannie always thinks about her father and the real bombs he is facing. When a friend's brother returns from the war, missing one leg, Jeannie has nightmares and worries and worries when Christmas comes with no letter from Daddy. The letter finally comes on New Year's Eve, and Jeannie hopes that this year (1944) the war will end and Daddy will come home. But it is almost two more years before the war ends and Daddy returns, just in time for Christmas. He is surprised to see her so grown up but assures her, "You were always with me, Jeannie-o."

The story is illustrated with full-page black-and-white pencil drawings on the right side of each double-page. The soft quality that typifies Kogan's illustration style reinforces the strong personal quality of this story. Though there are many details that reflect the story's period and location, the real subject is the emotions of one child. The majority of the pictures show the mother and daughter together, hugging, holding hands, and comforting and reassuring each other. Even when Jeannie's alone, she's still involved in the drama: she waits for Mama to come home, she works in the garden, and she helps with the scrap drive. The text and illustrations combine to show the real sense of loss and fear children experienced during the war as they waited for loved ones to return.

Stevenson, James. *Don't You Know There's a War On?* Greenwillow Books, 1992.

Source of Material: Author's childhood memories.

Location: Small town near New York City.

Dates: Early 1940s.

Grade: 2 to 5.

Stevenson's typical low-key humor is mixed with some of the fears children experienced during World War II. Though James's brother is in the navy, the war at first means only small changes and sacrifices to him: no gas for the car, no candy, and unusual kinds of food (Spam and home-grown kale). The neighborhood warden tries to enforce blackouts, and they are warned about saboteurs. James and a friend keep an eye on old Mr. Schmidt, in case he's a spy. All the boys collect tin foil and cans, watch for enemy planes, and brag about what they'll do when they are old enough to join the war. When James's father joins the army, the house suddenly seems empty and the war becomes more real. Father is running hotels for the army, and the family joins him for a week in Florida. There they have a wonderful time swimming and sight-seeing, but after they return home, the war continues on and on. Then one day James hears cars honking and whistles blowing, and everyone is celebrating. After a few weeks, James and his mother and brother meet Father at the station. "He saw us and he waved. That's when I knew the war was over."

The illustrations, in Stevenson's typical shorthand style, loosely define the time and place but leave the human characters as faceless figures. Still, his gesture drawings convey more with a few strokes than many others do with a hundred lines. They are a perfect match for his writing style, in which random details are combined to create a tangible memory.

Takashima, Shizuye. *A Child in Prison Camp.* Morrow, 1974.

Source of Material: Author's childhood memories.

Location: Vancouver, British Columbia.

Dates: 1941 to 1945.

Grade: 4 to 8.

After the Japanese attack on Pearl Harbor in December of 1941, the Canadian government joined the United States in the decision to remove all people of Japanese descent from the West Coast and send them to internment camps inland. They were stripped of civil rights and property, and all men over 18 were taken away.

In Shizuye Takashima's family, that leaves her mother, her older sister Yuki, and Shizuye to cope with selling what they can (for very little money), packing the rest, and waiting for the government to decide where to send them. Finally the word comes; their older brother David will remain in Toronto, but Mother and the sisters will join Father in a small village high in the mountains of British Columbia. The mountains are beautiful, but they share a small bungalow with another family, and there is no water or power. They are watched constantly by fellow Japanese hired by the Royal Canadian Mounted Police to keep order, but that doesn't prevent Father from complaining to the Red Cross about conditions and demanding improvements. There is no school until October, and Yuki will not be able to finish high school at all, since the government refuses to fund anything beyond Grade 8. Shizuye's school is taught by a handful of older girls who have completed correspondence studies but have no training in teaching. It is not the best, but school is school.

The men continue to complain to the Red Cross, and conditions gradually improve. They are finally given coal-oil lamps, then running water and the ability to build a community bathhouse. They clear land for gardens to help with the high cost of food, swim in a nearby lake, and celebrate O-ban, a festival for the dead. The next fall Yuki is able to go to a high school run by Catholic nuns, but Shizuye continues to find school dull and uninspiring. There is also growing conflict within the family. Those who choose to are allowed to return to Japan, and some families are already leaving. Father, who is very bitter, wants to go; he sees no future in a country that would take his rights and property and treat all of them so badly. Yuki is equally determined to stay. Canada is the only home she knows, and she would feel like a stranger in Japan. Mother is torn; she has no one in Japan, and her children are Canadian. Besides, the war is going badly in Japan. Would they be welcome?

The war and the debate go on and on as the people in the camp quarrel about the future. David has found a job and sends them gifts and encouragement. Quietly Yuki makes her own plans, and when she gets a job, she joins David in Toronto. Shizuye wonders what will happen to her family if Father decides to leave for Japan. Then news comes of the atomic bomb and the end of the war. Now the choice must be made: renounce Canadian citizenship and return to Japan or remain and be relocated. Finally, Father decides to go to Toronto. They have been in the camp almost three years, and as Shizuye looks at the beautiful mountains, she knows it has not all been hard and she will always remember these years.

The text is illustrated by an insert of watercolor paintings by the author, who is a well-known artist. The sketchy paintings show Shizuye and Yuki waiting for the train, carrying water through the snow, and bathing in the lake. Others show the mountains and community events such as O-ban dancing, the bathhouse, and a fire. Impressionistic rather than detailed, the paintings emphasize the beauty of the mountains and the closeness of a community determined to work together despite prejudice and conflicts beyond their control.

Uchida, Yoshiko. *Journey to Topaz: A Story of the Japanese-American Evacuation.* Illustrated by Donald Carrick. Charles Scribner's Sons, 1971.

————. *Journey Home.* Illustrated by Charles Robinson. Atheneum, 1978.

Source of Material: Author's personal experiences.

Locations: Berkeley, California; Topaz, Utah.

Dates: Early 1940s.

Grade: 5 to 8.

It is a quiet Sunday morning in Berkeley, California. Eleven-year-old Yuki Sakane is thinking about Christmas, her mother is cooking Sunday lunch, and her father is working in his beloved garden when they hear the news of Pearl Harbor. They dismiss the report as a hoax and are preparing to go on as usual when three FBI men arrive to search the house and take Father away for questioning. This is the beginning of years of fear, confusion, and exile for Yuki's family who, with other Japanese-Americans, are sent from their homes to internment camps. Father is sent to Montana, leaving Yuki's older brother Ken to help Mother sort and store their possesions, find a home for Yuki's beloved dog Pepper, and plan for a move into the unknown. Though he is given the opportunity to continue school at a university inland, Ken decides to stay and help his family. Their first new home is a horse stall at the Tanforan Racetrack, where Yuki becomes friends with Emi, who lives next to them with her grandparents. Tanforan is a nightmare with mud everywhere, no privacy, and almost inedible food. They are helped out by old neighbors from Berkeley until they are transferred to a more permanent camp in the desert of Utah.

The Topaz camp is a series of unfinished barracks that do little to keep out the dust and cold. Even when the buildings are complete, it is a bleak place with no vegetation to keep out the blowing sand. Emi contracts tuberculosis and is isolated in the hospital. While she is there, her grandfather, who is looking for arrowheads near the barbed wire that encloses the camp, is shot by one of the guards. Yuki becomes worried about her brother Ken, who is becoming silent and bitter and no longer even speaks of continuing his studies. She hopes that will change when her father is finally permitted to rejoin them just before Christmas. Then in February the army recruiters come, looking for volunteers for an all-Japanese unit. The recruiters say it is an opportunity for the Japanese to prove their loyalty, and though the people are still bitter, many young men decide to go. Ken and his best friend Jim are among the volunteers.

Spring is coming, and Emi is finally well enough to return home to her grandmother, but the camp atmosphere is changing. Groups of bitter agitators begin to turn their anger on the Japanese who worked with the Caucasian administration. They roam the camps at night, beating people. Father is warned that he is on their list, and when a stink bomb is thrown through their window, he gets special clearance to take the family to Salt Lake City. They promise to keep in touch with Emi and her grandmother and Mr. Toda, an old friend from Berkeley, and they leave the camp, returning to the uncertainties of the outside world.

Journey Home starts with the family in Salt Lake City, where Father and Mother have been able to find only menial jobs. Then news arrives from several places. Ken is wounded but will recover and be sent home, and the army has lifted its exclusion order for California so they can finally return to Berkeley. They return first to the Japanese church in Berkeley, where they help the minister create a hostel for returning Japanese. Though most old friends are happy to see them, the world is largely hostile to them and lacking in opportunties. After Emi and her grandmother join them, Father comes up with a plan. Another resident in the hostel, Mr. Oka, is trying to buy back his grocery store. Emi's grandmother also once had a grocery store, and Father knows about the import business. By pooling their resources, they could buy the business and live in the apartment above the store. It is a new start for them all and the business—despite an arson attack—begins to succeed when Ken finally comes home. He is on crutches, alone and withdrawn. Though he is slowly able to tell them how his best friend died saving the others, nothing seems to break though his despair. It is only when they realize that the neighbors who helped them recover from the arson attack lost their only son on Iwo Jima that Mr. Oka lets go of his bitterness and Ken is able to begin planning his future.

This is a dramatic story, but the real strength of the books lies in the variety of characters Yuki meets. Though this was a world of hate and fear, Yuki is protected by the love of her family and people such as her beloved neighbor, Mrs. Jamieson, their old friend Mr. Toda, and Emi's feisty grandmother. Though Uchida acknowledges the prejudice of the time, her story centers around people whose courage and commitment to honor protect them from lasting anger and bitterness.

Carrick's illustrations for *Journey to Topaz* have the soft line and somewhat abstract quality of Japanese brush paintings. He uses empty space and abstraction to convey Yuki's sense of loss and displacement. Robinson's illustrations, charcoal drawings on a canvas background, are both more realistic and harsher, showing the family's movement from place to place. Though they convey the bleak environment of the camp and the minimal housing later, the main emphasis is on the family and their friends.

Yolen, Jane. *All Those Secrets of the World.* Illustrated by Leslie Baker. Little, Brown & Co., 1991.

Source of Material: Author's childhood memories.

Location: Chesapeake Bay.

Dates: Early 1940s.

Grade: 1 to 4.

Janie is four and her cousin Michael five when her father boards the big ship and sails off to war. There are bands and flags and a hundred butterfly kisses from Daddy, but Mama cries all the way home. The next day Janie and Michael go to the shore of nearby Chesapeake Bay, take off their shoes, and wade in the water. Far away on the horizon are tiny specks that Michael says are ships taking soldiers across the sea. Janie doesn't understand. Daddy went on a *big* ship, and these specks are no bigger than her thumb. Then Michael tells her a secret of the world: things look small when they are far away. He runs away down the beach till he is no bigger than her hand, and she is suddenly afraid he will disappear like the ships. Janie remembers this secret two years later when Daddy returns, a stranger in brown with his arm in a sling. "You're so big, Janie," he said. "Lots bigger than I remembered." As she hugs him, she shares Michael's secret. "When you are far away, everything is smaller. But now you are here so I am big." He agrees and gives her a hundred butterfly kisses.

Leslie Baker's soft watercolor paintings capture the gentle innocence of this story in which a young child creates her own understanding of her father's absence. The clothing, automobiles, and even the style of the beach scenes take the viewer back to the time of World War II. Seen through the eyes of childhood, the ship's departure is a scattered, almost overwhelming, event that gives way to the quiet of her grandparents' home. This transition is echoed in the paintings, especially their colors. When Father returns, it is to the soft greens of a summer day.

SPECIAL PROJECTS AND ENRICHMENT ACTIVITIES

Background Sources

The activities in this section are designed to help children understand the way World War II and the nation's commitment to the war effort permeated every aspect of daily life. Because the books on the recommended reading list describe individual experiences, readers may want to consult some of the books that follow to get a more comprehensive picture of World War II.

Bailey, Ronald H. *The Home Front: U.S.A.*, [World War II]. Time-Life Books, 1987. **Grade:** 6 to Adult.

Duden, Jane. *1940s*, [Timelines]. Crestwood House, 1989. **Grade:** 4 to 8.

Harris, Mark Jonathan, Franklin Mitchell, and Steven Schecter. *The Homefront: America During World War II*. G. P. Putnam's Sons, 1984. **Grade:** 8 to Adult.

This Fabulous Century: 1940-1950. Time-Life Books, 1969. **Grade:** 6 to Adult.

Whitman, Sylvia. *V is For Victory: The American Home Front During World War II*. Lerner Publications, 1993. **Grade:** 5 to 9.

Although the Time-Life books listed above are written for adults, they are filled with photos and visual documents which will help students get a clear picture of the time. In addition, *The Homefront: America During World War II* contains interviews with ordinary citizens whose lives were changed by the war. *V is for Victory: The American Home Front During World War II* describes many aspects of daily life and is written for children. *1940's* gives a year-by-year summary of the decade and includes all aspects of life and culture. Together, they give a rich visual and emotional view of this time.

World War II Jackdaw

The term *jackdaw* refers to a bird that fills its nest with brightly colored objects it has gathered. Historic jackdaws are collections, based on historic events, that consist of primary resources (or facsimiles) and other bits of historic evidence that have been gathered together to create a firsthand view of a specific time.

ACTIVITIES

1. Talk to older relatives and friends and ask if they have any mementos of home life that they would like to donate to a World War II jackdaw. Some things you can look for include: unused ration stamps; recipes designed for rationed foods or substitutions for scarce foods such as butter and sugar; advertisements or price lists of goods or services; information or advertisements about scrap drives; airplane spotter cards, used to identify different kinds of aircraft; and advertisements that feature the war and the war effort.
2. Create a time line that shows how events of the war influenced what was happening at home. From the library, copy interesting news articles or documents about life on the home front. Look through popular magazines of the time and collect information on the popular culture: the songs, music, and dances. You might want to include in your jackdaw recordings of some of the music. Can you find advertisements for popular movies of the time? Nostalgia shops often carry old posters that advertised movies. Collect ads and articles on fashion and note how the war and shortages of material affected it. Look for references to the changed role of women, many of whom worked in factories while the men were in the army. Include these in your jackdaw.
3. Make a collection of articles about children during the war. Look for information about children collecting scrap metal and working in victory gardens. In what other ways did children help during the war?
4. Include a list of all the nonfiction books you have used for research in creating your jackdaw as well as recommended fiction that tells about the homefront.

Community Efforts: Sacrifices and Contributions

Rationing

In the books of recommended reading for this chapter, *But No Candy* (see p. 141), *My Daddy Was a Soldier* (see p. 143) and *Don't You Know There's a War On?* (see p. 144) describe the ways food rationing affected their lives. Not only did children have to do without candy and gum, they also ate different kinds of meat and cut down on their use of gasoline.

ACTIVITY

Talk to older relatives and friends who remember World War II. Ask them if they remember which foods and materials were rationed. What did they miss, and how did their families adjust to the shortages? Write down or record their experiences. You could combine these experiences into a report or a fictional story like *But No Candy* (see p. 141). Imagine you have been asked to give up foods such as candy, butter, and meat. Imagine there is a shortage of gasoline and your family could not drive very often. Write an essay or story about how you would make these sacrifices and what you might to do help.

Recycling

The EarthWorks Group. *50 Simple Things Kids Can Do to Recycle*. Illustrations by Michele Montez. EarthWorks Press, 1994. **Grade:** 4 to 8.

McVicker, Dee. *Easy Recycling Handbook: What to Recycle and How to Buy Recycled . . .Without All the Garbage*. Grassroots Books, 1994. **Grade:** 4 to 8.

Stefoff, Rebecca. *Recycling*. Chelsea House Publishers, 1991. **Grade:** 5 to 9.

During World War II, the materials needed to build weapons became very scarce, and it became a patriotic duty to save and collect tin cans, scrap metal, glass, and paper. The books listed above explain how important it is to recycle garbage and other ways to protect our environment.

ACTIVITY

How do you think collecting scrap for the war effort was the same as collecting materials for recycling today? Do you think children today care as

---

ACTIVITY cont'd.

much about protecting the environment as children in the past cared about helping with the war effort? Write an essay comparing these two activities: how are they the same, and how are they different?

Victory Gardens

Waters, Marjorie. *The Victory Gardens Kids' Book.* Houghton Mifflin, 1988. **Grade:** 4 to Adult.

Because there was a shortage of food during the war, citizens were asked to plant victory gardens and help grow some of their own food. *A Summer on Thirteenth Street* (see p. 140), *My Daddy Was a Soldier* (see p. 143), and *Don't You Know There's A War On* (see p. 144) all show how people planted gardens everywhere, even people who lived in the city and had little space. *The Victory Garden Kid's Book* describes a small garden, planted by kids, and gives advice on growing 30 easy-to-grow plants.

ACTIVITY

Use this and other books on gardening to plan a victory garden for your family. Where would you plant it? What sorts of food do you think you could grow? How would you take care of it? Draw a plan for your garden: where it will be located, what you will grow, and a schedule for taking care of it.

Internment Camps

Brimmer, Larry Dane. *Voices From the Camps: Internment of Japanese Americans During World War II.* Franklin Watts, 1994. **Grade:** 6 to 9.

After Japan bombed Pearl Harbor, families of Japanese origin in both the United States and Canada were forced to leave their homes and businesses and move into government internment camps. The book listed above tells about all aspects of these events, including the struggles for reparations that followed.

ACTIVITIES

1. Use this book and others to learn about these camps. What happened and why? Perhaps you can enrich your library research by interviewing older people who remember this time. What do they remember, and why

ACTIVITIES cont'd.

do they think the government took such an action against these people? How did they feel at the time, and how do they feel now? If possible, try to interview someone from one of the Japanese-American families involved. How did they feel then, and how do they feel now?

2. Do you think something like this could happen in Canada or the United States today? Write an essay explaining the reasons why you think it could or could not happen now.

3. Using your library, make facsimile copies of the headlines about the Japanese attack on Pearl Harbor and the reaction that followed. Look for headlines and articles that show the growing hysteria and prejudice against Japanese-Americans. Try to find a facsimile of one of the exclusion orders given to Japanese-American families.

4. Make a time line showing when Pearl Harbor was attacked, when the internment camps were established, how long they existed, and what happened when the war was over.

5. Make a map showing the location of the internment camps in the United States and Canada. Collect as many pictures as possible of life in the camps. Collect pictures and paintings made by the people who lived in the camps and compare them to the more official photos shown in magazines and newspapers.

CHAPTER

• • • • • • • • •

From Me to You: Passing On Traditions and Stories

This chapter is about collecting, saving, and remembering. Unlike other chapters, the titles recommended here include both books based on direct family memories and works of fiction. The source for books based on family stories is indicated in the annotation. The recommended works and the activities that follow each section illustrate the importance of different kinds of "memory triggers" and how they can create a sense of continuity within a family. Because many of these activities center on physical objects, such as photos, family heirlooms, and specific family stories, teachers will need to be aware of any students who may have no access to these resources. Students who are adopted, live in foster homes, or whose families find such activities intrusive will need alternative choices. Such students might find equal satisfaction in interviewing a willing volunteer and sharing that person's photos, heirlooms, and memories.

Family memories are passed on in a variety of ways. The books and activities in this chapter are centered around specific kinds of memory triggers. Generations can be traced, combining the formal structures of genealogy with the fascination of discovery. The resulting information can be used to learn about the different homes and different cities the family has lived in and everything that was involved in the decision to move. For many families, the strongest memory triggers are photo albums, scrapbooks, and collections of letters. Children should be encouraged to search for and explore the richness of these family treasures and use them to learn about family pets, family vacations, and other memorable events. Family storytelling, once the domain of family historians and folklorists, is now gaining recognition as a rich source of literature and formal public storytelling. It is also the most immediate way children learn about the lives of their parents and grandparents. Many children get their strongest sense of the past from visiting their grandparents and other relatives. As the books and activities show, these visits give children a glimpse into their parents' childhoods and the daily texture of life in the past.

Sometimes memories are passed on in the form of heirlooms—simple objects whose value lies in their ties to a memorable event or a loved person. These objects always come with a story attached, and usually the story is more valuable than the object. Tangible memory can also be formally collected in the form of memory boxes and paintings, creating physical evidence of personal memories. The books and enrichment activities are all designed to help children discover their own family heritage and share it, using writing and illustration.

RECOMMENDED READING WITH SPECIAL PROJECTS AND ENRICHMENT ACTIVITIES
Tracing the Generations

Children who live very much in the present can be confused by different generations in a family and the ways people are related to them. Still, they gradually become aware that their parents' connection to their grandparents is like the connection they feel to their own parents, and they begin to develop a sense of the bonds that tie generations together. The books in this section show the way individual stories overlap those of previous and following generations, and the activities help children find their place in the family tree.

Greenfield, Eloise, and Leslie Jones Little. *Childtimes: A Three-Generation Memoir.* Drawings by Jerry Pinkney and photographs from the author's family albums. Harper & Row, 1979. **Grade:** 6 to Adult.

In this book, Eloise Greenfield collected the childhood memories of three generations of women: herself, her mother, and her grandmother. The book tells not only the story of one African-American family, but the life of a Southern mill town. It traces Parmele's founding in the late 1880s to its decline in the 1930s, when the family of Eloise, the youngest narrator, was forced to move north to find work. Told as individual episodes in a somewhat random order, the book contains all the particular and tangible memories of childhood: games and chores, hungry times and good cooking, deaths and weddings. There is also a strong sense of the struggle of parents to maintain their own pride and impart a sense of pride to their children while under the dual burdens of poverty and deeply ingrained prejudice.

The first two-thirds of the book is centered on the Southern mill town where both parents worked at whatever jobs could be found and everyone shared in household chores. The depression sent the third generation north to

Washington, D.C., and Langston Terrace, a low-rent housing project with a strong sense of community and lots of other children to play with. Eloise describes this as a "good growing up place," where the neighborhood cushioned the blows of the outside world, and theatre and music were only a bus ride away. Annual visits to Parmele maintained the family's ties to their first home and the grandparents they left behind. These visits also kept alive their strong sense of family—a characteristic that permeates this memoir.

The voice of each of these women is individual, and the stories they tell are particular regarding time and place. These stories, however, merge into one seamless narrative, as one woman's childhood ends in marriage and the next child's story begins.

Three groups of photos and a handful of drawings by Jerry Pinkney provide visual connections to the narrative. Pinkney's drawings establish the basic settings: an early lumber mill, a turn-of-the-century train station, and a playground in the middle of a housing project. The family photos give faces to the characters described; however, the strongest imagery comes from the tangible memories of the three narrators.

Johnson, Angela. *Toning the Sweep.* Orchard Books, 1993. **Grades:** 6 to Adult.

Emily has been visiting her Grandmama Ola's home in the California desert every summer since she was two. Now she is 14, and this will be Emmie's last trip. Ola has cancer, and Emmie and her mother have come to take her back to Cleveland with them. To understand and remember her grandmother's life here in "the dry," Emmie borrows a camcorder, and while her mother and grandmother pack endless numbers of boxes, she begins to tape the people and places that are part of her grandmother's life. She learns the details of her grandfather's death in Alabama in 1964, the senseless murder of an African-American man that sent Ola fleeing across the country and left Emmie's mother filled with unresolved grief. She finds comfort in the laughter of "the aunts," the quiet calm of Ola's friend Martha Jackson, and the unspoken understanding from her own friend, David Two Starr. To deal with her own grief and loss, Emmie recreates an old ceremony to release the spirit and comfort the living, and she invites her mother to share it with her.

This book is filled with memorable characters, starting with Emmie. Like her grandmother, she is a free spirit who accepts and gives friendship easily and finds her own path to healing. Ola is extraordinary in her strength, her joy for life, and the way she chooses to live. Between them is Mama, who loves them both but cannot love the desert. She hated the prejudice that killed her father but never forgave her mother for taking her away from Alabama. Together these three women weave a pattern of grief, understanding, and forgiveness that will carry them through Ola's death.

Johnston, Tony. *Yonder.* Pictures by Lloyd Bloom. Dial Books for Young Readers, 1988. **Grade:** K to 3.

In a picture book using blank verse and repetitious phrases, Johnston tells how a young farmer creates a farm and watches his family grow, planting a tree to commemorate each important event. The hardworking adults and joyous children are shown against a colorful landscape of green rolling hills, trees, and sky. As wilderness gives way to fields, houses, and barns, the children grow and have children of their own, who listen wide-eyed to Grandpa's tales and sit beside the fire while Grandma knits. The last picture shows family and neighbors planting a tree in memory of Grandpa, who has died. The story is given visual unity by pictures of a plum tree that is shown in all seasons. Similarly, the recurring phrases of "yonder" and "There. Just over there" tie the story together and emphasize the continuity of this family.

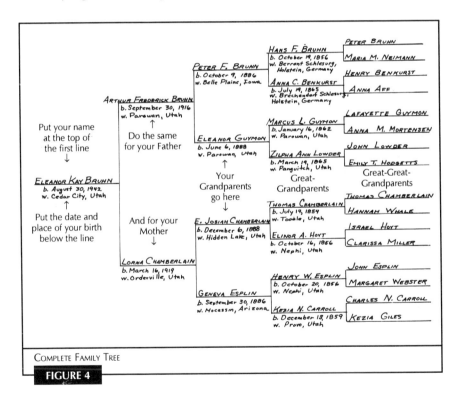

COMPLETE FAMILY TREE

FIGURE 4

ACTIVITIES

Family Trees. A good way to find out about your family is to make a family tree, or lineage chart (Figure 4). An example of a basic chart can be found on p. 27 of *Steven Caney's Kids' America* (see p. 42) or any of the books on

ACTIVITIES cont'd.

genealogy listed in Appendix 1. Use as many charts as you need, adding as many names as you can. Remember, you are moving back in time, from your memories to those of your parents and grandparents, so you will need their help filling in those names and dates. Find a good time to talk to members of your family and collect the information you need. Your parents and grandparents will be pleased by your interest, and you may find out some fascinating things as they remember their parents and grandparents. Make your family tree as complete as you possibly can with full names, birthplaces, and birth dates. You may also want to add marriage and death dates.

If you have pictures, you can make another kind of family tree using both names and pictures. If there is only one print of a picture, make copies of it for your family tree. Look for pictures that show the person's whole face clearly and separately. Put in as many pictures as you can find. When you have finished, look at the family tree carefully. Can you see how members of your family look like each other? How they look different? Do any of your ancestors remind you of someone else? Who do you think you look like?

Family Maps. One thing you may have discovered as you made your family tree is that your ancestors have lived in a lot of different places. Find a large outline map and use it to include all the places your family has lived. Starting with where you live now, mark all the places your family has lived, going back as many generations as you can. Collect as much information as you can about the changes in location. Why did the family move? What did they do in the new place? How long did they stay? Did your parents grow up in the same town, or did they meet somewhere else? If the map becomes too complicated, you may want to use one color for your father's family and another for your mother's.

Did you hear any interesting stories as you were collecting this information? Perhaps the person who told you the story will allow you to record it or write it down.

Remembering Family Houses

Among the strongest and most tangible memories are those of place—of houses and gardens and the streets that connect them to the outside world. Some families live in a single house for a lifetime or several lifetimes, collecting memories in one location. Others will move from house to house, each with its own story, each with its own memories. The stories and activities that follow show how houses and our memories of them can open a whole world of family stories.

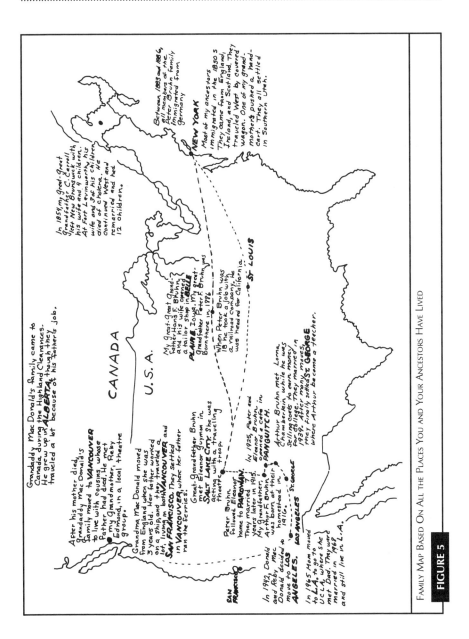

FAMILY MAP BASED ON ALL THE PLACES YOU AND YOUR ANCESTORS HAVE LIVED

FIGURE 5

Blegvad, Lenore. *Once Upon a Time and Grandma.* Margaret K. McElderry Books, 1993. **Grade:** 1 to 3.

When Grandma takes Emma and Luke to see the house and neighborhood where she lived as a child, they find it hard to imagine her as a little girl called Norrie, blowing bubbles on the fire escape, feeding sugar to the milkman's horse, throwing pennies to the organ grinder, and building a snowman right where they are standing. Even when Grandma shows them her name carved in a tree, they are not convinced. She finally proves it to them in a surprising way—demonstrating her skills as a tap dancer—and showing them that Norrie still exists, along with her memories of home and neighborhood. The author's pencil and watercolor illustrations show Norrie as a happy child enjoying her home in a city apartment and quiet neighborhood with tree-lined streets and a variety of visitors and activities.

Shelby, Anne. *Homeplace.* Illustrations by Wendy Anderson Halperin. Orchard Books, 1995. **Grade:** 2 to 6.

A grandmother tells her grandchild the story of their family home, starting with great-great-great-great-grandpa, who cut the logs to build the sturdy cabin that is added to as successive generations make this house their home. As time goes on, the changes in the house and it's furnishings are shown in a series of detailed color paintings surrounded by vignettes, showing all aspects of the life of this family. The stone fireplace is repaced first by an iron cookstove, then a microwave; the horses are traded for tractors and cars, and catalog orders are traded for trips to town. Wallpaper is added, colors are changed, but the family stays. They grow and change but always remain affectionate and happy in their home.

Rand, Gloria. *The Cabin Key.* Illustrated by Ted Rand. Harcourt Brace & Co., 1994. **Grade:** 2 to 5.

An unnamed little girl shares her joy on returning once more to her family's mountain cabin. She loves everything about it: the woodsy smell, the family treasures that they want to keep forever, the kerosene lamps, and great-grandmother's enameled tin dishes. She enjoys everything that makes life in the cabin special: carrying water from the creek, chopping wood, cooking in the fireplace, playing old records on a wind-up phonograph, and even going through the snow to the outhouse. The cabin described in this book has been in the Rand family for almost 60 years, and both the text and colorful illustrations are filled with love for this particular home and its place in the life of this family.

ACTIVITY

Your Own "House History." Make a personal map of all the houses you remember living in and where they were located (see Figure 6). Include as much information as you can. What did they look like? How were the rooms arranged? Were there porches or balconies? How were they heated? What furniture do you remember? What can you remember about the neighborhoods or locations and people who lived near you? Do you have

---

ACTIVITY cont'd.

photos of the houses? Draw pictures of each house; include yourself and your family in each picture. Perhaps you can write about the things you remember doing when you lived there.

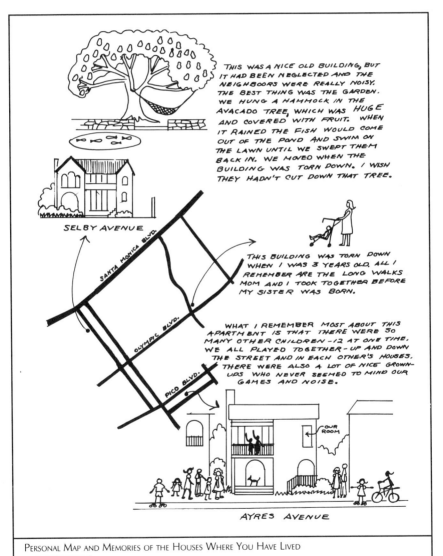

PERSONAL MAP AND MEMORIES OF THE HOUSES WHERE YOU HAVE LIVED

FIGURE 6

Family Storytelling

In most families, memories and stories are passed on directly in the form of stories. Such stories are told informally—sometimes at family gatherings with one story triggering another, and sometimes one-on-one with a grandparent or parent sharing memories with a child. Some families are blessed with a gifted storyteller whose special treatment of a memory gradually becomes the "official" version to be handed down from one generation to another. The books included in this section show how important these stories are and help children find ways to collect and share these important family treasures.

Dionetti, Michelle. *Coal Mine Peaches.* Illustrated by Anita Riggio. Orchard Books, 1991. **Grade:** 2 to 5.

Grandfather started telling stories when he was just a boy, working as a breaker in a coal mine. He told his brothers that in the summer it got so hot, peaches would grow from the coal. Later he would present small purple plums as coal mine peaches. He leaves the mines to go to New York, build the Brooklyn Bridge, and marry a beautiful young girl with long black hair. At the dinner table he entertains his five children with stories about themselves. And when his granddaughter comes to visit, he shows her the family pictures and tells her all the stories about himself and his children and the ones about her when she was little. One summer day he fills her hands with small dark plums and tells her all about coal mine peaches.

Anita Riggio's paintings with their broad strokes of color and period details show the passage of time, the growth of the family, the vigor of Grandfather's storytelling, and his granddaughter's appreciation of his gift for storytelling that "made lean times fat."

Igus, Toymi. *When I Was Little.* Illustrated by Higgins Bond. Just Us Books, 1992. **Grade:** K to 3.

As an African-American grandfather and his visiting grandson fish off the end of a river dock, the grandfather describes the way life used to be. Noel thinks Grandpa Will's descriptions of swinging into the river, buying blocks of ice for the ice box, and telling stories on the front porch sound like fun. But when he tries to imagine life without washing machines, televisions, or indoor toilets he decides he's glad he wasn't little when his grandfather was little. As Noel excitedly catches his first fish, his grandfather observes that while things *are* different now, "the important things are still the same."

The book's painted illustrations present reality in full color while Grandpa's memories are in the blacks and whites of old photos. These depict Grandpa as a boy in knickers carrying ice in a wooden wagon, his mama scrubbing clothes on a washboard, and the family gathered on the front porch or listening to a large wooden radio. The contrast of colors and life styles can help young readers understand how rapidly the world has changed since their grandparents' childhoods, and the stories, which are based on stories the author heard her father tell his grandchildren, provide a good introduction to oral history projects.

Johnson, Angela. *Tell Me a Story, Mama.* Illustrated by David Soman. Orchard Books, 1989. **Grade:** K to 3.

A little girl asks Mama to tell her stories about her childhood. She knows which ones she wants: stories that are already so familiar that she ends up telling most of each story herself. As the little girl tells about the mean old lady, the lost puppy, and a childhood train journey, Mama confirms each story with words of love and encouragement. Together they weave a portrait of a child with a quick temper, a kind heart, and loving parents—and a child listener who will feel the same love and pass these and other stories on to *her* children.

The full-page watercolor illustrations show three generations of an African-American family. Colorful paintings showing Mama's rural childhood and her loving parents alternate with pictures of the little girl's comfortable bedroom where Mama helps her into her pajamas and tucks her into bed.

Ketner, Mary Grace. *Ganzy Remembers.* Illustrated by Barbara Sparks. Atheneum, 1991. **Grade:** 2 to 6.

When a little girl goes with her grandmother to the nursing home to visit her great-grandmother Ganzy, she learns about the times when Ganzy was a little girl named Daphne. Ganzy is in a wheelchair now, but she remembers riding her horse to a one-room school, running away with her baby brother, a bird that built a nest in the pocket of Papa's overalls, and bathing in the creek.

The text and illustrations alternate between limited views of the nursing home and large paintings of Ganzy's childhood memories. This clearly demonstrates to the reader that Ganzy's childhood memories mean far more to Ganzy and her granddaughter than the present reality of the nursing home. The pale, sketchy watercolors illustrate the story but lack the graphic power to really pull the reader inside these memories.

Porte, Barbara Ann. *When Aunt Lucy Rode a Mule & Other Stories.* Pictures by Maxie Chambliss. Orchard Books, 1994. **Grade:** 2 to 5.

When Stella and Zelda ask Aunt Lucy to tell them a story, she tells them about a visit to her grandparents, the adventures she had, and the stories she heard. In the manner of real family storytelling, one story leads to another and the generations get mixed up a bit. Stella and Zelda learn about Great-Grandpa's walking stick, Great-Aunt Cissy's prodigious appetitite, a lady with a snake in her car, skinny dipping, hand fishing, and the time Grandma wore a flowered hat and was attacked by bees. Or was it Great-Aunt Cissy? After all this time, no one is really sure, but somehow that makes it an even better story.

The energetic, often comic illustrations don't accurately define the different time periods described, but they show a lively family that obviously enjoys one another and loves to share memories in the stories the author heard her own family tell.

Tate, Eleanor. *Front Porch Stories at the One-Room School.* Illustrated by Eric Velasquez. Bantam Books, 1992. **Grade: 4 to 6.**

One hot summer night when 12-year-old Margie and 7-year-old Cousin Ethel are bored, Margie's father takes them to the front porch of an old school for an evening of storytelling. He shares his memories of attending the all-black, one-room schoolhouse and his no-nonsense aunt who was the teacher. Like most informal story sessions, these stories wander from scary stories of ghosts and shadows to childhood memories of mischief and adventure: dogs in the school, walnut-throwing battles, a sudden flood, and the memorable day when Eleanor Roosevelt came to town. The stories themselves are based on a combination of actual experiences, stories the author heard in childhood, and the history of the Douglass School in Canton, Missouri. While the focus is on the past, another aspect of family storytelling is shown: the storytelling session ends with Ethel telling a story that clearly expresses her pain at her mother's disappearance three years earlier.

The colored painting on the cover shows the father telling stories to the two girls by the light of a fire set in a washtub. Black-and-white drawings in the text illustrate an event in each story. While the drawings clearly show the action, they are not strong on details of time and place.

ACTIVITY

Your Own Family Stories. Think about how your family shares stories and memories. Are stories told often, or are they reserved for a special time or place? Does everyone in your family take turns telling stories, or is one person the "official" storyteller? When different people tell about the same event, is the story the same or different? Write about your family, where stories are told, and who tells them.

Think about the stories you have heard about your family. Write down some of your favorite stories. Do you remember the event or the people, or did the stories happen long ago? Write one or more of the stories as you remember having heard them. Then write your own version, using your own words and pictures.

Think about your own life. What are some of the stories you may someday want to share with your children? Write the stories as you plan to tell them. You may want to illustrate the story to show how things happened.

┌───┐
| **ACTIVITY cont'd.** |
| |
| With other members of your group or class make a collection of |
| everyone's favorite family stories. You could add illustrations and make a |
| book to be shared. |
└───┘

Photo Albums, Scrapbooks, and Other Family Records

One of the important things about photos and scrapbooks is the way they capture specific moments and times. There is the fascination of seeing the adults one knows as children, the recognition that their lives were both the same and different from your own, and the fun of remembering past events. The books and activities in this section focus on photos as a powerful source of family stories and shared memories.

Caseley, Judith. *Dear Annie.* Greenwillow Books, 1991. **Grade:** K to 3.

Annie's collection of letters from Grandpa began with her birth, when he sent a card welcoming her to the world. At first Mama writes the answers, then Annie dictates them, and later on, she writes to Grandpa all by herself. She saves all of Grandpa's cards and letters in a shoebox, and one day she brings the box to school for show-and-tell. The children like her collection so much that they decide *they* want pen pals too. Now the class has a bulletin board filled with letters from all over the world, but nobody has as many letters as Annie: over 100 now, and Grandpa is still sending them every week.

  The simple-colored paintings that illustrate this book alternate pictures of Annie growing up with the cards and letters Grandpa sends her. Because the letters refer to time spent together, the cards are more than a collection of pictures; they are also the record of a loving relationship.

Myers, Walter Dean. *Brown Angels: An Album of Pictures and Verse.* HarperCollins, 1993. **Grade:** 4 to 8.

Walter Dean Myers has been collecting old pictures of African-American children for some time, and he chose a group of these photos as the basis for this book of poetry. Although the children in the photos are unknown to him, he has written about the way he imagined their lives to be based on his own life and the memory of the children he has known.

Vertreace, Martha M. *Kelly in the Mirror.* Illustrated by Sandra Speidel. Albert Whitman, 1993. **Grade:** 1 to 4.

Kelly, an African-American girl, feels bad when people say how much her younger brother and sister look like their parents—Kelly doesn't seem to look like anyone. Then when she is exploring in the attic, she finds the toys and clothes her mother had as a child. The hat and sweater fit perfectly, and she discovers an old photo album filled with pictures of Mama as a little girl. There is a picture of Mama wearing the sweater and hat, looking just like Kelly! The family is so pleased with Kelly's discovery that they take a picture of each child wearing something from the trunk.

Speidel's richly colored pastel pictures fill three-quaters of each double-page and show an attractive and loving family.

Zolotow, Charlotte. *The Sky Was Blue.* Pictures by Garth Williams. Harper & Row, 1963. **Grade:** 1 to 3.

As a little girl looks at the pictures in the family album, she and her mother notice that many things change. In each generation the clothes, the toys, and the house are different, and transportation changes too. Still, the mother reassures the child that the important things always stay the same: the sky is blue, the grass is green, there is wind in the trees outside, and mothers will always be there to hug their children at night.

Garth Williams's drawings reinforce the idea of changing life styles with precise details of dress, transportation, and architecture for each period. At the same time, the idea of constancy is depicted in the drawings of the little girls, who all remain looking much the same throughout.

Zolotow, Charlotte. *This Quiet Lady.* Pictures by Anita Lobel. Greenwillow Books, 1992. **Grade:** Preschool to 2.

In this picture book, a little girl moves about the house pointing out the pictures of her mother, starting with the one of her as a baby, smiling from her bassinette. In these pictures, the curly-haired toddler becomes a schoolgirl with wrinkled stockings and a Beatles lunch box, then a "flower child" with patched jeans and an Indian blouse. She graduates in cap and gown, is a bride "like a white flower," and, finally, is the quiet lady, "lovely and large." And looking at a picture in which her mother holds a smiling baby, the child says, "Here is where I begin."

The large pictures on the right side of each page are matched on the left by smaller, almost gray pictures of the child locating each family picture. Over the course of the book, it gradually becomes clear how important these photos are to the child, whose face is seen only on the last page.

ACTIVITY

Your Own Personal "Picture Hunt." Not all families have organized family photo albums, but almost everyone has family photos tucked away somewhere. Do a treasure hunt for old family photos, and look in a variety of places: boxes, desk drawers, old file cabinets, old school yearbooks, and family bibles. Ask your parents and other family members to help you collect as many family photos as possible.

ACTIVITY cont'd.

Look through the family photo album and the other photos you have found. Are there pictures of you when you were younger? Do any of the pictures remind you of events or people you would like to remember? Pick one special photo. Look at the photo and write about the event or person it shows. Add as many details as you can. You may want to use part of these memories to write a story. You could illustrate the story with the photo or draw a picture of the part of the story you remember best.

Now look at the pictures with an older family member. Ask that person about the people and places you don't recognize. Write down the information and keep it with the picture. You might tape record some of the stories this person remembers about the people or events in the picture. You may have to show the picture to several family members before you find someone who can tell you about it. You may even get several different stories about the same picture! Remember to handle the photos carefully and store them in a safe place when you are through. They are an important part of your family history.

Family Vacations

Much of childhood memory is a single continuum—one year running into another. But family vacations can provide the accent, the event that divides the year you went to Florida from the year you went to camp. For many children, the trip itself defines the experiences, as the family travels from one place to another, seeing new sights, eating new foods, and staying in new places. A family vacation is also an experience that is shared by the whole family, and part of the fun is remembering it together.

Bat-Ami, Miriam. *Sea, Salt and Air.* Illustrated by Mary O'Keefe Young. Macmillan Publishing Co., 1993. **Grade:** 2 to 5.

Miriam Bat-Ami describes her family's annual trips to visit her grandparents at the beach. In this family, the tradition begins with a trip to the attic to rummage through the old beach things, look through the old photo album, and remember. The drive to Nantasket seems endless, but as they get closer, Mom tells family stories and the air begins to change. Grandma is waiting on the porch, and they begin a week of "nowhere beach time" with swimming, playing in the sand, evening stories on the porch, and quiet moments with parents.

Young's colored drawings capture all the joys of this special time. The universality of a child's beach experience is combined with details, such as fancy plastic swim caps and cars with fins, which show that this particular memory is rooted in the 1950s.

Howard, Elizabeth Fitzgerald. *The Train to Lulu's.* Bradbury Press, 1988. **Grade:** 3 to 6.

In *The Train to Lulu's,* Elizabeth Howard uses first-person narrative to describe the excitement of the annual June train trips she and her younger sister Babs took to visit relatives in Baltimore. It's a long trip—nine hours—but the Traveler's Aid lady is reassuring, the conductors watch out for them, and Elizabeth and Babs know exactly what to do. They eat lunch in New Haven and dinner in Philadelphia. The girls draw and read and wait as the hours slowly pass. When they arrive in Baltimore, everyone is there to meet them: aunts, uncles, and cousins, including Lulu. They are going to stay at her house for the whole summer!

Khalsa, Dayal Kaur. *My Family Vacation.* Clarkson N. Potter, Inc., 1988. **Grade:** 2 to 6.

In this dynamic picture book, Khalsa remembers a long trip her family took by car, from the snows of New Jersey to the sunshine of Florida. These memories are centered around her collection of souvenirs: motel soaps, sugar packets, paper place mats, postcards, and a pink paper umbrella from a coconut drink. Other than switching cars midway through the trip, the events are those of a typical Florida vacation.

The brightly colored, flat illustrations show motels, tourist attractions, and restaurants, capturing perfectly Florida's flamboyance and the style of the 1950s.

Porte, Barbara. *When Grandma Almost Fell Off the Mountain and Other Stories.* Orchard/Richard Jackson, 1993. **Grade:** 2 to 6.

Like Khalsa, Porte remembers a family vacation in Florida, but Porte's memories seem to be from an earlier time, as her family's car features a running board and a strap children can hang onto when they stand up to see the sights. In Florida, they stay with relatives who own a hotel and have a wonderful time despite the children's many mishaps, including a broken swing, a near-drowning, a burnt hand, and the excitement of nearly running off the mountain in a thunderstorm.

The detailed, lively illustrations match the text, which vividly recalls the adventure of traveling long distances with accident-prone children.

Williams, Vera, and Jennifer Williams. *Stringbean's Trip to the Shining Sea.* Greenwillow Books, 1988. **Grade:** 2 to 6.

Here are the postcards and photos Stringbean Coe and his brother Fred sent home from a long trip they took one summer. Traveling in a truck with a homemade camper and kitchen on the back, they drove across the country from Kansas to the Pacific Ocean. The brevity of the postcard format leaves gaps for the reader to fill in, a device that gives unusual depth to a book that invites repeated readings. The reader experiences the affection of the family and the sense of family history that takes the boys to visit Grandpa's old home. They report in detail this visit, as well as the adventure of their first independent journey. You also learn that Stringbean's dog has followed them, that Fred begins to worry about money, and that a journey this long can try the patience of the most loving brothers. The trip itself and the wonderfully detailed "postcards" give a rich and entertaining view of this vacation memory.

ACTIVITY

Your Family's Favorite Vacations. All the above are stories about family vacations the authors took when they were children. What do you remember about vacations your family has taken? Do you have photos or postcards from vacation trips? Did you bring back any souvenirs? Write about a particular vacation you remember. Who went on the vacation with you? Where did you go? How did you travel? Where did you stay, and what did you do? What adventures do you remember? What did you like best, and what did you like least? What might be the best way to illustrate your story? Drawings? Photographs? Maps?

In *Stringbean's Trip to the Shining Sea*, Stringbean's trip is shown in the form of postcards saved in a family album. Look at the book carefully; check the pictures and the information on the front of the postcards as well as the stamps on the back. Think about the ways all these are used to tell the story of this trip. Design a postcard or series of postcards to illustrate a trip you have taken.

You could also write about your trip using the letters you sent home or a journal you may have kept during the journey. You could illustrate the story with pictures, photos, or a map showing your travel route and all the places you visited.

Visiting Grandparents and Other Assorted Relatives

For many children, the most tangible experience of family memory comes when they visit their grandparents or other relatives and see for themselves the homes their parents grew up in, thus sharing some of the experiences from their childhood. These homes are filled with remnants of the past, and a few questions are often all that are necessary to learn the stories behind them. As the stories in this section show, these visits are memorable events, and the memories linger long after childhood.

Allen, Thomas B. *On Grandaddy's Farm.* Alfred A. Knopf, 1989. **Grade:** 1 to 6.

This stunning picture book recalls the summers the author and two cousins spent on his grandfather's farm in Tennessee. Granddaddy is a brakeman for the railroad and is away four days at a time but lets the children know what needs to be done while he's gone. While they do chores, Granny puts in a full day and keeps them well fed and well behaved. When Granddaddy returns, the children help him with big jobs like bringing in the hay, but there's still time for fun things like jumping into the pile of new straw and swimming in the creek. On Sunday, other relatives join them for an afternoon of good food and games.

The quiet, low-key text is given rich dimension by Allen's softly colored drawings on textured gray paper. Though much of the background is lightly sketched, important details—such as the buildings that make up the farm and the strong horses and chickens—are precisely drawn. Though the story is set in the 1930s, there is a timeless quality about this farm; the men and boys wear overalls and the girl simple dresses, but Granny wears long dresses, aprons, and a sunbonnet. The family is often seen from behind or at a distance, but the portrait of Granddaddy sitting at Sunday service is breathtaking, drawn with precision and tangible love. This book is a particularly vivid tribute to the author's grandparents and the summers he spent on Granddaddy's farm.

Crews, Donald. *Bigmama's.* Greenwillow Books, 1991. **Grade:** 2 to 6.

In this picture book, Donald Crews remembers childhood summers spent visiting Bigmama, who was not big, but Mama's Mama. He travels by train with his mother, brothers, and sisters for three days and two nights. They all eagerly await the first glimpse of Bigmama's house and their grandparents waiting on the porch. After their arrival and greetings with hugs and kisses, they take off their shoes and socks and start a tour to make sure nothing has changed. First they inspect the house and its pedal sewing machine, wind-up record player, kerosene lamps, and Sears, Roebuck catalogs. Then it's off the back porch to explore the yard, the sheds, and the barn and stable. They then take the familiar path to the pond that has plenty of water for fishing and swimming. Their cousins come to dinner, and everyone is so busy talking about what they did last year and what they are going to do this year that they hardly have time to eat. The last page shows the adult author in a city, remembering and imagining, "I might wake up in the morning and be at Bigmama's with the whole summer ahead of me."

The text of this picture book is filled with joyous energy, and the watercolor illustrations show the house and farm in precise detail. Crews has departed from his typical flat, abstract illustration style to show his grandparents' house as he experienced it then and remembers it today. It is all there: the wide porches on the house, the well and pumps, the cluttered toolshed, and the various animals scattered about. While the depictions of individual characters are not very strong, the sense of joy and eagerness is clearly shown in the body language of the children. Though the details are particular to this family, the story will ring true to anyone who has returned, filled with happy anticipation, to a familiar place.

Flournoy, Valerie. *Tanya's Reunion.* Pictures by Jerry Pinkney. Dial Books for Young Readers, 1995. **Grade: K to 3.**

In this sequel to *The Patchwork Quilt* (see p. 175), Grandma's family is planning a family reunion at the old family farm in Virginia. Grandma and Tanya have been invited to go early to help with the arrangements, and Tanya is thrilled until they actually arrive at the farm. Grandma is happy to be back in her old home, but Tanya is homesick and disappointed—nothing is the way she imagined it. To make things worse, it begins to rain and Grandma is too busy making lists with Aunt Kay to remember their Saturday baking time. But she's not too busy to take time to help Tanya see the farm through her eyes and share memories of the time when, "We had the land and the land had us." Now Tanya is ready to explore the barn with cousin Keisha, help pick apples for apple pie, and even discover a momento of Grandma and Grandpa's life on the farm to add to the family history collection being assembled in the parlor.

Jerry Pinkney's masterful water-color paintings subtly capture the contrast between the two households, especially the ramshackle charm of the old farm, where the fences lean a little, the fields are overgrown, and the furniture is a collection from many generations. The sense of family love is strongly conveyed in paintings that show Grandma hugging her younger sister, everyone crowded together in the kitchen, and Tanya and Grandma sitting on the porch swing, looking at the rain. This lovely book is a tribute to the importance of special places in the history of a fmaily and the way these traditions are passed onto new generations.

Hershey, Kathleen. *Cotton Mill Town.* Illustrated by Jeanette Winter. E. P. Dutton, 1993. **Grade: K to 3.**

As her visit to her grandmother comes to an end, a young girl lists one by one all the things she loves about the cotton mill town where Grandmama lives. It is a beautiful place with flowering cotton fields, woods, a pond to swim in, and a hammock for reading and dreaming. Grandmama shows her how to pick berries and takes her fishing. They work together at the peach farm, pulling out the too-ripe culls. When it's time to go back to the city, Mama lets her choose one of Missy's kittens to take home, a white kitten that she names Cotton, to remind her of this place.

The quiet reverie of this text based on the author's childhood memories is balanced by Jeanette Winter's boldly colored illustrations. Ultramarine blue, dark green, and lavender are the dominant colors. Flowers, fruits, and fish are in contrasting red and orange tones. The vigor and abstraction of these illustrations keep the book fresh and save it from sentimentality.

Pinkney, Gloria Jean. *Back Home.* Illustrated by Jerry Pinkney. Dial, 1992.

————. *Sunday Outing.* Illustrated by Jerry Pinkney. Dial, 1994. **Grade:** 2 to 5.

Back Home, a picture book based on the author's childhood, describes a visit to the place, Ernestine was born and her mama grew up, and *Sunday Outing* tells of the planning and sacrifice that made the trip possible. One of Ernestine's favorite things is to go with her Great-Aunt Odessa to the North Philadelphia Station and watch the silver passenger trains roll in while Aunt Odessa tells stories about Ernestine's Great-Uncle Ariah, the train man. When her relatives from Lumberton, North Carolina, invite Ernestine for a visit, she imagines herself boarding the steps and waving good-bye. But her parents are saving to buy a house, and the only way they can afford a train ticket is for each of them to make a sacrifice. When Ernestine offers to give up new clothes for school, everyone else finds something they can do without and she's on her way, riding her favorite train back to the place she was born.

Back Home starts with her arrival, when she recognizes Uncle June Avery right away. Everything is just as she imagined it would be, except her cousin Jack, who makes fun of her fancy clothes and city ways. Aunt Beaula finds her a pair of overalls that her Mama wore at her age, but Jack still finds ways to make her feel out of place and uncomfortable. Then Uncle June takes her to see the old house where she was born, and though she remembers nothing of her life there, she decides to return one day and fix it up. She looks at her mother's scrapbook, puts flowers on Grandmama's grave, and finally makes friends with Jack before she goes home. At the end, she leaves the overalls behind for next summer.

Both of these picture books are lushly illustrated with Jerry Pinkney's watercolors. The backgrounds and clothing show in meticulous detail the time and place of the story, but the paintings' spontaneous, "painterly" quality is never lost. The characters are fully realized portraits of real people with tangible emotions. The illustrations add richness and dimension to the telling of this memory.

Tiller, Ruth. *Cinnamon, Mint & Mothballs.* Illustrations by Aki Sogabe. Browndeer Press, 1993. **Grade:** 1 to 5.

Using haiku form, Tiller relates her memories of a visit to Grandmother's house with its empty barn and cellar and a pantry that smells of cinnamon, mint, and mothballs. There is a bathtub with claw feet, a squeaky red cistern, and a fireplace in her bedroom. As she drifts off to sleep, she is aware of a nocturnal world of creeping creatures, croaking frogs, and Grandmother's yellow tomcat who greets her in the morning.

Aki Sogabe's cut paper illustrations evoke early Japanese woodcuts and echo the richness and restraint of the text.

ACTIVITY

Your Visits to Grandparents and Other Relatives. The books listed above are all about visiting grandparents or other relatives. Each one is a little different. *On Grandaddy's Farm* and *Bigmama's* are about doing a lot of different things while visiting. *Cotton Mill Town* and *Cinnamon, Mint & Mothballs* are poetic lists of favorite things. If you were writing about your own grandparents, which of these styles of writing would be best? Write a story or poem about visiting your own grandparents using a style that best expresses your own emotions.

Sometimes when you visit relatives, you are also visiting a house that someone in your family has lived in for a long time. Think of how the house tells you about your family and its history: Who slept in the bedrooms? How old is the furniture? Who are the people in the photographs? Are there old toys, pictures, or other things from when your parents were children? Ask about these things and any other interesting objects you see. Think about how visiting your relatives helps you learn about your family, and write down some of the stories they tell you. Write about objects you have learned about and the people who owned and used these things.

Draw a picture of a favorite relative's house and the things you like best about visiting it. Remember to include people, pets, and anything else you particularly want to remember.

Family Heirlooms

Many family stories are centered around simple objects that are valued not for what they are, but for the memories they evoke. In each of the books that follow, an object or collection of objects is used to introduce the stories associated with them. Such stories give insight beyond specific events into the continuing story of the family itself. Students are then encouraged to search out their own family heirlooms and share the stories that go with them.

Aliki. *Christmas Tree Memories.* HarperCollins, 1991. **Grade:** K to 4.

It's Christmas Eve, and the family is gathered around the tree, sharing memories. Some of the ornaments on the tree are very old, but many have been made by the family and each has its own story. There are memories of blizzards, chicken pox, and the crochet stars made after a sledding accident. Some ornaments were made at school or at the museum. Others came about when a big group went to the country and gathered corn husks to make wreaths and eggs to decorate. The starfish Santa came from a day at the beach, the candle drip fish was made one New Year's Eve, and the pine cone angel and walnut cradle were made at Grandma's house. Some are gifts from special friends that remind them of happy times together. Looking at the tree together creates a quiet feeling of "good, beautiful memories."

Aliki's color paintings are small, quiet vignettes of the family eating Christmas cookies and pointing out particular favorites, and the full-page paintings on each right-hand page illustrate the dynamic memory that goes with each ornament.

Bonners, Susan. *The Wooden Doll.* Lothrup, Lee & Shepard, 1991. **Grade:** 2 to 5.

Stephanie has long been fascinated by the wooden doll her grandparents keep on top of the china cupboard. But Grandma tells her the doll is Grandpa's, and Grandpa thinks she's too little to be trusted with the heirloom. On the day she defiantly climbs a chair and bring down the doll, she discovers its secret. Inside are a whole family of dolls, one inside the other, and Stephanie's name is carved on the bottom. When she confesses that she has played with the dolls, Grandpa tells her about his life on a farm in Poland, how he came to leave his family, and how the doll was given to him by his mother, whose name Stephanie shares. The doll will be hers and she can play with it, but for now it will stay at Grandpa's house. This story was based on Bonners' childhood and her fascination with the wooden nesting doll her grandfather brought with him from Poland.

Clifton, Lucille. *The Lucky Stone.* Delacorte, 1979. **Grade:** 3 to 6.

Tee loves sitting on the front porch with her great-grandmother and hearing stories about when she was a girl. They both love telling and hearing about the lucky stone and all its owners. The first to use the stone was Mandy, a slave girl who was so frightened of a beating that she ran away and hid in a cave. She used the stone to let the other slaves know where she was hiding, and they helped her get food for more than a year, until emancipation. Mandy passed the stone to her daughter Vashti, and it was reaching for the stone that saved Vashti from a lightning strike during a revival meeting. Vashti passed the stone to Great-Gran in exchange for a cool drink of water, and the luck worked for Great-Gran the day she met her husband. Then Great-Gran gets sick and goes to the hospital, and when Tee sneaks in to see her, Great-Gran tells her to look on her dresser. In an envelope with her name she finds the lucky stone. Tee knows what she wants from the lucky stone, and sure enough, Great-Gran comes home the next day! The day after that, she gets a beautiful valentine from the very boy she has been watching so much at school.

This short novel is illustrated with black-and-white drawings on nearly every page showing each of the girls who owned the stone. There are excellent depictions of the revival meeting under the trees, Great-Gran and her friend at the Silas Greene show, and Great-Gran's fear when she is chased by a dog. Running throughout are pictures that show Tee's and Great-Gran's obvious love for each other.

Cohen, Ron. My *Dad's Baseball*. Lothrop, 1994. **Grade:** 3 to 6.

"Grandma's attic is big and every inch of it is stuffed with memories," but this day holds a special surprise: the baseball Dad caught at the first baseball game he attended. Though he's a Milwaukee Braves fan, young Ron is thrilled with his first game, the dizzying size of Yankee stadium, the sounds and colors, and the noise of the crowd. Then Yogi Berra hits a home run straight to them, and when Ron crawls under the seats to hide from the pandemonium, the ball is suddenly there in his hands. The next day when his uncle takes him to get the ball signed, Ron reluctantly hides his Braves cap, only to have it fall out as he reaches for the ball. Yogi advises Ron to always be himself; after all, "Who knows, I could be playing for the Braves one day." Now, 37 years later, Yogi's signature is still as sharp and clear as the memory, and now that the ball has been found, Ron can give it to his son.

The full-page pastel paintings give a clear portrait of the 1950s, a time when TVs were small, cars had fins, and baseball stadiums were the center of many a young boy's life.

Flournoy, Valerie. *The Patchwork Quilt*. Pictures by Jerry Pinkney. Dial Books for Young Readers, 1985. **Grade:** 2 to 6.

This story is about the creation of a family heirloom that will go on to become a cherished part of this family's heritage. Tanya is the youngest child and only girl in her family and the one with the most time to talk to Grandma. At first, she's the only one who understands why Grandma wants to make a quilt. Though Mama is not sure about the project at first, Grandma keeps on, gathering scraps from Jim's favorite blue pants, Tanya's African princess costume, and Mama's Christmas dress. With Tanya's help, Mama finally understands why this family quilt—Grandma's masterpiece—is so important, and she begins to help with the sewing. When Grandma gets sick, Tanya doesn't know what to do, but she knows the quilt is important so she starts working on it. Mama helps when she can, and one night the boys help cut the squares, but Tanya works on the quilt every day as winter turns to spring and Grandma slowly gets stronger. Then one day Tanya comes home to find Grandma working on the quilt, adding some special finishing touches. A few days later it is finished and spread out for the whole family to admire and remember how it was made. In the last row of patches, delicately stitched, is the dedication, "For Tanya from your Mama and Grandma."

Jerry Pinkney's delicate watercolor illustrations show a comfortable home and a warm and loving African-American family. Though the father and brothers are depicted, this is really a story about three generations of women and Grandma's gentle determination not to let the old ways be forgotten. Together, she and Tanya find a way to tell this family's story.

Galbraith, Kathryn Osebold. *Laura Charlotte.* Illustrated by Floyd Cooper. Philomel, 1990. **Grade:** K to 3.

Though Mama has told it many times before, Laura's favorite story is the one about Charlotte. So once again Mama tells her about that day, long ago, when Mama turned five years old. She and Grandma were making a cake when a package arrived. Inside the box was an elephant with soft gray flannel ears and a tiny, tiny flannel tail. It was a beautiful elephant that Mama's grandma had made just for her. Mama picks the prettiest name in the world for her, and from that day on Charlotte and she are best friends, doing everything together. Charlotte is left outside one night, and before she is rescued, Dinah the cat chews off one of her ears. But they are both brave while Grandma sews on a new ear. When Mama is too old to play with Charlotte, she keeps her on her pillow, safe at home, and when she is older still, she wraps her up and puts her away. When her daughter is born, she is named Laura Charlotte, and now Charlotte is Laura's best friend and Laura plays with her. As she goes to sleep, Laura thinks of Great-Grandmother who made Charlotte, Grandma who made the birthday cake, and Mama who ate it. "Circled by love, she hugged Charlotte closer and closed her eyes."

Floyd Cooper's paintings show an idyllic world of open meadows and glowing skies and a little girl whose joy at her gift is both appealing and believable. The beauty of the child and setting move the story dangerously close to the sentimental, but this is offset by Cooper's strong sense of design and feeling for the core of reality in this child and her open-hearted love for her toy.

Kirkpatrick, Patricia. *Plowie: A Story From the Prairie.* Illustrated by Joey Kirkpatrick. Harcourt Brace & Company, 1994. **Grade:** 2 to 6.

When her father's plow unearths a tiny porcelain doll, a lonely little girl eagerly claims it as her own and names it Plowie. Plowie becomes her companion, sharing her life and adventures. Always there is the mystery: Where had the doll come from? Who had lost her? How long had she been in the ground?

As the girl grows, the doll changes from daily friend to cherished treasure, and though she still sleeps in a tobacco tin stuffed with calico, her home is on a special shelf. Later, generations of children and grandchildren beg to hold her and hear her story once again. Now almost 100 years later, Plowie wears a pink calico dress and lives in a china hutch, but children still admire her. They still listen to the story of how she was found and wonder at the mystery.

The somewhat primitive but detailed watercolor illustrations show farm life at the turn of the century and the changes time brings as Plowie moves through three generations of the same family. The author and artist are grandchildren of the little girl, and many of the illustrations have the quality of vivid memory. The book clearly shows the importance of this particular heirloom and its connection to a beloved grandmother.

Oberman, Sheldon. *The Always Prayer Shawl.* Illustrated by Ted Lewin. Boyds Mills, 1994. **Grade: 2 to 5.**

Adam is a young Jewish boy living in a Russian village and learning Hebrew and Jewish traditions from his grandfather. When revolution and war come, Adam's parents feel they must leave, but his grandfather is too old and chooses to remain. He gives Adam the prayer shawl he got from *his* grandfather, and Adam promises his grandfather, "I am always Adam and this is my always prayer shawl. That won't change."

The shawl travels to a new world where Adam goes to a regular school, learns English, grows up, and marries. Everything about his life is different, but every Saturday, year after year, Adam puts on the prayer shawl. As they wear out, he replaces the fringes, the collar, and the cloth. When his grandson, Adam, comes to visit and asks about his childhood, he tells him about the village, his grandfather, and about the prayer shawl that will someday be young Adam's. Like his grandfather, he tells young Adam that some things change and some don't.

Illustrator Ted Lewin has conveyed the passage of time, not only in the details of background and costume, but by portraying Adam's childhood in black and white and his adult life in color. This gives the early scenes the quality of faded photos, while the present is shown in close and accurate detail. This is a strong statement of the power of family tradition and belief.

Polacco, Patricia. *The Keeping Quilt.* Simon & Schuster, 1988. **Grade: 1 to 6.**

The keeping quilt was made by Great-Gramma Anna's mother from the clothes the family brought with them from Russia. "We will make a quilt to help us always remember home . . . It will be like having the family in backhome Russia dance around us at night." The quilt is covered with colorful animals and flowers, and the border is Anna's babushka. The quilt then begins its journey through the generations. It is the tablecloth for Sabbath prayers and other family celebrations, the wedding *huppa* for three generations of daughters, and a quilt for babies and the aging Anna. The quilt, a beloved heirloom, filled with memory, will go next to the author's own daughter.

For the illustrations, Polacco has employed her vigorous style and dynamic line but reduced the color and toned down the more comic elements found in other works. The illustrations are all in black and white, except for Anna's colorful Russian clothes and the quilt that is made from them. While the quilt remains the same cherished object, everything around it changes: the family circumstance, the location, even the traditions that define each successive wedding. This is a story of mothers and daughters, generational change, and shared traditions and memory.

Whelan, Gloria. *Bringing the Farmhouse Home.* Illustrated by Jada Rowland. Simon & Schuster Books for Young Readers, 1992. **Grade:** 2 to 6.

The summer after Grandma dies, her children and grandchildren gather at the farmhouse to share memories and the contents of the farmhouse. As they divide everything into five separate piles, each thinks of a favorite thing. Is it the rocking chair Grandpa made, the family bible, the cuckoo clock, or the big yellow bowl Grandma used to mix cookie dough? Sarah's mother wants the platter with pink roses that was used for birthday cakes, but Sarah longs for Grandma's quilt and all the memories it holds. After a potluck dinner, each of Grandma's children draws a number to determine the pile they can keep, and they begin to exchange items with each other. At the end, Sarah's mother has the platter she wanted, but Aunt Edna has the quilt and the only thing she'll exchange is the platter. Mom makes the trade, and Sarah gratefully hugs the quilt as they all load up their treasures and memories. Everyone kisses and hugs and they "bring the farmhouse home."

This book shows the power of family heirlooms to bring back memories of happy times and the importance of a loving family in creating these memories. The full-color illustrations evoke Norman Rockwell's works but are less exaggerated. The paintings, though somewhat sentimentalized, show the variety and confusion of a memorable day and the powerful love of this family, all from a child's point of view.

ACTIVITY

Your Cherished Treasures: Personal Heirlooms. All the above stories are about heirlooms. An heirloom is an object that has been passed down from one family member to another. The heirloom is a reminder of people or happy times from the past. Unlike other family treasures, heirlooms often have no value other than the memories they convey. Do you have something like that in your family? Find out what you can about the object, where it came from, and why it is important in the story of your family. Write about the object and those who previously owned it. Illustrate your story with a photo or picture of the heirloom.

ACTIVITY cont'd.

Each of the books listed above tells how important certain objects were to immigrants, reminding them of their families at home. These objects, called *heirlooms,* were passed down from one generation to the next. Does your family have any heirlooms that were brought by immigrants from their place of origin? Who owned them, and why were they important? How is the heirloom passed through the family? Who will inherit it next?

After you have found out as much as you can about your family heirloom, write about it. You can use the books listed above as a model for a fictional story, or you could write a simple history of the item and why it is important to your family. Perhaps your story could be in the form of a diary kept by the heirloom, in which the heirloom tells about the different places it has been and the different people who have owned it.

Make a pictorial presentation telling about your heirloom and its history. This could be in the form of a picture, a collage, or any other visual design that conveys the history of the heirloom and its importance to the family.

Do you have something that is so special you would want to pass it on to your children? Write about your personal heirloom and why it is important to you. Illustrate your essay with a photo or picture of your heirloom.

The Memory Box

The stories that follow are about a way of formally structuring family or personal memories. In these stories, family heirlooms are gathered in a single place as a way of preserving important events for future generations. Students are then encouraged to create their own memory boxes as a way of sharing their memories with others.

Bahr, Mary. *The Memory Box.* Illustrated by David Cunningham. Albert Whitman & Co., 1992. **Grade:** 3 to 8.

Zach knows this is going to be a great vacation: three weeks of fishing on the lake with Gramps and eating Gram's cooking. Then Gramps tells him about the memory box. It is a special box made by an older and younger person together. The box stores family tales and traditions so that memories are saved forever. Gramps asks Zach to help him make his memory box, and when Zach agrees, Gram gives them a carved box, a gift from their wedding day. For the rest of the vacation as they sit and fish or watch the wildlife around the cabin, they remember things and Gram writes the memories on paper scraps. Grandpa adds old photos and souvenirs. Over time Zach notices little changes in Grandpa; it seems as if his body is there, but his mind is somewhere else. Then one morning Gramps is gone and Zach finds him barefoot and confused in the woods. That morning Gram tells Zach why the memory box is so important. Gramps has Alzheimer's, and he will soon forget many things that are important to him. The memory box is for Gram and Zach and Zach's mother. With it, Gramps can show them what he remembered when he could still remember. When Zach goes home, Gram asks him to keep adding things to the memory box and bring it next summer; "We'll need it, you and I."

David Cunningham's paintings, which fill the right side of each double-page, show a crisp idealized world of wood and lake and emphasize the affectionate interaction among the three main characters, whose serene world is about to change.

Clifford, Eth. *The Remembering Box.* Illustrated by Donna Diamond. Houghton Mifflin, 1985. **Grade: 3 to 6.**

Joshua is nine now and has been going to his Grandma Goldin's for the Sabbath since he was five years old. It is a special time for both of them. When he was little, they played games and went for long walks, but for Joshua the best part was always reading time and storytelling time. The best stories are when Grandma Goldin looks through her remembering box, a trunk filled with all kinds of things, each with its own story. There is the willow stick an ancestor used to find water in the old country, a bag filled with ribbons saved from special occasions, and Grandma's *knippel,* the old sock that holds unexpected treasure. Of course, not all of Grandma's memories are in the box. The silver candlesticks made by Grandfather Shimon are polished and used each Sabbath, and the letter Joshua wrote when he was in first grade is framed in the living room. And Joshua's memories of their times together are in his mind and heart. Just before Joshua's tenth birthday, Grandma gives him his own remembering box. In it are some of his favorite memories and one more story, to carry him into the time when Grandma will no longer be there to share her memories with him.

Each chapter of this short novel is enhanced by portraits of Grandma Goldin and Joshua. The illustrations of Grandma's stories are abstract silhouettes, but Grandma is a real person who can cry and dance and give encouragement and comfort to her earnest young grandson.

ACTIVITY

Making Memory Boxes. Make your own memory box. Find a strong box and decorate it so you will know it is special. What will you put in this box? How will you save your special memories? As written stories? As pictures, photos, recordings, or perhaps another way altogether? Keep the box in a safe place so you can look through it and add memories from time to time, perhaps on your birthday or another special occasion.

ACTIVITY cont'd.

Plan a memory box for someone close to you and save some memories to put in this box. Think of the best way to share these memories: as stories, drawings, a recording, or an album of special photos. A memory box makes a special gift for a birthday, anniversary, or other occasion.

Tracking Time

In *The Hundred Penny Box*, an aged woman uses a hundred pennies to help her track the years of her life. The activities that follow show students how the creation of a personal time line can be used to connect personal memories with other events of the time.

Mathis, Sharon Bell. *The Hundred Penny Box*. Illustrated by Leo and Diane Dillon. The Viking Press, 1975. **Grade:** 3 to 6.

Michael is fascinated by Great-Great-Aunt Dew who is 100 years old. She won't learn Michael's mother's name and has trouble remembering who he is, but when Michael takes the pennies from her hundred penny box (one for each year of her life) and counts them out, she can remember what happened each year of her life. As they count the pennies, Aunt Dew tells Michael about her childhood during Reconstruction and about her husband, family, and neighbors: the whole story of her life. Michael can't understand why his mother wants to throw out the old box or why she interrupts their games to make Aunt Dew take naps. Despite his mother's anger, he is determined to save the old broken box for Aunt Dew who tells him, "When I lose my hundred penny box, I lose me." As the story ends, Michael is with Great-Great-Aunt Dew, guarding her treasure and listening to her sing her long song, "Precious Lord, Take My Hand."

The Dillons have illustrated this story of love and conflict in shades of black and sepia. Despite the low-key abstract nature of the paintings, there is a strong sense of the house and Aunt Dew's room with its brass bed and sheer curtains. You see Aunt Dew's age, Michael's eager fascination, and his mother's frustration. Two of the paintings show Aunt Dew telling stories, surrounded by the shadowy figures of the past. This is an effective means of conveying the reality of the stories.

ACTIVITY

Your Own Personal Time Line. In *The Hundred Penny Box*, Aunt Dew used her collection of pennies to help her remember her life. You can do the same by making a time line of your life (see Figure 7). Find a long sheet of

I WAS BORN FEBRUARY 7	1981	RONALD REAGAN IS PRESIDENT
WE MOVED (I DON'T REMEMBER)	1982	
MY FAVORITE T.V. SHOW WAS "SESAME STREET"	1983	1ST FLIGHT OF THE CHALLENGER WITH SALLY RIDE - 1ST U.S. WOMAN IN SPACE BOMB KILLS 237 MARINES IN LEBANON
I BEGAN NURSERY SCHOOL	1984	SUMMER OLYMPICS IN LOS ANGELES
I HAD CHICKEN POX ON MY BIRTHDAY, AND I GOT MY FAVORITE "SNOOPY" DOG FROM MY SISTER.	1985	
I REMEMBER SEEING IT ON T.V. → I BEGAN KINDERGARTEN AND MET MY BEST FRIEND JULIE	1986	THE CHALLENGER EXPLODES CHERNOBYL NUCLEAR DISASTER
I HAD A BIG BIRTHDAY PARTY AT THE PARK AND INVITED MY WHOLE CLASS	1987	IRAN CONTRA AFFAIR BEGINS
1ST GRADE - I LEARNED TO READ	1988	OLYMPIC GAMES GEORGE BUSH ELECTED PRESIDENT
MY FAVORITE T.V. SHOWS WERE "PERFECT STRANGERS" AND RERUNS OF "THREE'S COMPANY"	1989	EXXON VALDEZ OIL SPILL CHINESE STUDENTS KILLED IN TIENEMAN SQ.
THIS WAS VERY NEAR MY SISTER'S COLLEGE. WE DROVE → UP LATER TO MAKE SURE SHE WAS O.K.	1990	SAN FRANCISCO EARTHQUAKE
I BEGAN ICE SKATING LESSONS WE DISCUSSED THIS AT SCHOOL →	1991	PERSIAN GULF WAR GROWING UNREST IN YUGOSLAVIA CLARENCE THOMAS HEARING
I GOT A DOG FOR MY BIRTHDAY! HER NAME IS ASHLEY, AND I LOVE HER!	1992	WINTER OLYMPICS L.A. RIOTS!! SUMMER OLYMPICS
THIS WAS SCARY - THE STREETS → WERE BLOCKED - THEY CLOSED MY SCHOOL AND ALL YOU COULD SEE ON T.V. WAS LOOTING AND FIRES	1993	
I WENT TO A LOT OF BAR AND BAT MITZVAH PARTIES FOR FRIENDS		
A LOT OF THINGS FELL AND WERE → BROKEN, BUT OUR HOUSE WAS OK AND NO ONE IN MY FAMILY WAS HURT.	1994	L.A. EARTHQUAKE !!! WINTER OLYMPICS (MY FAVORITE)
I SAW "PHANTOM OF THE OPERA" WITH JULIE MY FAVORITE T.V. SHOW IS "X-FILES" I GRADUATED FROM MIDDLE SCHOOL	1995	THE O.J. SIMPSON TRIAL BOMBING OF THE FEDERAL BUILDING IN OKLAHOMA

SAMPLE TIME LINE (BASED LOOSELY ON THE LIFE AND INTERESTS OF MY OWN 14-YEAR-OLD DAUGHTER)

FIGURE 7

ACTIVITY cont'd.

paper—a roll of shelf paper works well for this project. Draw a straight line down the center and divide it into sections, one for each year of your life, and label each mark with the year and your age. Now think about the things that have happened to you and write them down above the line in the appropriate year. You can include significant events, but you might also want to write about a special toy, your friends, hobbies, and anything else that is special in your life. Talking to your parents and friends may help you remember some things. You might want to include the popular songs, television shows, toys, and foods you remember for each year of your life.

Look at an almanac or other book that lists important news events that have occurred during your life. Write these below the line in the appropriate year. Do you remember any of them? You might want to also list them above the line with your personal memories; this way you can tell how you remember these events or how you felt about them. Are you surprised about anything you found? Did things happen at the time or in the way you remember them? Did the pictures in the almanac or books help you remember things you have forgotten?

If this is a class project, compare the things you remember with the things your friends remember. How are they the same, and how are they different?

Now get a longer sheet of paper and use it to portray the life of someone older (your parents, a relative, or an older friend). Divide it into yearly sections and start by writing down everything you already know, such as birthdates, marriage dates, etc. Using an almanac, list the major events and popular culture for each year in the space below the time line. Then conduct an informal interview by taking notes or recording the information. Ask, "What are the most significant events in your life? When did each occur? What is the first thing you remember?" You can add this information during the interview or put it in later. Ask what the older person or persons remember about the news events you listed. Where were they, and what were they doing at the time? Do they remember the popular songs and movies? Do those help them remember something else? Is their memory of an important event in *your* lifetime different from yours? You might want to illustrate the time line with photos or ads from each year. A personal time line makes a terrific gift for a birthday or anniversary, especially if it is illustrated.

The Many Origins of Family Stories

Inspiration for family stories can be found in a number of places: stories handed down through the generations, family diaries and letters, and fragmentary memories that linger long after the details have been forgotten. The books in this section illustrate the ways writers use these ideas, and the activities encourage students to find and develop their own stories.

Josephs, Anna Catherine. *Mountain Boy.* Illustrations by Bill Ersland. Raintree, 1985. **Grade:** 3 to 6.

His brothers are away fighting on both sides of the Civil War, leaving 14-year-old Tommy Zachary to help care for his bedridden father. Tommy's father is a well-known Union sympathizer, and when a group of Union soldiers asks for their help, Tommy volunteers to lead them over the mountains to Tennessee. It is the middle of winter, and the soldiers, who have escaped from a prison camp, are being tracked by bloodhounds. They travel for 52 days, hiding in caves, building shelters of chestnut bark, and gathering what food they can find without firing a gun. Though Tommy is tired and homesick, he keeps his promise, then returns home safely. Though he never gets the education the Union soldiers promised him, he has a full and adventurous life.

This story is realistically illustrated with full-page, precise paintings that show each aspect of the story: the mountain cabin, the soldiers' escape, and the long trek through the snow.

Lyon, George Ella. *Cecil's Story.* Illustrated by Peter Catalanotto. Orchard/ Richard Jackson, 1991. **Grade:** 3 to 6.

In terse prose, Lyon tells the story of a boy who is left with neighbors while his mother goes to care for his father, who was wounded in the Civil War. Weeks go by as the boy worries and imagines life without his father. When they return, Papa is missing one arm, but he is still the Papa who taught the boy to fish and hunt, and he is still strong enough to lift him with one arm.

The brief text is enlarged by Catalanotto's watercolor paintings, which fill the pages with light and color. The paintings alternately show a thoughtful boy pursuing his daily tasks and the things the boy worries about. He knows he can chop wood and care for the livestock, but though he goes through every move in his mind, he's not sure he's strong enough to plow. Catalanotto's illustrations have an almost cinematic quality in the way they move in and out of the boy's world. Overlapping, transparent images are used to create a sense of time and imagination. This book is an effective example of a fragmentary story creating a unified picture book.

Polacco, Patricia. *Pink and Say.* Philomel Books, 1994. **Grade:** 3 to 6.

The author/artist tells the story of Sheldon Russell Curtis in Sheldon's own words, re-creating the story as nearly as possible to the way Sheldon told it to his daughter and the way it was passed through several generations of the family to her. Sheldon, known to his family as Say, was only 15 years old when he was left for dead after a Civil War battle in Georgia. He was rescued by

Pinkus Aylee, an equally young soldier who is separated from his unit, the 48th Colored. Though Pinkus, a runaway slave, fears the marauders who are everywhere, he pulls and carries Say across the country to the cabin of his mother, Moe Moe Bay. She hides and protects them while Say recovers and they compare their experiences before and during the war. Say is impressed by Pink's ability to read, and he shares his one special experience with Pink and Moe Moe: he touched Lincoln's hand just before Bull Run. They are preparing to return to the front when the marauders come, murdering Moe Moe Bay. Two days later the boys are captured and sent to Andersonville, where they are forcibly separated. Pinkus is hanged within hours, but Say survives the months of imprisonment and returns home, where he fathers seven children and lives a long life. The story is passed through the generations, and at the end, just as Say did to Pink, the teller puts out a hand and says, "This is the hand that has touched the hand, that has touched the hand, that shook the hand of Abraham Lincoln."

The story is illustrated in a rather muted version of Polacco's dynamic style.

Turner, Ann. *Katie's Trunk.* Illustrations by Ronald Himler. Macmillan Publishing Co., 1992. **Grade:** 3 to 6.

Katie and her family can feel the rising tension in the air and the way neighbor children who were once friends hiss the word *Tory* when they pass. The rebels are arming and their power is growing, and one hot summer day Papa comes running with the warning. The rebels are coming and the family must hide in the woods. As they crouch there, Katie's anger grows, and before they can stop her, she runs back, determined to protect their house. When the rebels arrive, her courage fails and she hides in Mama's wedding trunk, burying herself under the dresses. As the rebels search for money, she realizes there is no air and she cannot breathe. Just then one of the rebels, a neighbor, opens the trunk and a hand touches her. There is a pause, then he shouts out, calling the rebels away and leaving the lid open. Though they face an uncertain future, Katie knows she will always remember that act of kindness.

Himler's watercolor illustrations show in detail the Revolutionary War setting, adding to the dramatic impact of this story based on an ancestor's diary.

ACTIVITY

Finding Stories in Your Own Family. Each of the above four books are based on a family story that was passed down in one form or another. *Cecil's Story* started with a chance remark during a family outing to the Cumberland Gap that an ancestor had died near there. George Ella Lyon then had to

---

ACTIVITY cont'd.

research and find the story for herself. The story in *Pink and Say* has been passed through the family from one generation to the next, and *Katie's Trunk* was based on a journal that had been in Ann Turner's family since the Revolutionary War. Nine-year-old Anna Catherine Josephs had heard the story of *Mountain Boy* from her grandparents many times. She wrote it for a school-assigned heritage story that later won Raintree's Publish-a-Book contest.

Family stories can be found in many places: in the stories your parents and grandparents tell you, journals and letters left by your ancestors, and the research you do for your family tree. Add to these stories your imagination about what it would be like to be in that time or place and what you would do in the circumstances, and you have the beginnings of a great short story, picture book, or novel. Stories written by children about the history of their families can be found in *Stone Soup*, a magazine that publishes children's writings.

Finding Family Stories in Local History

These two picture books are based on fragments of pioneer history that Sanders found while researching the early history of Portage County, Ohio. The first describes a family who arrives at their destination during a terrible storm, only to find that the established village they had been led to expect is an unbroken woods. Helped by neighbors, they begin to make a new life in a new place. *Warm as Wool* centers around a mother's struggle to establish a flock of sheep and turn their wool into warm clothes for her family. As the author explains in *Aurora Means Dawn*, many of his stories grow "from a seed of fact: a diary, a soldier's log, a letter, a newspaper clipping, or some other historical account."

Sanders, Scott Russell. *Aurora Means Dawn*. Illustrated by Jill Kastner. Bradbury, 1989. **Grade:** 2 to 5.

————. *Warm as Wool*. Illustrated by Helen Cogancherry. Bradbury, 1992. **Grade:** 2 to 5.

ACTIVITY

As you investigate the history of your town or county, look for these seeds of fact. They can be combined with what you have learned about how people lived in an earlier time; add your own imagination to this to create stories about the past. Remember that although some things were different then, many things are still the same, and pioneer families, for example, shared many of your feelings.

Finding Family Stories in Journals and Diaries

All of the books listed below are based on journals or diaries. *My Prairie Year, Only Opal,* and *Celia's Island Journal* are diaries kept by girls in the past who lived in the country, far away from friends and neighbors. *No Words to Say Goodbye* is a modern journal, kept by a young Soviet immigrant.

Boulton, Jane. *Only Opal: The Diary of a Young Girl.* Illustrations by Barbara Cooney. Philomel, 1994. (See Chapter 1.) **Grade:** 2 to 6.

Harvey, Brett. *My Prairie Year: Based on the Diary of Elenore Plaisted.* Illustrated by Deborah Kogan Ray. Holiday House, 1986. (See Chapter 2.) **Grade:** 3 to 6.

Kopelnitsky, Raimonda, and **Kelli Pryor.** *No Words to Say Goodbye: A Young Jewish Woman's Journey from the Soviet Union to America: The Extraordinary Diaries of Raimonda Kopelnitsky.* Translated by William Spiegelberger. Hyperion, 1994. (See Chapter 4.) **Grade:** 6 to Adult.

Krupinski, Loretta. *Celia's Island Journal.* Written by Celia Thaxter; adapted and illustrated by Loretta Krupinski. Little, Brown & Co., 1992. (See Chapter 4.) **Grade:** 2 to 6.

ACTIVITY

In the past, many people, including children, kept journals, writing down important events and private thoughts. Ask your parents if anyone in your family kept a journal that you might read. If you are lucky enough to find a family journal, you might also find a story in the journal. After you read it, write the story in your own words. If there are no journals in your family, write an imaginary one using what you know about the life of one of your ancestors. Use as many real events as possible, and try to imagine how it would feel to live in that time and place.

Write a journal about your own life. Remember, it's your personal journal, so you can write down whatever you think is important. Write about things that happen, the way you feel, and special ideas. If you find you enjoy it, keep going. Journals are an important and fascinating record of a person's life, and many well-known writers started by writing personal journals when they were young.

Using Family Stories in Storytelling

Davis, Donald. *Listening for the Crack of Dawn.* August House. Audiocassette, 120 minutes. **Grade:** 5 to Adult.

————. *Miss Daisy.* August House. Audiocassette, 58 minutes. **Grade:** 5 to Adult.

————. *The Southern Bells.* August House. Audiocassette, 55 minutes. **Grade:** 5 to Adult.

Klein, Susan. *Through a Ruby Window: A Martha's Vineyard Childhood.* Susan Klein, Audiocassette in 2 vols. 55 minutes each volume. **Grade:** 6 to Adult.

May, Jim. *The Farm on Nippersink Creek: Stories from a Midwestern Childhood.* August House. Audiocassette, 110 minutes. **Grade:** 6 to Adult.

Parent, Michael. *Sundays at Grandma's.* Virginia Arts Records. 45 minutes. **Grade:** 3 to 6.

Stivender, Ed. *Raised Catholic (Can You Tell?).* August House. Audiocassette, 111 minutes. **Grade:** 6 to Adult.

Torrance, Jackie. *My Grandmother's Treasure.* August House. Audiocassette, 60 minutes. **Grade:** 3 to Adult.

More and more storytellers are using stories they heard from their families or simple events from their own lives to create the stories they share with others. Many of these stories are available on audiocassette such as those listed above. Though August House is the primary source for such stories, many storytellers also make their tapes available directly or through storytelling festivals held throughout the country.

ACTIVITY

After you have listened to some of these stories, compare them to stories you have heard in your family. Try telling one of your own family stories to your friends. As you tell it, think about which parts of the story are the most interesting and which parts can be left out. How much description do you need to explain the setting? What are some ways you can convey the different characters in the story. Practice telling the story different ways until it feels right to you, then try telling it to a larger audience. Plan a storytelling festival with your group in which you all share stories with each other. You might also want to record your story as a way to share it with others.

APPENDIX 1

·········

Oral History and Genealogy Techniques

RECOMMENDED READING

Akeret, Robert U. *Family Tales, Family Wisdom: How To Gather the Stories of a Lifetime and Share Them With Your Family.* William Morrow & Co., Inc., 1991. **Grade:** 7 to Adult.

This book is an adult-level how-to on the craft of personal storytelling. Akeret explains how to make optimum use of memory triggers such as old photographs, letters, and other memorabilia to encourage the sharing of memories. He also shows how to organize stories around themes in different family storytelling sessions. This program, "Elder Tales," could form the basis of oral history programs at all levels.

Beller, Susan Provost. *Roots for Kids: A Genealogy Guide for Young People.* Betterway Publications, 1989. **Grade:** 4 to Adult.

A complete how-to on genealogy for all beginners, not just young people. Beller shows step-by-step how to start with a basic family group sheet, documenting not only family members but their birth dates, marriages, and deaths. She moves on to family pedigree charts that connect the family groups and suggests a variety of sources to fill in the information gaps. She lists numerous resources, both informal and official, that show how to combine oral interviews, local histories, and official records (census records, property deeds, and military records) to create a family genealogical document. The book is based on a 12-week program the author developed for fourth-graders. She leads the readers through the protocols of dealing with record keeping officialdom—all the way from making sure your hands are clean to listing in advance the records you will need. There is also an excellent chapter on oral history techniques. There are extensive appendices that show the format of genealogical records, abstracts, and U. S. census forms from 1790 to 1910, as well as sources for the worksheets and forms used in the field.

Brown, Cynthia Stokes. *Like it Was: A Complete Guide to Writing Oral History.* Teachers & Writers Collaborative, 1988. **Grade:** 8 to Adult.

Using her own oral history projects as examples, the author goes through the steps of collecting oral history: transcribing the material and editing or writing from this source. The examples range from articles to full-length biographies, as well as multiple-voice narratives clustered around a single theme. There is a separate chapter on conducting oral history in the classroom, a suggested list of projects that work well in a classroom setting, and a sample unit plan. There is an extensive list of resources and two examples of extended oral history projects.

Caney, Steve. *Steven Caney's Kids' America.* Workman, 1978. **Grade:** 4 to 8.

This book consists of projects for children to re-create—projects that encourage children to become part of the spirit of America, its history, ingenuity, and life styles. The introduction describes it as "a rediscovery of those bits of America's past that are fun to know today." The first chapter demonstrates basic genealogy, including a variety of ways to chart your findings. There are lists of the meaning of common surnames and directions on how to create a coat of arms as a family symbol. The book is a treasure trove of project ideas centered on America's historic and cultural heritage.

Hilton, Suzanne. *Who Do You Think You Are?: Digging for Your Family Roots.* Westminster Press, 1976. **Grade:** 6 to Adult.

This book is a detailed how-to of the variety of resources that can be used for genealogy. After starting with a basic pedigree chart and ideas on gathering information from living relatives, Hilton goes on to suggest a variety of information sources. The pictures and the many quotes and anecdotes enliven the text and make the search worthwhile and entertaining. Hilton gives ideas about specific genealogical problem areas: adopted children, divorced parents, Native Americans, African-Americans, and a variety of immigrant populations. One of the more entertaining chapters deals with the problem of ancestors with less-than-perfect records. The author points out that persistence in learning about your ancestors will lead to some fascinating stories. The combination of enthusiasm, crisp writing, and useful ideas makes this an excellent introduction to genealogical research.

Noren, Catherine. *The Way We Looked: The Meaning and Magic of Family Photographs.* Lodestar/E. P. Dutton, 1983. **Grade:** 5 to Adult.

Author and documentary photographer Noren shows how to look at those old family photographs and interpret what you see. There are clues in the subjects' eyes, poses, clothes, and backgrounds that reveal not only time and place but how the subjects felt about each other. There are discussions on where to find photos and how to assemble them so that they document important events in a personal and revealing way.

Oryx American Family Tree Series. The Oryx Press, 1996. **Grade:** 6 to Adult.

This series contains student guides to historical, cultural, and genealogical information on twelve different ethnic groups, ranging from Polish American to Mexican American. These books also contain instructions on how to correctly conduct genealogical research for each ethnic group.

Perl, Lila. *The Great Ancestor Hunt: The Fun of Finding Out Who You Are.* Clarion Books, 1989. **Grade:** 3 to 7.

This book is an introduction to genealogy and the gathering of family histories. Using simple language and examples that will appeal to children, it shows how to do basic genealogical research and suggests ways to collect family photos, heirlooms, and the stories that go with them.

Sitton, Thad, George L. Mehaffy, and O. L. David, Jr. *Oral History: A Guide for Teachers and Others.* University of Texas Press, 1983. **Grade:** 12 to Adult.

In the wake of the *Foxfire* phenomenon, teachers became increasingly interested in an active approach to the study of history; this book addresses that interest. The book shows how the active approach to history can be combined with language arts studies. It also surveys a number of successful projects and gives guidelines and models for developing similar programs. Project options show oral history's adaptability in a variety of physical and social environments. The technical input shows how to prepare students, conduct the actual interviews, and document the findings. The final section demonstrates some of the results of such research. Geared for adults, specifically teachers, this guide is a thorough, if somewhat dense, introduction to the rich possibilities of this approach to history.

Stillman, Peter R. *Families Writing.* Writers Digest Books, 1989. **Grade:** 7 to Adult.

This book is filled with ideas on how families can use writing to communicate, share, and save memories for each other. Stillman sees this not as a formal oral history project but an ongoing process that takes place in the form of journals (both private and family), letters, written gifts, newsletters, stories, poems, and even family bulletin boards. The ideas and samples should inspire even reluctant writers to try one or another of these models, fulfilling what Stillman calls "the very old, very decent reasons to write, among them *to make a mark, to leave a record, to tell a story.*"

Weitzman, David. *My Backyard History Book.* Little, Brown & Co., 1975. **Grade:** 5 to Adult.

This is a strong introduction to collecting personal family stories. It leads logically through the research and personal process and suggests sources of information and ways to collect stories from family members. Above all, the reader senses the author's enthusiasm and commitment to personal history making.

Westin, Jeane Eddy. *Finding Your Roots: How Every American Can Trace His Ancestors—At Home and Abroad.* J. P. Tarcher, Inc., 1977. **Grade:** 8 to Adult.

This book is filled with ideas and resources for finding records of ancestors. Starting with the clues found in family names, the author discusses the ways immigrants came to this country, where the records are likely to be found, and how to contact various agencies and research organizations to create a genealogical record. A rich bibliography is followed by six useful appendices of research sources. Designed for the serious researcher, it recommends many resources that might otherwise be overlooked.

Wolkman, Ira. *Do People Grow on Family Trees? Genealogy for Kids and Other Beginners (The Official Ellis Island Handbook).* Illustrations by Michael Klein. Workman, 1991. **Grade:** 4 to Adult.

Written for older children but useful for any novice, this handbook enthusiastically tells how to collect all aspects of family histories. Specific how-to information on creating a genealogy chart, locating information, and preserving family photos and other documents is mixed with a general survey of the immigrant experience and the forces that brought families to the New World. The book's format, in which text is broken with photos and charts, makes the book attractive to children. The organization of the material makes this book useful for teachers as well as young ancestor hunters.

Zeitlin, Steven J., Amy J. Kotlin, and Holly Cutting Baker. *A Celebration of American Family Folklore: Tales and Traditions from the Smithsonian Collection.* Yellow Moon Press, 1993. **Grade:** 6 to Adult.

This delightful collection shows the full range of stories that can be collected within the family and how such stories can define a time, a place, or a memorable personality. The text is categorized; there are stories about family members, stories told to children, family expressions, customs, and family photography. The collected stories of five different families are included, and the final section tells how to collect your own family folklore. This volume provides guidelines for family history projects and examples of the kinds of materials that can be found.

SOME SUCCESSFUL ORAL HISTORY PROJECTS

Foxfire. Rabun County High School, Clayton, Georgia. **Grade:** 5 to Adult.
One of the earliest and most successful uses of oral history in education, *Foxfire* is a magazine that began as a single experimental publication in 1967 and evolved into an organization that actively collects and preserves the artifacts and memories of life in Appalachia. More than 25 years later, *Foxfire* magazine continues to be the work of Rabun County high school students and is a fundamental part of the language and social studies curriculum. It has generated a number of hardcover anthologies and a play/television film. (It has also inspired numerous similar projects in a wide range of circumstances, both rural and urban that are still going on today.)

Frommer, Myrna Katz, and Harvey Frommer. *It Happened in Brooklyn: An Oral History of Growing Up in the Borough in the 1940s, 1950s, and 1960s.* Harcourt, Brace & Company, 1993. **Grade:** 6 to Adult.
To create this book the authors interviewed over 100 people about the full range of the experience of growing up in Brooklyn. The book is divided into clear sections: childhood experience, school, life in the neighborhood, recreation, religion, and family life. Within each chapter, individual paragraph-length memories are illustrated by a wide range of photographs from the period. What emerges is a vivid portrait of crowded apartments, small businesses that gave personalized service, schools that expected much of students, and a vigorous neighborhood where anything was possible.

Ginns, Patsy Moore. *Snowbird Gravy and Dishpan Pie: Mountain People Recall.* J. L. Osborne, Jr., Artist. University of North Carolina Press, 1982. **Grade:** 6 to Adult.
This collection documents firsthand accounts of early mountain life in North Carolina, ranging from the 1880s to the Depression era. Each selection includes that narrator's name, year of birth, and county, and the recollections cover family life, child life, work, community events, religion, and medicines—plants and herbs. Tellers share stories about memorable animals and local ghosts and include some traditional mountain stories. The selections range from short paragraphs to a page or two, but most are a page or less. The crisp pen-and-ink illustrations show roads, streams, tree-covered hills, and traditional farm buildings and mills. These fragmentary memories merge to create a portrait of home and family life around the turn of the century.

Schwartz, Alvin, editor. *When I Grew Up Long Ago: Family Living, Going to School, Games and Parties, Cures and Death, A Comet, A War, Falling in Love and Other Things I Remember.* Drawings by Harold Berson. J. P. Lippincott, 1978. **Grade:** 4 to 8.

This delightful book demonstrates the range of responses one can expect from an oral history project. The book contains several thousand passages chosen from 156 interviews and covers the full range of human memory: family, food, clothes, school, games, punishments, home remedies, birthdays, holidays, songs, and stories. There are also reminiscences about disasters, wars, a comet, and an eclipse. The book includes suggestions on how to conduct interviews. The table of contents suggests a range of topics, and the responses suggest many questions.

APPENDIX 2

•••••••••

Collecting Local History

RECOMMENDED READING

Cooper, Kay. *Who Put the Cannon in the Courthouse Square?* Illustrated by Anthony Accardo. Walker & Co., 1985. **Grade:** 5 to 9.

Written as a source book for local history projects, this guide starts with suggestions on how to define and limit questions in local history. It then goes on to suggest sources for the answers. Cooper recommends looking at local names, landmarks, industries, historic events, and natural disasters. She also suggests ways that generic topics such as community helpers can be the focus of research. She then moves on to the various sources at all levels that can be used for research. The book concludes with examples of interesting local history projects at various levels.

Jungreis, Abigail. *Know Your Hometown History: Projects and Activities.* Watts, 1992. **Grade:** 3 to 8.

This is a relatively simple book outlining a series of projects that can involve young people in the history of their local community. Starting with local geography, projects include students developing their own communities with the aid of maps, models, interviews, and historic research. The basic projects are adaptable to a number of community models and can be used for a variety of age groups.

Kyvig, David E., and Myron A. Marty. *Nearby History: Exploring the Past Around You.* American Association for State and Local History, Nashville, Tennessee, 1982. **Grade:** 10 to Adult.

An adult, academic approach that lists all the potential resources for collecting local history, this book gives suggestions for research, preservation, and development of a written record to guide others. It also includes sample forms for requesting information and nominating sites for the National Register of Historic Places. There are also sample forms for requesting the addresses of regional branches of the national archive, state archives, humanities councils, historical societies, and preservation offices. Though a bit dense for students, it's a useful guide to potential resources, and it shows how to locate and use diverse materials to create an accurate picture of the past.

Weitzman, David. *My Backyard History Book*. Little, Brown & Co., 1975. **Grade:** 4 to Adult.

———. *Underfoot: An Everyday Guide to Exploring the American Past*. Charles Scribner's Sons, 1976. **Grade:** 8 to Adult.

My Backyard History Book begins with family history and personal stories, but the second part moves out into the community and is filled with projects and ideas related to local history. Weitzman shows how history can be discovered in different places all over the community: old objects around the house, antique stores, cemeteries, old catalogs, telephone books, and the original centers of towns. He demonstrates how to look at old buildings and preserve them with rubbings, photos, and models. Filled with fascinating illustrations and brimming with the author's obvious enthusiasm, this book is a strong introduction to the study of local history.

Underfoot: An Everyday Guide to Exploring the American Past is an advanced, adult version of the previous title with much more detail. While the reading level and content will be difficult for children, the book is full of ideas that a teacher could use to motivate students and help them find new resources and hidden treasures in their family and community.

APPENDIX 3

Recommended Titles by Ethnic Origin, Dates, and Location of Story

ETHNIC ORIGIN

African-American

Clifton, Lucile. *The Lucky Stone*, 174
Crews, Donald. *Bigmama's*, 170
Flournoy, Valerie. *The Patchwork Quilt*, 171, 175
———. *Tanya's Reunion*, 171
Greenfield, Eloise. *Childtimes*, 155
Haskins, Francine. *I Remember* 121, 113
Howard, Elizabeth Fitzgerald. *Aunt Flossie's Hats (And Crab Cakes Later)*, 114
———. *Chita's Christmas Tree*, 114
———. *The Train to Lulu's*, 168
Hurmence, Belinda. *My Folks Don't Want Me to Talk About Slavery*, 8
Igus, Toymi. *When I Was Little*, 162
Johnson, Angela. *Tell Me a Story, Mama*, 163
———. *Toning the Sweep*, 156
Lester, Julius. *To Be a Slave*, 8
Lyons, Mary E. *Stitching Stars: The Story Quilts of Harriet Powers*, 44
Mathis, Sharon Bell. *The Hundred Penny Box*, 181
Myers, Walter Dean. *Brown Angels*, 165
Nickens, Bessie. *Walking the Log: Memories of a Southern Childhood*, 86
Pinkney, Jerry. *Back Home*, 172
———. *Sunday Outing*, 172
Polacco, Patricia. *Chicken Sunday*, 122
———. *Pink and Say*, 184

DATES

1860s

Brink, Carol. *Caddie Woodlawn*, 28
——. *Magical Melons*, 28

1867–1930s

Broker, Ignatia. *Night Flying Woman*, 52

1870s

Pelloski, Anne. *First Farm in the Valley*, 89
Standing Bear, Luther. *My Indian Boyhood*, 55
Wilder, Laura Ingalls. *Little House Series*, 38
——. *On the Banks of Plum Creek*, 38

1880s

Greenfield, Eloise. *Childtimes* (pt. 1), 155
Howard, Ellen. *The Cellar*, 78
——. *The Chickenhouse House*, 78
——. *Sister*, 78
Lehmann, Linda. *Better than a Princess*, 6, 25
——. *Tilli's New World*, 6
Wilder, Laura Ingalls. *By the Shores of Silver Lake*, 38
——. *The Long Winter*, 38
——. *The Little Town on the Prairie*, 38, 50

1880s–1950s

Houston, Gloria. *My Great-Aunt Arizona*, 77, 101

1889

Harvey, Brett. *My Prairie Christmas*, 29
——. *My Prairie Year*, 29, 187

1890s

Bartone, Elisa. *Peppe the Lamplighter*, 1
Baylor, Bryd. *The Best Town in the World*, 68, 101
Cooney, Barbara. *Hattie and the Wild Waves*, 111
Howard, Ellen. *Edith Herself*, 78
Stroud, Virginia. *Doesn't Fall Off His Horse*, 56

1893–1896

Keith, Harold. *The Obstinate Land*, 31

1910–1911

Levinson, Riki. *Watch the Stars Come Out*, 9, 25
———. *Soon Annala*, 9

1912–1919

Taylor, Sydney. *All-of-a-Kind Family* (series), 127

1910–1925

Kherdian, David. *The Road from Home*, 4
———. *Finding Home*, 4

1910s–1945

Cech, John. *My Grandmother's Journey*, 3

1914–1917

Strait, Treva Adams. *The Price of Free Land*, 36

1917

Lehrman, Robert. *The Store that Mama Built*, 7

1918

Houston, Gloria. *Littlejim*, 77

1919–1920

Hesse, Karen. *Letters from Rifka*, 3

1920s

Bresnick-Perry, Roslyn. *Leaving for America*, 2
Jones, Adrienne. *A Matter of Spunk*, 115
Lim, Sing. *West Coast Chinese Boy*, 12
McDonald, Megan. *Potato Man*, 120
———. *The Great Pumpkin Switch*, 120
McLerran, Alice. *Roxaboxen*, 82
Polacco, Patricia. *Bee Tree*, 91
Valla, Lawrence. *Tales of a Pueblo Boy*, 57
Yep, Laurence. *The Star Fisher*, 15

1930s

Allen, Thomas. *On Grandaddy's Farm*, 169
Arrington, Francis. *Stella's Bull*, 68

Bell, Bill. *Saxaphone Boy,* 110
Greenfield, Eloise. *Childtimes* (pt. 3), 155
Hendershot, Judith. *In Coal Country,* 75
Kurelek, William. *A Prarie Boy's Summer,* 80
———. *A Prarie Boy's Winter,* 80
Peck, Robert Newton. *A Day No Pigs Would Die,* 88
———. *Soup* (series), 89
Pelloski, Anne. *Stairstep Farm,* 89
Rossiter, Phyllis. *Moxie,* 93
Smothers, Ethel. *Down in the Piney Woods,* 98
Stevenson, James. *When I Was Nine,* 126
———. *Higher on the Door,* 126
———. *Fun, No Fun,* 126
Tate, Eleanor. *Front Porch Stories at the One-Room School,* 164

1938–1943
Levitin, Sonia. *Journey to America,* 11
———. *Silver Days,* 11

1940s
Carrier, Roch. *The Boxing Champion,* 70
———. *A Happy New Year's Day,* 70, 100
———. *The Hockey Sweater,* 70
Hendershot, Judith. *Up the Tracks to Grandma's,* 76, 101
Hest, Amy. *Love You Soldier,* 141
Houston, Gloria. *But No Candy,* 141
Rosenblum, Richard. *My Block,* 123
———. *Brooklyn Dodger Days,* 123
Stevenson, James. *Don't You Know There's a War On?,* 144
Thomasis, Antonio de. *The Montreal of My Childhood,* 128
Yolen, Jane. *All Those Secrets of the World,* 148

1941–1945
Houston, James. *Farwell to Manzanar,* 142
Mohr, Nicholasa. *Nilda,* 121
Ray, Deborah. *My Daddy Was a Soldier,* 143
Takashima, Shizuye. *A Child in Prison Camp,* 145
Uchida, Yoshiko. *Journey to Topaz,* 146
———. *Journey Home,* 146

1942
Hall, Donald. *The Farm Summer 1942,* 139

LOCATION

Poland

Bonners, Susan. *The Wooden Doll*, 174
Hesse, Karen. *Letters from Rifka*, 3

Russia

Bresnick-Perry, Roslyn. *Leaving for America*, 2
Cech, John. *My Grandmother's Journey*, 3
Hesse, Karen. *Letter from Rifka*, 3
Oberman, Sheldon. *The Always Prayer Shawl*, 177

Russia/Ukraine

Kopelnitsky, Raimonda. *No Words to Say Goodbye*, 5, 187

Switzerland

Levitin, Sonia. *Journey to America*, 11

United States

Appalachian Region

Houston, Gloria. *Littlejim*, 77
———. *My Great-Aunt Arizona*, 77, 101
Rylant, Cynthia. *Appalachia: The Voices of Sleeping Birds*, 94, 101
———. *The Relatives Came*, 94, 100
———. *Waiting to Waltz*, 94
———. *When I Was Young in the Mountains*, 94

Great Plains

MacLachlan, Patricia. *Three Names*, 81
Standing Bear, Luther. *My Indian Boyhood*, 55

New England

Hall, Donald. *The Man Who Lived Alone*, 75, 101

South

Lester, Julius. *To Be a Slave*, 8
———. *My Folks Don't Want Me to Talk About Slavery*, 8
———. *Our Song, Our Toil*, 8
Nickens, Bessie. *Walking the Log: Memories of a Southern Childhood*, 86

Southwest

Valla, Lawrence Jonathan. *Tales of a Pueblo Boy*, 57

Wisconsin

Brink, Carol Ryrie. *Caddie Woodlawn*, 28
———. *Magical Melons*, 28
Kherdian, David. *Finding Home*, 4
Pelloski, Anne. *Willow Wind Farm*, 90
———. *Stairstep Farm*, 89
———. *Winding Valley Farm*, 90
———. *First Farm in the Valley*, 89
Wilder, Laura Ingalls. *Little House in the Big Woods*, 38

Wyoming

Scott, Lynn H. *The Covered Wagon and Other Adventures*, 35

INDEX

· · · · · · · · · · ·

by Virgil Diodato